LONDON

D0259897

SPIRALGUIDE

 Publishing

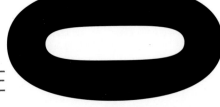

Contents

Written by Lesley Reader
Magazine by Fiona Dunlop and Steve Watkins
Where to sections by Elizabeth Carter
Revised and updated by Steve Watkins

Revision managed by Bookwork Creative Associates
Series Editor Karen Rigden
Series Designer Catherine Murray

Published by AA Publishing, a trading name of AA Media Limited, whose
registered office is Fanum House, Basing View, Basingstoke, Hampshire RG21
4EA. Registered number 06112600.

ISBN: 978-0-7495-6593-0

All rights reserved. No part of this publication may be reproduced, stored in
a retrieval system, or transmitted in any form or by any means – electronic,
photocopying, recording or otherwise – unless the written permission of the
publishers has been obtained beforehand. This book may not be sold, resold,
hired out or otherwise disposed of by way of trade in any form of binding or
cover other than that in which it is published, without the prior consent of
the publisher.

The contents of this publication are believed correct at the time of printing.
Nevertheless, AA Publishing accept no responsibility for errors, omissions or
changes in the details given, or for the consequences of readers' reliance on
this information. This does not affect your statutory rights. Assessments of the
attractions, hotels and restaurants are based upon the author's own experience
and contain subjective opinions that may not reflect the publisher's opinion or a
reader's experience. We have tried to ensure accuracy, but things do change, so
please let us know if you have any comments or corrections.

A CIP catalogue record for this book is available from the British Library

© AA Media Limited 2000, 2002, 2004, 2006, 2008, 2010
New edition 2010
Maps © AA Media Limited 2000, 2002, 2004, 2006, 2008, 2010

Cover design and binding style by permission of AA Publishing
Colour separation by AA Digital Department
Printed and bound in China by Leo Paper Products

Find out more about AA Publishing and the wide range of services the
AA provides by visiting our website at theAA.com/shop

A04026

Enabled by | OS Ordnance Survey®

This product includes mapping data licensed from
Ordnance Survey ® with the permission of the Controller
of Her Majesty's Stationery Office.
© Crown copyright 2010. All rights reserved. Licence
number 100021153.

The Magazine

A great holiday is more than just lying on a beach or shopping till you drop – to really get the most from your trip you need to know what makes the place tick. The Magazine provides an entertaining overview to some of the social, cultural and natural elements that make up the unique character of this engaging city.

Life on the
RIVER THAMES

Ancient and gentle, the River Thames meanders through the city of London and the lives of Londoners. This cappuccino-coloured waterway splits the city in two geographically. Once frequented by trade ships and barges, nowadays trendy houseboats and reveller-filled night cruises have taken over.

Stretching for 346km (215 miles) from Gloucestershire to the Thames Estuary, beyond Canvey Island, the Thames is the second-longest river in the United Kingdom (after the River Severn). Its tidal route through central London takes it past Hammersmith and Chelsea, below the Houses of Parliament and the Tower of London, before it winds towards Greenwich.

Liquid History
The Thames has played a major part in the history of London. Neolithic settlements have been unearthed along its length; it suffered an intensive period of attack from the Vikings and enjoyed glorious heydays under the Tudors and Stuarts. In 1929, this colourful past led Parliamentarian John Burns to describe the river as "liquid history".

By the 18th and 19th century, the port of London was flourishing, thanks to the expanding British Empire, and the Thames was the major trade artery into southern England. The 20th-century progression of the rail and road network around Britain and, later, the advent of gigantic container ships needing deep-water ports put paid to the viability of the East London docks and trade along the Thames.

River Sights

Wander along Cheyne Walk in Chelsea and you will find a charming houseboat village – the best non-city lifestyle London has to offer.

Further east, on either side of Westminster Bridge, are two of the city's most iconic landmarks. The grand Houses of Parliament feature London's famous bell, Big Ben (► 97) in its clock tower. Across the river, there is no mistaking the London Eye, erected to celebrate the Millennium.

Just beyond Greenwich, the Thames reaches what is perhaps the most important structure, in terms of security, along its length. The Thames Barrier was completed in 1982 and serves to protect London from high tides and powerful tidal surges. The threat of rising sea levels, caused by climate change, means that, even with the barrier, the river has never posed a greater threat to London's existence.

The London skyline at dusk (top); the Thames Barrier (below right)

WILD THAMES

The River Thames is now one of the cleanest city waterways in the world. Salmon, Dover sole, sea trout and bass, along with an occasional seal, dolphin or porpoise, can be found swimming in it. Above water, you will likely see black cormorants, herons and swans. As part of the regeneration of the river, two "bubbler" boats operate, pumping oxygen into the water when the levels become critically low.

Pub Life

The variety of watering holes, from quirky and quaint to modern gastro, reflects the pivotal role that pubs play in London's social life. The jostling atmosphere of a traditional pub offers a welcoming retreat to enjoy a pint. Many gastropubs, however, have raised the stakes in terms of pub grub.

Olde Worlde

If there is one thing that the UK does better than any other country in the world, it is the traditional pub. In London, one of the oldest pubs is the Lamb and Flag (33 Rose Street, WC2) in Covent Garden. Immediately upon entering, the low door jambs give a clue to its age, around 300 years old. With wonky walls, wonky floors and restricted space, the pub oozes authentic charm. Other traditional pubs worth seeking out are the Trafalgar Tavern (Park Row, SE10) in Greenwich, for its setting above the Thames, and the delightful, gallery-fronted George Inn (Borough High Street, SE1) in Borough. Charles Dickens used the latter as inspiration for his novels.

Downright Strange

If quirky is your thing, then one of the most surreal pubs is Waxy O'Connor's (14–16 Rupert Street, W1), between Piccadilly and Leicester Square. Its most outstanding feature is a tree growing through the middle of one of its rooms. Add in some strange medieval-themed murals and heavenly arches and you may be forgiven for thinking you have stumbled into a church service. Another quirky offering worth checking out is the

PUB ETIQUETTE

Pubs operate a system of first-come, first-served, and you order drinks at the bar. You cannot buy alcohol unless you are at least 18 years old, and it is an offence to buy it for anyone under 18 (16 and 17 year olds with an adult may drink beer, wine or cider with a table meal). You may be challenged about your age so carry legal ID (a passport is fine). Many pubs allow children into their premises though they may be restricted to certain areas. Many also close at 1am on Thursday, Friday and Saturday. Smoking is banned inside.

Left: A quiet time at the Churchill Arms in Kensington

Below: The King's Head, Crouch End

VICTORIANA RULES

These pubs preserve the etched glass screens (snob screens), mirrors, tiles, wood panelling and lofty ceilings of Victorian times:
- Red Lion (2 Duke of York Street, SW1
  Tube: St James's Park, Green Park
  ✚ 197 E1)
- Dog & Duck (18 Bateman Street, W1
  Tube: Tottenham Court Road ✚ 197 E2)
- The Lamb (94 Lamb's Conduit Street, WC1
  Tube: Russell Square ✚ Off map 200 B5)
- Paxton's Head (153 Knightsbridge, SW1
  Tube: Knightsbridge ✚ 195 F2)

Churchill Arms (119 Kensington Church Street, W8), near Notting Hill Gate tube, where you will find a disturbingly large collection of chamber pots hanging from the ceiling and, on the walls, random memorabilia, ranging from photos of the Queen and Churchill to boxes of butterflies.

New Food Order

Food offerings at pubs used to be a little patchy in both concept and quality. The gastropub revolution has not only seen the fare change beyond recognition, but it has also forced traditional pubs to improve. In the gastropub expect finely cooked, beautifully presented culinary fusions served up with designer ale, all in a distinctly sophisticated environment. The Warrington (93 Warrington Crescent, W9), owned by chef Gordon Ramsay, is a prime example of how good the gastropub can be.

FESTIVE SPIRITS

Whether you want to celebrate the Chinese New Year, keep those Irish eyes smiling on St Patrick's Day or samba in the streets, London has a cultural festival to bring out your best party spirit. These are the pick of the best and the good news is that they are all free of charge.

Carnaval del Pueblo

This flamboyant August gathering, based in Burgess Park near Peckham, is the largest Latin American festival in Europe. A parade leaves London City Hall and winds its way to the park, where live music and dancing keep the Latin action going into the night.
www.carnavaldelpueblo.co.uk

The New Year's Day Parade

Featuring over 10,000 performers from more than 20 countries, the parade begins from Parliament Square in Westminster when Big Ben strikes noon. It heads past Trafalgar Square and eventually onto Piccadilly. Temporary grandstands line much of the route, but you will need to arrive early to secure a seat; more than half a million people attend.
www.londonparade.co.uk

Chinese New Year

Dancing dragons, lions and acrobats combine with Chinese music and fireworks to help London celebrate the Chinese New Year. London's Chinese community dates back to the 18th century and is focused on the labyrinth of streets south of Shaftesbury Avenue.

Events happen in Leicester Square and Trafalgar Square, along Shaftesbury Avenue and in Chinatown itself (the area around Gerrard Street). The date for Chinese New Year varies and each year is named after an animal. The upcoming dates and animals are

- 2010: 14 February (Tiger)
- 2012: 23 January (Dragon)
- 2011: 3 February (Rabbit)
- 2013: 10 February (Snake)

www.london.gov.uk/chinainlondon/newyear/

Chinese New Year, Chinatown (top); Notting Hill Carnival (right)

St Patrick's Day

The Irish have long formed a significant community in London; they were the powerhouse behind the rapid expansion of the city in the 18th and 19th centuries. On 15 March London's St Patrick's Day events include a marching band parade, from Piccadilly to Whitehall, via Trafalgar Square, where a music and dance festival takes place. Every Irish pub in the city will also be joining in with the fun. www.london.gov.uk/stpatricksday

Eid in the Square

Held to celebrate Eid al-Fitr, the end of the Muslim fasting month of Ramadan, Eid in the Square takes place in Trafalgar Square. Live music, traditional food and Asian arts and crafts are on offer throughout the day. Dates for Eid al-Fitr vary; upcoming ones are:

- 2010: 9 September
- 2011: 30 August
- 2012: 19 August
- 2013: 8 August

www.eidinthesquare.com

NOTTING HILL CARNIVAL

This is London's most famous festival. Exuberant, colourful and, at times, edgy, it is the largest street festival in Europe. With its roots firmly in the Caribbean, the carnival has come a long way from its humble beginnings in 1964; nowadays more than 1 million people attend. The highlights are spectacular street parades, where dancers and performers of the Mas (short for masquerade) groups swirl to infectious calypso rhythms. The carnival takes place over the August Bank Holiday weekend, with the main parades on Monday (www.nottinghillcarnival.biz).

DOUBLE
Destruction

London's two infernal nightmares, the Great Fire and the Blitz, three centuries apart, both left smouldering ruins. Yet, phoenix-like, out of the ashes arose new approaches to urban living that transformed the face of the capital.

London's Burning

It was 2 September 1666. Flames crackled and cinders whirled into the night sky, the king's bakery in Pudding Lane was on fire and 80 per cent of the city of London was about to go up in smoke. It was not the first time this medieval town had seen a fire, but this one was to be by far the most destructive. As the flames raged, the Lord Mayor dithered, unwilling to rouse himself, and announced dismissively that "a woman might piss it out". That woman unfortunately did not materialize, and the fire spread to warehouses filled with combustible materials. The blaze took hold.

Rebuilding the City

Even the efforts of King Charles II, his brother the Duke of York and armies of firefighters were to little avail and four nights later, when the wind abated and the fire died down, more than 13,000 houses had been consumed, along with 76 churches, 44 livery company halls, the Guildhall, the Royal Exchange and St Paul's Cathedral. Remarkably, there were only nine deaths, but 100,000 became homeless.

The king issued new building regulations: all new construction was to be in brick or stone and all streets were to be wide enough for carriages to pass along them. This Rebuilding Act was the first of much legislation over the next two centuries, designed to regulate the standard of housing. Although architect Sir Christopher Wren's plan for a model urban layout was rejected on grounds of practicality, some improvements were made, notably a continuous quay between the Tower of London and London Bridge. Rebuilding took about 10 years – not counting St Paul's and 50 or so churches, all designed by Wren – but the most important spin-off was the drift to the suburbs, to Southwark or to Westminster. The old City of London lost its hold, its population plummeted, and the embryo of suburban London took shape.

Right: Sir Christopher Wren
Below: The London's Burning exhibit at the Museum of London

WARTIME SHELTERS

Although thousands of steel bomb shelters were issued to Londoners who had gardens, many East Enders used the public shelters. The largest was an underground goods yard in Stepney, where 16,000 people would spend their nights in overcrowded conditions. Far better in terms of facilities was a network of caverns at Chislehurst, Kent, where electric light, bunk-beds, lavatories and an old piano all added to the rousing atmosphere of solidarity. But top of the popularity stakes were the Underground stations. Tickets were issued for regulars, bunk beds set up and impromptu sing-songs took place. At times, around 177,000 people came here each night.

Above: Firemen tackle a Blitz fire near St Paul's Cathedral

Left: Many Londoners sheltered in Underground stations during the Blitz

Survivors

Not every City church succumbed to the flames of the Great Fire. Among the survivors in the Bishopsgate area were St-Botolph-without-Bishopsgate, the tiny St Ethelburga and, above all, the remarkable St Helen's, once part of a 12th-century Benedictine nunnery. However, all three were to suffer extensive damage in 1993 when an IRA bomb blasted out Bishopsgate. To the west, the beautiful medieval church of St-Bartholomew-the-Great, much restored in the 19th century, also escaped the fire, together with London's oldest hospital, St Bartholomew's ("Barts").

London Blitz

Blackouts and wailing sirens were the prelude to London's World War II drama: the Blitz. The aerial assault began on 7 September 1940, when some 320 Luftwaffe bombers flew up the Thames to unleash their

devastation on the East End. The bombing continued mercilessly for 57 consecutive nights, then intermittently for a further six months, with more than 27,000 bombs and countless incendiaries dropped on the city. By November more than 11,000 people had been killed and 250,000 were homeless. Initially the East End, Docklands and the City were the targets, but attacks on central London soon followed. The last raid came on 10 May 1941, when 550 bombers hammered the capital for five hours, destroying the Chamber of the House of Commons (among other buildings) and killing more than 1,400 people.

After the war, priority was given to planning new satellite towns and filling the craters that

> The bombing continued for 57 nights, then intermittently for a further six months

pockmarked the urban landscape. The late 1950s and 1960s witnessed a building bonanza of offices and public housing, with tower blocks often overshadowing a Wren church or a Regency terrace. Slum clearance, too, gave way to high-rises, but it took two decades and inner city riots during the 1980s before these concrete jungles were recognized as non-viable. Like them or not, they're part of London's history and have created a social patchwork across the capital.

Urban
GREEN

The British love for all things rural is undeniable and the fact that the capital, despite rising pollution and traffic, manages to preserve this aspect must stem from some psychic feat of collective will-power. The parks of central London are bucolic havens carved out of the general mayhem. With a short break in the clouds, Londoners are out there, bikini-clad on deckchairs, strolling or playing football.

In summer London's parks fill with people

Hyde Park

Set between Kensington Palace and Park Lane, Hyde Park (pictured left) is perhaps the most iconic of London's parks. Vast and spacious, wonderful, tree-lined walkways circumvent and criss-cross the park, while the immense Serpentine lake splits it in two. If you feel like cooling off in the heat of summer, the Serpentine Lido offers a chance for a quick dip or, at 100m (110-yards) long, a serious swim. Near to the Lido is the intriguing Diana, Princess of Wales Memorial Fountain. Constructed from Cornish granite, the water flows around the oval bed in two directions before collecting in a peaceful pool. For those wanting to voice an opinion, the legendary Speakers' Corner beckons.

🚇 Hyde Park Corner, Marble Arch, Lancaster Gate

St James's Park

At just over 23ha (57 acres), St. James's Park is relatively small compared to London's other green spaces. What it lacks in size though, it makes up for with quality and location. Nestled alongside Buckingham Palace, The Mall, with St James's Palace and Clarence House, runs along its northern edge. Inside, paths fringe the lovely lake, home to the charming, wooded Duck Island. The park was a particular favourite of King Charles II, who used to while away the hours playing with the ducks. Pelicans and many other waterfowl can also be spotted around the island. Tucked away on the island's southern side is a small cottage. Once an office for the Ornithological Society, it is now used by the London Historic Parks and Gardens Trust. For great views of Buckingham Palace, take a stroll across the lake on Blue Bridge.

🚇 St James's Park

UP THE GARDEN PATH

Less obvious gardens in London that are open to the public include:

- Fenton House (Windmill Hill, Hampstead, tel: 020 7435 3471, www.nationaltrust.org.uk Tube: Hampstead), a 17th-century house with a walled garden containing roses, an orchard and a vegetable garden.
- Ham House (Ham, Richmond, tel: 020 8940 1950, www.nationaltrust.org.uk Tube: Richmond), a 17th-century mansion with formal gardens.
- Roof Gardens (99 Kensington High Street, W8, tel: 020 7937 7994, Tube: High Street Kensington). This is one of London's greatest bucolic gems, built in 1938 above a department store to be the largest of its kind in Europe. Three thematic gardens are Spanish (fountains), Tudor (red-brick structures) and English (streams, ducks and flamingos). It is now home to an events centre, a private members' club and Babylon at the Roof Gardens restaurant (tel: 020 7368 3993).

BLOOMING MANIA

■ The Chelsea Flower Show takes place every year in late May and is traditionally part of the London social season. No other flower show can rival it in status.

■ The National Gardens Scheme organizes access to nearly 200 private gardens all over the capital. These are open at varying times between February and October. Information leaflets are available at tourist offices (► 35) or check out www.ngs.org.uk

Greenwich Park

Set on a steep hill overlooking the River Thames and the National Maritime Museum, Greenwich Park is the oldest of the Royal Parks and a UNESCO World Heritage Site. The park is very popular with both walkers and runners, especially at weekends. At the southern edge, near Blackheath, there is a more densely wooded area, where you may see a small herd of deer. Nature aside, the park's star attraction is the Royal Observatory. Designed by Sir Christopher Wren under commission from King Charles II, it features the line demarking zero degrees longitude – the Prime Meridian. Observations from the observatory were, until 1954, used to calculate the world time standard, Greenwich Mean Time.
🚇 North Greenwich 🚆 Greenwich.

Hampstead Heath

The wildest of London's rural areas, Hampstead Heath is a nature lovers' delight. Just 6.5km (4 miles) north of Trafalgar Square, between Hampstead and Highgate, the heath is a favourite place for Londoners to go walking, running and kite flying. It is rumoured that Parliament Hill is so called because Guy Fawkes looked down from here while waiting for his explosives to ignite under Parliament. The hill provides panoramic views over the city, including St Paul's Cathedral and the Millennium Wheel. The heath hosts around 30 ponds, woodland, meadows and many ancient trees and hedgerows, which help support a variety of wildlife, including kingfishers, reed warblers and woodpeckers. On the northern side of the heath lies the resplendent Kenwood House.
🚇 Hampstead, Golders Green 🚆 Hampstead Heath.

Holland Park

One of the prettiest and most secluded parks is a favourite with residents of Kensington and Notting Hill. In 22ha (54 acres) of grounds, wilderness and order are juxtaposed. The park attracted a colony of wealthy artists to its fringes in Victorian days. Today, art exhibitions take place at the Ice House or the Orangery Gallery. Families gather at the tea-house, squirrels and peacocks roam in the woods of the northern half, and nannies watch over their charges in the playground of the formal gardens. The Kyoto Japanese Garden offers a meditative retreat northwest of Holland House.
🚇 Holland Park

Regent's Park

The most northerly of the royal parks is the work of John Nash, "a thick squat dwarf with round head, snub nose and little eyes" (his own self-appraisal). Appearances aside, this visionary architect came up with the prototype for England's garden suburbs and cities, combining urban and rural to lure the nobility to what was then considered far north of the fashionable West End. The circular park is edged by the Outer Circle of highly desirable, white stuccoed residences. Within this lies the Inner Circle of botanical glories, with their diverse and fragrant rose-gardens and an open-air theatre, which optimistically stages Shakespeare productions on summer evenings. The open, northern section is where ball game players vie with the zoo's mountain goats for attention.

🚇 Regent's Park

Battersea Park

On 80ha (198 acres) of land where the Duke of Wellington and Lord Winchelsea once fought an uneventful pistol duel (they both deliberately missed), Battersea Park was created in 1858. It catered for "tens of thousands of mechanics, little tradesmen, apprentices, and their wives and sweethearts". Today, its location directly across the river from Chelsea makes it an obvious escape for the people who live and work there, among others, interior decorators and antiques dealers from the King's Road. On the park's eastern edge looms Battersea Power Station, closed since 1983 and rumoured to become a huge leisure complex. As well as a charming children's zoo, the park also boasts the Peace Pagoda, a two-tier building by the Thames, erected in 1985 by Japanese Buddhists.

🚆 Queenstown Road rail station is nearest to the park

Top: The tranquil Kyoto Japanese Garden, Holland Park
Middle: A statue in Queen Mary's Gardens,
Kensington Park
Left: Spring flowers in bloom in St James's Park

SUSTAINABLE GOLD

The countdown is on to the next Olympics in 2012, when the planet's greatest athletes will descend on London to play out the dramas of the biggest sporting show on Earth. The spectacular stadiums of the 2008 Beijing Olympics will be hard to match, but London is rising to the challenge with an exciting and sustainable redevelopment project.

Brand New Arenas

The main hub for the event will be Olympic Park in the Lower Lea Valley, near Stratford in the Docklands of East London. There are five big construction projects in the park: the Olympic Village, the Olympic Stadium, a media centre, an aquatics centre and a velodrome.

Much of the planning and design has centred on regenerating the East London area and leaving a sustainable legacy for the surrounding communities. Post-event, the Olympic Park will be transformed into one of Europe's largest urban green spaces.

Local Legacy

The 80,000-seat Olympic Stadium will later be downscaled to a capacity of 25,000 to make it usable for local sporting, cultural and entertainment events. The Olympic Village will be converted into homes and the local

LONDON'S OLYMPIC HERITAGE

The Olympics have come to London twice before. In 1908 only the now demolished Olympic Stadium at White City was built, as London hosted at short notice when an eruption of Mount Vesuvius ruled out Rome. Just over 2,000 athletes took part from 22 countries. By 1948, the first Olympics since the start of World War II, the number of athletes competing had doubled and 59 countries participated. The main events took place in Wembley Stadium.

transport network, including the Docklands Light Railway, is being improved and extended. Post-Olympics, the aquatics centre will be open to the public and used as an elite swimmer training centre, while the velodrome will have a road-cycling circuit and mountain-bike track added. This ensures that London will reap the rewards of its Olympic adventure.

Citywide Action

Although much of the action will be taking place in the Olympic Park, some sports will utilize other venues around the city. Rowing and flatwater kayaking will take place on Dorney Lake, at Eton College, near Windsor.

Volleyball aficionados can head to the Earls Court exhibition centre, while the triathlon and 10km open swim will take place in Hyde Park. Road-cycling events will be in Regent's Park and the archery will be held at Lord's Cricket Ground. Equestrian events are planned for Greenwich Park, while gymnasts and basketball players will grace the North Greenwich Arena. Perhaps the most surreal scene will be created by scantily clad beach volleyball players throwing themselves around in the sand before the buildings of Horse Guards Parade, near Downing Street!

Acclaim for the UK teams' successes in the 2008 Olympics and Paralympics (above)

The mark of
FAME

Literary, arty, musical, political or a thinker…the metropolis bristles with blue plaques posted on the former residences of its illustrious inhabitants. The plaque scheme, now run by English Heritage, started in 1867. To qualify for a plaque, the famous person must have been dead for more than 20 years or passed the centenary of their birth and, of course, have a building in London associated with them.

Creative Londoners

London has inspired thousands of writers over the centuries. Long established as popular areas for the city's literati are the northern districts of Hampstead, Camden Town and Islington. Some houses have even been home to more than one famous inhabitant, as at 23 Fitzroy Road, Primrose Hill (Tube: Chalk Farm), once occupied by the Irish poet W B Yeats and later by the American poet Sylvia Plath. Plath was drawn to Yeats's blue plaque when passing and decided that it was "the street and the house" for her. Within minutes of persuading some builders to let her in, she was at the agents, negotiating the lease for the top-floor apartment.

From left to right: A blue plaque to Handel; author Charles Dickens; Karl Marx, author of *Das Kapital*; the plaque on the house once occupied by musician Jimi Hendrix

OTHER NOTABLE PLAQUES

- **John Keats** (1795–1821), Wentworth Place, Keats Grove, NW3
  🚇 Hampstead
- **D H Lawrence** (1885–1930), 1 Byron Villas, NW3 🚇 Hampstead
- **Samuel Taylor Coleridge** (1772–1834), 71 Berners Street, W1
  🚇 Goodge Street
- **Florence Nightingale** (1820–1910), 10 South Street, W1
  🚇 Hyde Park Corner
- **Charles Dickens** (1812–70), 48 Doughty Street, WC1 🚇 Russell Square
- **Sir Winston Churchill** (1874–1965), 28 Hyde Park Gate, SW7
  🚇 High Street Kensington

George Orwell (1903–50), in keeping with his socio-political concerns, lived closer to the pulse of less erudite streets, gravitating between Camden Town and rent-free rooms above a bookshop in South End Green where he worked. He later moved to 27 Canonbury Square in Islington (Tube: Highbury and Islington), at the time a far from gentrified address. Another socially concerned writer, H G Wells (1866–1946), meanwhile lived in style overlooking Regent's Park from 13 Hanover Terrace (Tube: Baker Street). When negotiating the lease he said, "I'm looking for a house to die in". This he did 10 years later, having survived the world war that he had so grimly predicted.

Drawn to Chelsea

Chelsea has seen a stream of luminaries ever since Sir Thomas More, Henry VIII's Lord Chancellor, built his stately house in Cheyne Walk in the 16th century, though this is now long gone. Exoticism and scandal always went hand in hand here, but Chelsea's notoriety really took off in Victorian times when custom-built artists' studios became the rage. At this time, Oscar Wilde (1854–1900) penned plays at 34 Tite Street (Tube: Sloane

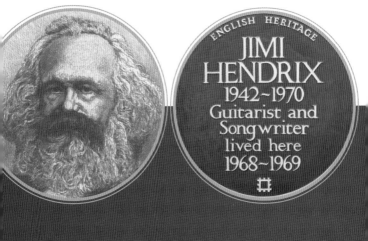

Left: Sir Winston Churchill in RAF uniform in 1948
Right: Irish wit and dramatist Oscar Wilde, photographed *c.*1891

Square). Though Wilde's wife and children lived here, he was partying madly with his boyfriend "Bosie", a double life perfectly reflected in his novel *The Picture of Dorian Gray*.

Before the American John Singer Sargent (1856–1925) became London's most fashionable portraitist from his Tite Street home, his compatriot James Whistler (1834–1903) was painting Chelsea's riverscapes from 96 Cheyne Walk. Whistler was not the first, however, as the great landscape painter J M W Turner (1775–1851) had already been inspired into abstraction from the windows at No 119.

In the 20th century Chelsea continued to attract creative souls and it was in Cheyne Row that Ian Fleming (1908–64) pounded out his first James Bond novel, *Casino Royale*, on a gold-plated typewriter while T S Eliot (1888–1965) lived below. The latter's chequered marital life was exposed at 24 Russell Square in Bloomsbury, where for 40 years he worked for the publishers Faber & Faber (Tube: Russell Square). Literary hopefuls who mounted the steps often spotted Eliot's first wife, Vivienne, who would arrive wearing placards saying "I am the wife he abandoned".

THE BLOOMSBURY GROUP

London's literary coterie par excellence was the Bloomsbury Group. Members included writers Clive Bell and E M Forster, painters Roger Fry, Lytton Strachey and Vanessa Bell, and her writer sister, Virgina Woolf (1882–1941). Virginia and her husband, Leonard Woolf, marked the group's heyday in 1924 when they moved the Hogarth Press from Richmond to Tavistock Square, in Bloomsbury, in the shadow of London's university. It was scandal all the way, including Woolf's lesbian love affair with Vita Sackville-West.

Political Exiles

With democracy stamped on the nation's soul and tolerance on its psyche, it is hardly surprising that numerous politicos on the run made London their base. Napoleon III (1808–73), Bonaparte's nephew, found himself exiled in London twice over and in 1848 lived at 1 King Street, in the gentlemanly heart of St James's (Tube: Green Park). He became so inspired by the parks of the English capital that on his coronation as emperor he ordered his city architect to set about copying them in Paris. Nearly a century later, another Gallic exile, General Charles de Gaulle (1890–1970), was notoriously less of an anglophile, despite an equally salubrious address at 4 Carlton Gardens (Tube: Charing Cross). This was his base for organizing the Free French forces while broadcasting to resistance fighters before a triumphal return at Liberation.

Communist Writers

At the other end of the spectrum was Karl Marx (1818–83) who, after expulsion from Germany, settled in London to pursue a rocky, often impecunious existence. From 1851

It was in Cheyne Row that Ian Fleming pounded out his first James Bond novel

to 1856 he lived in what was then a seedy Soho, at 28 Dean Street (Tube: Tottenham Court Road), later writing much of *Das Kapital* in the British Museum's Reading Room. He was buried in Highgate Cemetery beneath a gigantic bust bearing the words "Workers of the World Unite".

Marx's wealthier compatriot, supporter and fellow thinker, Friedrich Engels (1820–95), was also buried in Highgate Cemetery after spending much of his life in London. From 1870 to 1892 he lived at 121 Regent's Park Road, a desirable address overlooking the park (Tube: Camden Town). Communist theoreticians continued to be inspired by no less than Vladimir Ilyich Lenin (1870–1924), who in 1905 lived at 16 Percy Circus (now the Royal Scot Hotel, Tube: King's Cross), near the London Patriotic Society where he worked. This 1737 building now houses the Marx Memorial Library (37a Clerkenwell Green, Tube: Farringdon).

football
CRAZY

Fast, flowing and rarely short of drama, the game of football has never been so popular and football fans in London are spoiled for choice. Events here have played a significant role in transforming football from a disorganized pastime into the professional game that has swept across the world.

A New Code

The origins of football are hard to pinpoint. References to it, or similar activities, exist in many ancient cultures, including Chinese texts dating from 2BC. Some of the first written references to football in London appear in the 14th century.

In 1863, the modern game began to take shape, thanks in principal to the work of Ebenezer Cobb Morley. He helped create the Football Association, which first codified the game, at a meeting in the Freemason's Tavern, near Covent Garden. The original tavern was demolished, but the Freemason's Arms (81–82 Long Acre) stakes its claim as the pub where the FA was founded. The FA is still based in London, in Soho Square.

Oldest Teams

Fulham Football Club was the capital's first professional team, making the transition from amateur status in 1879. The current team plays at

LONDON'S PREMIERSHIP TEAMS

Arsenal
Ground: Emirates Stadium, N5
Ticket office: 020 7619 5000

Chelsea
Ground: Stamford Bridge, SW6
Ticket office: 0871 984 1905

Fulham
Ground: Craven Cottage, SW6
Ticket office: 020 7384 4710

Tottenham Hotspur
Ground: White Hart Lane, N17
Ticket office: 0844 844 0102

West Ham
Ground: Boleyn Ground (Upton Park),
E13. Ticket office: 0870 112 2700

Left: Wembley Stadium Arch
Bottom left: Arsenal v Chelsea FA Cup semi-final match at Wembley Stadium in 2009

Craven Cottage, its home for more than 114 years. It is one of London's most charming football grounds and still retains the red-brick work in the Johnny Haynes stand and Cottage sections of the stadium.

One of the city's most successful teams, Arsenal, turned professional in 1891, when they were known as Woolwich Arsenal. In 1913, they moved to Highbury and changed their name to their current one. They played at Highbury for 93 years before moving in 2006 to the spectacular Emirates Stadium, in Holloway.

Wembley Stadium

London's most famous football ground, Wembley Stadium, is owned by the FA and was built for the British Empire Exhibition, which began in 1924. A year earlier, however, the stadium's first event was the FA Cup Final. English football's finest moment happened at Wembley in 1966, when the national team beat Germany 4–2 in the World Cup Final.

In 2000, the original stadium was demolished. The new stadium, retaining the original towers, has an impressive arch and finally opened to host the 2007 FA Cup Final.

London's Best
for Free

It may be one of the world's most expensive cities, but London has a surprisingly rich array of enthralling things you can enjoy for free, from music and art galleries to markets or simply great views.

Best Music

To get a free dose of music, one of the best places is Covent Garden (➤ 150–151), where, on a sunny day in the Piazza, you'll hear street entertainers play anything from Vietnamese xylophones to Peruvian flutes or a home-grown electric guitar. Inside the market, on the lower floor outside the Crusting Pipe wine bar, there are often live performances of classical music and opera. Lunchtime is one of the best times to catch a show. There are also excellent, free lunchtime classical concerts at St Martin-in-the-Fields (➤ 53), at Trafalgar Square. The Barbican Centre (➤ 86) holds free jazz concerts in the bar on Sunday lunchtime.

Best Galleries and Museums

For art lovers there are some wonderful galleries in the city offering free access. It is well worth taking in the Tate Modern (➤ 100–101), Tate

Britain (➤ 92–93) and the National Portrait Gallery (➤ 60). Virtually all of the city's best museums are free to enter for the permanent displays. The Natural History Museum (➤ 124–126), the Victoria and Albert Museum (➤ 117–120) and the venerable British Museum (➤ 142–145) are just a few of the ones not to miss if you have the time.

Best Markets

There are some superb markets to peruse. Bermondsey Market (SE1, ✚ 202 B1) glitters with silverware, paintings, odd furniture and obsolete objects. Open from Thursday to Sunday, Camden Markets (➤ 152) is for anyone hankering after street fashions, crafts, jewellery or furniture. Saturday is the best time to visit Portobello (➤ 131) for everything from fruit and vegetables to specialist bric-a-brac, young designer fantasies and antiques – fake or sublimely real. For delicious, fresh produce, head to award-winning Borough Market (➤ 110). Free food samples are always on offer.

Best Bridge Views

Take a breather from London's hectic pace by the River Thames and enjoy some superb views from the various bridges. Albert Bridge (Tube: Sloane Square) is a magically illuminated suspension bridge between Battersea Park and Chelsea. Take the Chelsea Harbour development and Cheyne Walk to the north and monumental Battersea Power Station to the east. Blackfriars Bridge (Tube: Blackfriars, ✚ 201 D3) is the widest bridge on the Thames. It offers views of the expanding skyline of Southwark to

the south – including Tate Modern, St Paul's Cathedral, high-rises in the City to the north, the South Bank Centre, Waterloo Bridge and Westminster to the west. From the iconic Tower Bridge (➤ 76–77) you can see waterside lofts replacing wharves, as well as HMS *Belfast* on the south bank, and the dwarfed turrets and walls of the Tower of London.

Covent Garden (opposite); Tate Britain (top); Borough Market (left)

LIVE SOUNDS

Rock, indie, jazz, soul, blues, country, samba; no matter what your musical tastes are, you can indulge your passion most nights of the week thanks to the bewildering choice of live music venues, from glitzy clubs to cosy pubs, around the city.

Jazz It Up
If jazz is your thing, then you really are spoiled for choice. One of the most glamorous venues to get your fix is at Ronnie Scott's Jazz Club (47 Frith Street, W1) in Soho. Opened over 50 years ago by the late tenor saxophonist Scott and Pete King, it has hosted some of the jazz greats, from Zoot Sims to Kenny Garrett. For something more intimate, the atmospheric 606 Club (90 Lots Road, SW10) in Chelsea popular with aficionados.

Mix It Up
For an eclectic mix of styles in an intimate, but somewhat downbeat, setting head to the famous 12 Bar Club (22 Denmark Street, WC2) near Tottenham Court Road. It features four acts every night of the week and it is not unknown for big names to turn up and play secret gigs. Another great place to catch a variety of sounds is Barfly (49 Chalk Farm Road, NW1) in Camden. Over the years, it has secured an impressive reputation for featuring upcoming bands, with Coldplay, the Kaiser Chiefs and Oasis playing there early in their careers. Also in Camden, The Dublin Castle pub (94 Parkway, NW1) is another cool venue for catching up-and-coming acts.

Big Bands
One of London's most respected larger venues is the Roundhouse (Chalk Farm Road, NW1) in Chalk Farm. Originally a steam engine turning shed, it holds more than 3,000 people for concerts. It is on the radar for most big bands coming to London and has featured Jimi Hendrix, Pink Floyd and the Rolling Stones.

Finding Your Feet

First Two Hours

Heathrow and Gatwick are the principal airports serving London. However, Stansted and London City Airport are increasingly busy with traffic from continental Europe.

From Heathrow

Heathrow (code LHR) lies 24km (15 miles) west of central London and is served by good road and rail connections. All the services below go from all five terminals and are well signposted.

■ The **London Underground** (tel: 020 7222 1234; www.tfl.gov.uk/tube), Piccadilly line, serves Heathrow from 5am to 12:20pm (Monday to Saturday) and 5:50am to 11:25pm (on Sunday). The journey to central London takes about an hour and can get very crowded in the rush hour, but is the most convenient, best-value option.

■ The **Heathrow Express** (tel: 0845 600 1515; www.heathrowexpress.com) is a high-speed train to Paddington station. It runs from 5:10am to 11:40pm every 15 minutes and the journey takes around 15 minutes – it's fast but expensive.

■ Pick up a black metered **taxi** outside any terminal. Expect around an hour's journey time and £40 to £70 on the meter by the time you get to central London. Don't forget to allow for a 10 per cent tip for the driver.

From Gatwick

Public transport from Gatwick (code LGW), which lies 43km (27 miles) south of the city centre, includes an express train service.

■ **Gatwick Express** (tel: 0845 850 1530; www.gatwickexpress.com) train service runs to Victoria station in central London. It runs every 15 minutes most of the day and hourly most of the night with the last train at 1:35am and service resuming at 4:35am; journey time is 30 to 35 minutes. An alternative train service is provided by First Capital Connect, which goes to St Pancras International (tel: 0845 026 4700).

■ **National Express** (tel: 0871 781 8181) operates coaches from 5:15am to 10pm to Victoria coach station. The journey takes up to 1 hour 15 minutes.

■ **Taxis** operate from outside the terminal – journey time to central London is usually more than 1 hour 15 minutes and prices are around £80.

From Stansted

Stansted (code STN), small and modern, lies 56km (35 miles) northeast of central London.

■ **Stansted Express** (tel: 0845 850 0150; www.stanstedexpress.com) train service runs to Liverpool Street station, every 15 to 30 minutes, from 6am (5:30am Monday, Friday, Saturday and Sunday) to 12:30am (1:30am Friday, Saturday and Sunday). The journey time is about 45 minutes.

■ **National Express** (tel: 0871 781 8181) to Victoria coach station operates 24 hours a day. The service runs every 20 minutes and takes around 1 hour 45 minutes.

■ There's a **taxi** booking desk inside the terminal and it costs around £99 into central London. The journey takes between 1 and 2 hours.

From London City Airport

London City Airport (code LCY) is the most central of the capital's airports, lying just 9 miles (14.5km) east of central London.

- The best option is the **Docklands Light Railway** (tel: 020 7363 9700). Trains to and from Canary Wharf, Canning Town, Bank and other stations operate every 8 to 15 minutes and the journey takes 8 to 22 minutes; fares from £1.60.
- Black metered **taxis** wait outside the terminal and the journey time is about 30 minutes into Liverpool Street. The cost will be around £25, but expect to pay around £30 for journeys to central London, which can depend very much on the traffic.

Train Arrivals
International train services (Eurostar, tel: 0870 518 6186) from France (Lille and Paris) and Belgium (Brussels) arrive at St Pancras International Terminal where you connect with the Underground system.

Getting Around

Buses and the Underground (London's metro system, also called the Tube) operate 5am–12:30am (Sunday 7:30am–11:30pm) on most routes, after which a network of night buses operates until early morning. The system is divided into zones – six for the Underground and four for the bus system. These are marked on bus and Underground maps displayed at stations. On both buses and the Underground you must have a ticket valid for the zone you are in or you are liable for an on-the-spot fine. For London transport enquiries visit www.tfl.gov.uk

Travelcards and Bus Passes
If you plan to do a lot of travelling over a day or a week, buy a pass that gives unlimited travel during that period. Make sure it covers all the zones you need – most of the places in the main part of this guide are in Zones 1 and 2.
- **Travelcards** are valid on buses, the Underground, the Docklands Light Railway and some National Railways' services in the London area off peak (after 9:30am during the week and any time at weekends or on public holidays). Off-peak Travelcards and other off-peak tickets are much cheaper than peak tickets. **Accompanied Child Day Travelcards** are also good value. All Travelcards can be purchased at Underground stations, London Travel Information Centres and National Railways' stations, or newsagents shops displaying an Oyster Ticket Shop logo.
- A weekly or monthly pass will usually be issued as an **Oyster card**, London's smart Travelcard system.

The Underground
The Underground (Tube) is easy to use, though travellers with disabilities or those with baby strollers may find it less convenient. The system operates on 12 lines, which are colour-coded on maps and signs. Follow signs for the line you need and the direction you want to travel (north, south, east or west).
- **Tickets and Travelcards** can be purchased from machines or ticket offices in Underground stations.
- If you are going to make three or more Underground trips in one day, or a mix of bus and Underground trips, then **consider buying a Travelcard**.
- An **Oyster card**, which can be topped up as needed is a cheaper option if you will be making a number of trips in central London spread over several days. They are available from Underground stations or designated Oyster Card shops.

Buses

An extensive bus network operates in London. Though good for travelling short distances, buses tend to be slower on longer journeys.

- Payment is increasingly by **pre-paid ticket**. There are machines by main bus stops or buy tickets in bus and rail stations and some newsagents.
- The older style of buses, which have a back entrance and a conductor to take fares, are now only used on two routes – **Routemaster Heritage Tours**.
- On all other buses you enter via the door at the front to show your ticket or pass and get off through the **doors nearer the back**.

Docklands Light Railway (DLR)

Docklands Light Railway is an above-ground train system operating from Bank Underground station to Lewisham in the south, Stratford in the north and Beckton in the east. Most visitors use it to get to Greenwich. For tickets the DLR is part of London Underground, and Travelcards are valid.

Taxis

Black cabs (many now painted in gaudy colours) are available from outside stations and hotels, but you can also hail them from the roadside.

- Cabs **available for hire** will have the yellow "For Hire" sign lit.
- All taxis **are metered** and the fare will depend on journey time; there are surcharges after 10pm. Drivers expect a 10 per cent tip.
- To ring for a taxi, **Radio Taxis** (tel: 020 7272 0272) and **Dial-a-Cab** (tel: 020 7426 3420) are both 24-hour services.
- **Black Taxi Tours of London** (tel: 020 7935 9363; www.blacktaxitours.co.uk) offer a 2-hour, tailor-made sightseeing tour.

Sightseeing Buses

Several companies operate private bus routes that cover the main tourist sights. The tour is usually in open-topped buses with a commentary in several languages. It's a hop-on, hop-off service. For more information contact:

Big Bus Company (tel: 020 7233 9533; www.bigbustours.com)
The Original London Sightseeing Tour (tel: 020 8877 1722; www.theoriginaltour.com)

Car Hire (Rental)

A car can be a liability in London; traffic is congested and parking expensive and elusive. Parking illegally can result in a parking ticket or having your car immobilized by a wheel clamp. It's only really worth renting a car for an excursion from the city.

Alamo (tel: 0870 400 4562; www.alamo.co.uk)
Avis (tel: 0844 581 0147; www.avis.co.uk)
Europcar (tel: 0870 607 5000; www.europcar.co.uk)
Hertz (tel: 0870 844 8844; www.hertz.co.uk)

Driving

In the United Kingdom, you need a full driving licence or an International Driver's Permit (available from motoring organizations in your own country).

- Traffic in the United Kingdom drives on the **left**.
- It is obligatory to wear **seat belts**.
- The **speed limit** in built-up areas is 30mph (48kph); 60mph (97kph) on single carriageways; and 70mph (113kph) on dual carriageways (divided highways) and motorways (expressways).
- There are stringent laws against **drinking and driving**.
- Private cars are banned from **bus lanes** – watch out for signs informing you when they are in operation.

Congestion Charging

A congestion charge system operates in central London. Every private car in the zone is charged £8 per day between 7am and 6pm Monday to Friday, excluding public holidays. Pay online (www.cclondon.com), by phone 24 hours a day (tel: 0845 900 1234), in person at outlets throughout the UK, including fuel stations and shops, or by credit or debit card at self-service machines at car parks inside the zone and other selected locations. You can also pay by SMS text message if you pre-register. When you pay, you need your vehicle registration. You can pay before midnight on the day or up to 90 days before your journey into the zone. The charge rises to £10 if paid on the day after travel. Digital cameras check licence plates and those in breach of regulations are fined at least £60 if paid within 14 days, £120 thereafter. The Western Extension to the zone will be removed no earlier than 2010.

Tourist Office

London Tourist Board (LTB) runs a very comprehensive and easy-to-use website: www.visitlondon.com

Britain and London Visitor Centre

✉ 1 Lower Regent Street ☎ 0870 156 6366 🕐 Mon 9:30–6:30, Tue–Fri 9–6:30, Sat–Sun 10–4 (summer 10–5)

Admission prices

The cost of admission for museums and places of interest mentioned in the text is indicated by the following price categories:

Inexpensive under £3	**Moderate** £3–£6
Expensive £6–£10	**Very expensive** over £10

Accommodation

London is an expensive city and its hotels reflect this. The capital is popular, and with not enough beds to go round, prices for hotel rooms are forced ever higher.

Hotels

The hotels listed on pages 36–38 are the pick of the bunch: what they offer in terms of service, character, charm and standard of facilities is second to none. More hotel and B&B listings can be found by clicking the Hotels and B&B link at the AA website: www.theAA.com

Bed and Breakfasts

Bed and breakfasts (B&Bs) can be a less expensive alternative to hotels. At their simplest, B&Bs offer a bedroom in a private house with a shared bathroom, but further up the scale are rooms with private bathrooms in beautiful old houses.

Budget Accommodation

For travellers on a budget, London can present something of a challenge.

■ **Youth hostels** run by the Youth Hostel Association (YHA) are a good starting point. You do not need to be a member of the Association to stay, but joining saves you £3 per night on the price. Membership costs around £16 or £10 for under 26s (tel: 0870 770 8868 in UK; 00 44 1629 592700 outside UK; www.yha.org.uk).

■ **Inexpensive hotel chains** worth considering include Travelodge (www.travelodge.co.uk) and Premier Inn (www.premierinn.com).

■ During the summer, usually from the end of June to mid-September, **university halls of residence** are rented to non-students. These are slightly more expensive than youth hostels, but you get a single room (and even a few doubles) with shared facilities. The **Imperial College of Science and Technology** (15 Prince's Gardens, SW7, tel: 020 7594 9507. Tube: South Kensington) is one of the best located, being close to the South Kensington museums.

Seasonal Discounts

July, August and September are the capital's busiest months, though Easter and pre-Christmas are also popular periods, when room prices and availability are at a premium. In the winter months, especially November, January and February, rooms may be discounted. The period between Christmas and New Year is also relatively quiet (many hotels offer special rates after Boxing Day and before New Year's Eve – but you have to ask for them).

Accommodation prices
Prices are per night for a double room:
£ under £75   ££ £75–£150   £££ £150–£250   ££££ over £250

Abbey Court Hotel ££–£££

Located in Notting Hill and within easy reach of Kensington, this elegant town house is in a quiet side road. Rooms are individually decorated and furnished to a high standard and there is room service of light snacks. Breakfast is taken in the conservatory.

🚹 194 A4 ✉ 20 Pembridge Gardens, Kensington, W2 ☎ 020 7221 7518; www.abbeycourthotel.co.uk
🚇 Notting Hill Gate

The Academy £££

This cosy, light, Bloomsbury hotel – not far from the British Museum – has been carved out of four Georgian town houses. Bedrooms in particular have been thoroughly updated and are now fully air-conditioned; studio rooms are the most spacious and the best equipped. Food is good too: the breakfast buffet is a cornucopia of fresh fruits, compotes, warm rolls and croissants, while the various lunch and dinner menus offer food with a Mediterranean slant.

🚹 197 E3 ✉ 21 Gower Street, WC1 ☎ 020 7631 4115; www.theetoncollection.com
🚇 Goodge Street

The Amsterdam Hotel ££

Although just a couple of minutes from Earl's Court Underground station, this town house is set in a peaceful street. The hotel retains the house's original character while providing every modern comfort. Walls in the lobby and the stairs are crowded with modern prints and a stylish use of pastel colour and fabrics distinguishes the 28 bedrooms. Guests have the use of a kitchenette.

🚹 Off map 194 A1 ✉ 7 Trebovir Road, SW5 ☎ 020 7370 5084; www.amsterdam-hotel.com
🚇 Earl's Court

Apex City of London Hotel £££

Situated just a few minutes walk from the Tower of London, this award-winning hotel is ideally placed for exploring the city. The 179 rooms have tasteful modern decor and a high level of features, including free WiFi connection. There is also a small gym and an excellent restaurant, the Addendum, that's worth visiting for non-residents.

🚹 202 B4 ✉ 1 Seething Lane, EC3 ☎ 020 7702 2020; www.apexhotels.co.uk
🚇 Tower Hill, Aldgate

Ashlee House £

A stylish and rather funky hostel just two minutes' walk from King's Cross Station, and close to plenty of good clubs and restaurants. It is also in a good position for access to most of the city's major landmarks, with Covent Garden and Piccadilly Circus just a stone's throw away. This is a safe, clean place to stay, making it very popular with backpackers. Single, twin and larger rooms are available and breakfast is included in the price.

🔲 Off map 200 C5 ✉ 261–265 Grays Inn Road ☎ 020 7833 9400; www.ashleehouse. co.uk 🚇 Tube 🚉 King's Cross

Claridge's £££–££££

Claridge's has for more than a century enjoyed the patronage of visiting royalty, heads of state and dignitaries. A major refurbishment has brought the hotel's facilities right up to date, though outwardly little appears to have changed. Bedrooms now have the latest service systems and telecommunications, as well as a privacy button alongside those for maid, valet and floor waiter. Suites and *de luxe* rooms are outstanding.

🔲 196 C2 ✉ Brook Street, W1 ☎ 020 7629 8860; www.claridgeshotel.com 🚇 Bond Street

Gate Hotel ££

This Georgian house is set in one of the trendiest streets in one of the most fashionable parts of the capital. Portobello Road antiques market (held on Saturday, ► 131) is on the doorstep. Although bedrooms are small, they lack for nothing, with a refrigerator, TV, radio, phone, minibar and bathroom. Continental breakfast only is served in the bedrooms.

🔲 194 A4 ✉ 6 Portobello Road, W11 ☎ 020 7221 0707; www.gatehotel.co.uk 🚇 Notting Hill Gate

Goring Hotel £££–££££

One of the few top hotels in the capital to be independently run, the Goring is a wonderful example of a good old-fashioned British hotel and, as such, is very popular. Guests are drawn by the blue-blooded appeal of the classic decor, the exemplary staff (many of whom have worked there for years) and the excellent facilities, which run to fully air-conditioned bedrooms and power showers.

🔲 198 C3 ✉ Beeston Place, Grosvenor Gardens, SW1 ☎ 020 7396 9000; www.goringhotel.co.uk 🚇 Victoria

Hampstead Village Guesthouse £–££

Antiques, bric-a-brac and family memorabilia clutter, albeit in a charming manner, this detached Victorian house just off Hampstead High Street. Most rooms have attached bathrooms, and all have welcome trays. Breakfast is served in the garden (weather permitting). Hampstead Underground station is just minutes away, so the place is handy for central London.

🔲 Off map 197 D5 ✉ 2 Kemplay Road, NW3 ☎ 020 7435 8679; www.hampsteadguesthouse.com 🚇 Hampstead

Hart House Hotel ££

This delightful, well-cared-for hotel occupies a Georgian terrace just off Oxford Street. Much of its original late 18th-century elegance has survived careful restorations, and modern comforts abound. The smart ensuite bedrooms are furnished and equipped to a high standard.

🔲 196 A3 ✉ 51 Gloucester Place, W1 ☎ 020 7935 2288; www.harthouse.co.uk 🚇 Baker Street

London County Hall Premier Travel Inn Metro ££

The rooms here are simple but functional, neatly designed and quite comfortable. All have bathrooms and will accommodate up to two adults and two children (under 15). So, if all you really want is a bed for the night in the heart of central London (right next to the London Eye and opposite the Houses of Parliament, though sadly with no views in this direction), then you can't beat the value-location equation that this chain hotel offers. It occupies the modern part of the old County Hall, formerly the headquarters of the Greater London Authority.

➕ 200 B2 ✉ County Hall, SE1
☎ 0870 238 3300; www.premierinn.co.uk
Ⓣ Westminster

London Marriott County Hall
£££–££££

Like its neighbour, the Premier Travel Inn Metro (➤ above) the Marriott occupies part of the old County Hall, and has a great location next to the London Eye. Housed in the grand older wing of the building, it has an unbeatable view across the River Thames to the Houses of Parliament. Rooms are smartly laid out and thoughtfully equipped with the business traveller in mind. The hotel spa will revive you after a day of business or leisure around town.

➕ 200 B2 ✉ County Hall, SE1
☎ 020 7928 5200; www.marriott.com
Ⓣ Westminster

London Vicarage Hotel ££

Located in one of London's most exclusive areas, this hotel is a real bargain. The 17 bedrooms are a good size and the tall Victorian house retains a strong period feel and many original features. Eight of the bedrooms have attached bathrooms, the others share the spotlessly maintained shower room and lavatory located on each floor. The price includes a traditional hot English breakfast.

➕ 194 B3 ✉ 10 Vicarage Gate, Kensington, W8 ☎ 020 7229 4030;
www.londonvicaragehotel.com
Ⓣ Kensington High Street

Mostyn Hotel ££–£££

Just a short walk from Marble Arch and Oxford Street, this hotel is in a good location for accessing many sights. Although some of the architectural style has been retained from its 18th-century heritage, this is a thoroughly modern hotel. The bedrooms are well equipped and comfortable and there is a good restaurant.

➕ 196 A2 ✉ 4 Bryanston Street, W1
☎ 020 7935 2361; www.mostynhotel.co.uk
Ⓣ Marble Arch

The Ritz ££££

César Ritz opened the hotel in 1906 following the success of the Hotel Ritz in Paris. It remains one of London's most fashionable hotels, distinguished by an exterior that is pure Parisian elegance and an interior that has been restored in belle époque style. French period furniture, colourful chintzes and gilt detailing to the moulded-plaster walls, together with modern facilities like DVD players, provide exceptional levels of comfort in the bedrooms.

➕ 199 D5 ✉ 150 Piccadilly, WI
☎ 020 7493 8181; www.theritzlondon.com
Ⓣ Green Park

Thanet Hotel ££

This family-owned and -run Georgian town house is right in the heart of Bloomsbury, with the British Museum a short walk away. The 16 bedrooms are pleasantly decorated and each has a shower room. Back rooms are quieter. The price includes a hot English breakfast, which is served in the cheerful breakfast room. Thanet Hotel is tremendous value for money in an area not noted for good, individual places to stay.

➕ 200 A5 ✉ 8 Bedford Place, WC1
☎ 020 7636 2869; www.thanethotel.co.uk
Ⓣ Russell Square

Twenty Nevern Square ££–£££

This slightly odd but nonetheless lovely hotel, in a Victorian town house tucked away in peaceful Nevern Square, is a short stroll from the Earl's Court Exhibition Centre. The 20 bedrooms are all individually decorated and boast interesting features, including some flamboyantly carved furniture. The staff are helpful and there is a lovely breakfast room.

➕ Off map 194 A1 ✉ 20 Nevern Square, SW5
☎ 020 7565 9555; www.twentynevernsquare.
co.uk Ⓣ Earl's Court

Food and Drink

London is regarded as one of the restaurant capitals of the world, boasting food styles and chefs from all corners of the globe, and finding a restaurant table on a Saturday night is no easy task.

Evolving Trends

The explosion of new restaurants, even pubs, serving excellent food means that there is a wider choice of places to eat than ever before. Fusion cooking, incorporating ideas from all over the world, plus an entirely new school of modern Italian cooking, and the reworking of traditional British dishes into lighter cuisine have all made their mark. And to crown it all, some of the finest French cuisine to be found in the capital is being created by British chefs. For the food lover there has never been a better time to visit London.

Movers and Shakers

In the 1990s, two men from widely different backgrounds influenced the London dining scene more than anyone else. Businessman Sir Terence Conran blazed the way with the Blue Print Café at the Design Museum and the stylish **Bibendum** on the Fulham Road (▶ 132). With the South Bank's **Gastrodome**, which also includes **Le Pont de la Tour, Cantina del Ponte** (▶ 108) and **Butler's Wharf Chop House**, and the mega-restaurants **Quaglino's** (▶ 64), **Floridita** (▶ 156) and **Bluebird** (▶ 132) at the King's Road Gastrodome, he has transformed dining habits in fashionable districts.

For a long time Marco Pierre White was considered the *enfant terrible* of the London restaurant scene. He has retired from the stove to build a restaurant empire that includes the **Mirabelle** (▶ 63), in Mayfair. His brand of complex modern British cooking still has many fans in the capital.

But both restaurateurs have been eclipsed by the success of a chef who once worked with Marco Pierre White: Gordon Ramsay. The Scot opened **Restaurant Gordon Ramsay** (▶ 133) in 1998 and has since developed some of the most highly regarded eateries in London, including the Boxwood Café in the Berkeley Hotel and the restaurant at **Claridge's** (▶ 37). His protégés have revitalized some of London's finest (and most expensive) restaurants: Angela Hartnett at The Connaught and Marcus Wareing at Petrus.

As well as Ramsay, any list of homegrown talent should include celebrity chef Jamie Oliver, founder of the restaurant Fifteen, and Fergus Henderson of **St John** (▶ 87). Jamie Oliver has successfully influenced government policy on school food, while Fergus Henderson has reintroduced traditional, even if unfamiliar, British dishes – roast marrow bone is a signature dish – to the London palate.

Up and Coming

With big bucks dominating the West End, the burgeoning restaurant scene has pushed out the boundaries of fashionable London. To check the latest openings, look in the *Evening Standard* newspaper every Tuesday when restaurant critic Fay Maschler digests the pick of the crop. Saturday and Sunday editions of *The Times* and *The Independent* newspapers also carry good reviews of restaurants, which are generally London based.

Be prepared to travel out of the centre in search of the latest hit restaurant – Clerkenwell and Farringdon, for example, are rich hunting grounds. These areas were once deserted after dark, but are now booming. with stylish bars, shops and galleries jostling for space. Ethnic restaurants, such as **Moro** (▶ 85) and **Tas** (▶ 109), do well outside the West End.

Bars and Pubs

You'll find all sorts of bars and pubs across London, from the traditional to more themed affairs. Many serve food and make a good, slightly less expensive option for daytime meals or snacks. Licensing laws have changed and many pubs remain open until late on some nights (➤ 8–9). Some bars and pubs have live music every night or on weekends.

All across London, gastropubs – pubs where eating good food is as much of a priority as drinking – are going from strength to strength. Pioneers, such as **The Eagle** (➤ 84), introduced inventive menus to the pub environment, and new gastropubs now open regularly. Many make a point of offering exciting wine lists and beers from independent brewers.

Drinkers will find that each London neighbourhood has its own character: traditional pubs line old-fashioned Borough High Street, south of the Thames, while trendy bars have followed nightclubs into the East End's Brick Lane. On both sides of Oxford Street, in Soho especially, there are hundreds of pubs and bars to choose from.

Budget Eating

In general, you would be lucky to get a decent meal and a glass of wine for less than £15 a head in London. But inexpensive eateries do exist. Pizza and pasta places can be good value. The well-distributed **Pizza Express** group is always a good choice. The **Pret-à-Manger** chain has captured Londoners' hearts with its sandwiches, wraps, salads, pastries, and even sushi, made freshly each day. Don't forget most pubs serve inexpensive food.

Ethnic restaurants are also a good bet. If you head for Chinatown (➤ 154–155; 159), many noodle bars and cafés serve inexpensive one-plate meals. Some Japanese restaurants in central London now offer value set-lunch deals. The South Indian restaurants in Drummond Street (Tube: Warren Street/Euston Square) are good for vegetarians.

Prices
Expect to pay per person for a meal, excluding drinks and service:
£ under £25   ££ £25–£50   £££ over £50

Afternoon Tea

Afternoon tea in a grand hotel is the ultimate treat. It's an excuse to dress up (nearly all the hotels listed here adhere to a jacket-and-tie code) and partake in a very British institution. It is also expensive and the bill for two people will be somewhere between £35 and £70. It is advisable to make reservations at the following establishments.

Brown's Hotel

Tea in the Drawing Room here is a cosy experience; it's like spending the afternoon in a country house. There is a splendid Victoria sponge cake, as well as delicate sandwiches and fresh scones with jam and cream. Reservations essential.
✚ 197 D1 ✉ 33–34 Albemarle Street, W1
☎ 020 7518 4155; www.brownshotel.com
⊚ Mon–Fri 3–6, Sat–Sun 1–6 Ⓛ Green Park

The Dorchester

The Promenade, where tea is served, is soothing and luxurious, with deep armchairs and thick carpets. A piano plays in the background and tea brings mouthwatering pâtisserie. Reservations advisable.
✚ 198 B5 ✉ 54 Park Lane, W1
☎ 020 7629 8888; www.dorchesterhotel. com ⊚ Daily sittings at 2:30pm and 4:45pm
Ⓛ Hyde Park Corner

The Ritz

The Palm Court, with its opulent Louis XVI decor, is the quintessential location for tea at the Ritz. This very touristy afternoon tea is an unforgettable experience. Reservations for any of the sittings is required six weeks in advance (three months for weekends).

➕ 199 D5 ✉ Piccadilly, W1 ☎ 020 7300 2345; www.theritzlondon.com 🕐 11:30, 1:30, 3:30, 5:30, 7:30 🚇 Green Park

The Savoy

The Savoy is the most accessible of the capital's grand hotels, with tea served in the stately Thames Foyer. To the sound of a tinkling piano, an exquisite array of food is served, including miniature sandwiches, scones with jam and cream, and a selection of cakes and pastries.

➕ 200 B3 ✉ The Strand, WC2 ☎ 020 7836 4343; www.fairmont.com/savoy/ 🕐 Mon–Fri 2–3:30, 4–5:30, Sat–Sun 12–1:30, 2–3:30, 4–5:30 🚇 Charing Cross, Embankment

The Waldorf Hilton

It's no longer possible to take tea in the hotel's famous Palm Court but the restored 1930s Waring & Gillow panelling in the new Homage Pâtisserie provides an stunning backdrop. Among the rich fabrics and period furniture, the focal point is a "jewel box" counter displaying fine pastries by day and serving champagne cocktails by night.

➕ 200 B4 ✉ Aldwych, WC2 ☎ 020 7836 4083; www.hilton.co.uk/waldorf 🕐 Daily 2:30–5:30 🚇 Covent Garden

Fish and Chips

Fish and chips (french fries) is the one dish tourists to London want to try most. Forget fusion, modern British cooking and the rest of the food revolution, here are four top-quality "chippies".

Expect to pay around £10 per main course if you dine in, around £6 for a fish-and-chip takeaway (takeout).

Fish Central

Regarded by many as the capital's best fish-and-chip shop, all manner of piscine delights are listed here, from sea bass to sole to the traditional cod. Make a reservation to be sure of a table.

➕ Off map 201 E5 ✉ King Square, 149 Central Street, EC1 ☎ 020 7253 4970; www.fishcentral.co.uk 🕐 Mon–Sat 11:30am–2:30pm, Mon–Thu 5pm–10:30pm, Fri-Sat 5pm–11pm 🚇 Angel, Old Street

North Sea Fish Restaurant

This is where the cabbies (taxi drivers) come for their fish and chips. They usually occupy the back room, while the rest of the clientele sit in the front, among the pink velvet upholstery and stuffed fish. Portions are gigantic, and the fish is very fresh. Reservations are recommended for dinner.

➕ 197 F5 ✉ 7–8 Leigh Street, WC1 ☎ 020 7387 5892 🕐 Mon–Sat 12–2:30, 5:30–11 🚇 Russell Square

Rock and Sole Plaice

This claims to be the oldest surviving chippie in London, opened in 1871. The Covent Garden location draws a pre-theatre crowd to the restaurant and reservations are recommended for dinner. A takeaway (takeout) service is also available until midnight.

➕ 200 A4 ✉ 47 Endell Street, WC2 ☎ 020 7836 3785 🕐 Daily 11:30–11 (Sun 12–10) 🚇 Covent Garden

Sea Shell

Sea Shell is probably the most famous of London's fish-and-chip shops. It is certainly very popular with visitors to the city – you should be prepared to wait as reservations are not taken for parties of fewer than six people.

➕ Off map 196 A3 ✉ 49–51 Lisson Grove, NW1 ☎ 020 7224 9000; www.seashellrestaurant.co.uk 🕐 Mon–Fri noon–2:30, 5–10:30, Sat 12–10:30, Sun 12–4 🚇 Marylebone

Shopping

A wave of change has swept through the city's retailers, and you will find an enthusiastic mood and glimpse a new modernism in London's shopping streets. Traditional institutions and long-established stores, however, continue to provide top-quality goods and deserve time on any visit.

Fashion

The capital's shops cater for a wide variety of tastes and pockets, whether you are looking for designer labels, a top-quality made-to-measure suit or moderately priced high-street fashion.

■ High-street chain stores sell good quality clothes at moderate prices. **Oxford Street** (➤ 66), **Covent Garden** (➤ 159) and **Chelsea** and **Kensington** (➤ 134, 135) have the best choice.

■ Boutiques and smart department stores are the best bet for **designer names**, and lovers of designer labels will have fun finding their favourite names on either **Bond Street** (➤ 65) or **Sloane Street** (➤ 134).

■ For classical fashion, **Burberry** have three central locations in Brompton Road, New Bond Street and Regent Street. **Savile Row** (➤ 65), offers made-to-measure gentlemen's wear; it also contains new-wave tailors.

■ To find everything under one roof try the fashion-orientated department stores: **Harrods** (➤ 116), **Harvey Nichols** (➤ 134), **Liberty** (➤ 65) and **Selfridges** (➤ 66).

■ Seek out young alternative fashions, as well as retro and vintage clothing at **Camden Markets** (➤ 152) and **Carnaby Street**.

■ For a one-stop base that offers a wide range of shops with both high-street and designer labels, consider visiting the **Westfield** centre at Shepherds Bush/White City. Make a day of it and visit one of the on-site eateries.

Art and Antiques

A thriving commercial art scene has both antiques and art from the London of a bygone age, as well as pictures so fresh the paint is still drying.

■ The **galleries of Mayfair**, primarily Cork Street and Bond Street, show established names and sure-fire investments, with plenty of late 20th-century work.

■ Many young artists have warehouse studios in the **East End** and a number of galleries here show exciting work at attractive prices. Listings magazines contain weekly updates of exhibitions and studio shows.

■ If antiques are your passion, the auction houses of **Sotheby's**, on New Bond Street (Tube: Bond Street), **Christie's** in South Kensington (Tube: South Kensington) and, to a lesser extent, **Bonham's** in Chelsea (Tube: Knightsbridge) provide the best hunting grounds.

■ The **King's Road** (➤ 135) in Chelsea and **Kensington Church Street** (➤ 134–135) are two long stretches of road lined by shops stuffed with furniture, ceramics, memorabilia and jewellery – eye-catching displays make for interesting window shopping.

Contemporary Furniture

Habitat, **Heal's** and **Conran** are still popular for furniture, but are definitely resting on their design laurels; these days they are generally considered to be middle-of-the-road, disguised as modernist. Two places selling furniture designs that are bang up-to-date are **SCP** (135–139 Curtain Road, EC2, tel: 020 7739 1869. Tube: Old Street) and **Viaduct** (1–10 Summers Street, EC1, tel: 020 7278 8456. Tube: Farringdon).

Specialist Food Shops
- The **Conran Shop** at Brompton Cross (Tube: South Kensington) and Conran's **Bluebird** in the King's Road (▶ 132) are terrific for stylish food.
- Historic **Fortnum & Mason** (▶ 65) stocks a fabulous range of teas and a choice of 50 types of marmalade, among other luxury foods.
- **Harrods** food hall (▶ 116), with its lush displays and own-brand comestibles, is irresistible to Londoners and tourists alike.

Markets
- Antiques hunters have to be at **Portobello Road Market** (▶ 131) at the crack of dawn, but if you're hunting for clothes or are just plain curious you can afford to visit at a more leisurely hour.
- **Portobello Road Market** and **Camden Markets** (▶ 152) are probably the best places for second-hand and unusual designer clothes.
- **Borough Market** (▶ 110) is hugely popular with shoppers who are looking for good food and unusual flavours.

Department Stores
- For general gift ideas, household goods and clothes, try the following department stores: **Debenhams** and **John Lewis** (both on Oxford Street); **Peter Jones** on Sloane Square (also part of the John Lewis group) and **Marks & Spencer**, in particular its flagship store at 458 Oxford Street. At the luxury end of the market are **Harrods** (▶ 116), **Harvey Nichols** (▶ 134) and **Liberty** (▶ 65).

Entertainment

The choice of entertainment in London is vast, and listings magazines are invaluable for detailing what's on, whether it's theatre, movies, art exhibitions or gigs. *Time Out*, which is published every Tuesday, covers the whole spectrum of entertainment and is the best buy. The Thursday editions of the *Evening Standard* (London's evening newspaper) and Saturday editions of national newspapers such as *The Times* and *The Independent* also have listings magazines.

Music
Diversity sums up the London music scene, and supports a serious claim to the title of music capital of Europe. Classical music is celebrated by five symphony orchestras, as well as various smaller outfits, several first-rate concert halls and high standards of performance. The ever-changing pop music culture that is the driving force behind London fashion, and stylish restaurants and bars can feature more than a hundred gigs on a Saturday night alone, from pub bands to big rock venues.
- If you enjoy classical music, the **Proms**, an annual festival at the Royal Albert Hall, is held from mid-July to mid-September (▶ 136).
- In summer, informal **open-air concerts** are held at Kenwood House (tel: 020 8348 1286. Tube: Hampstead) and in Holland Park (▶ 18, 136).
- The **Royal Opera** at Covent Garden (Floral Street, WC2, tel: 020 7304 4000. Tube: Covent Garden), stages elaborate productions with performances by the major stars. Alternatively, try the **English National Opera** (London Coliseum, St Martin's Lane, WC2, tel: 0871 911 0200. Tube: Leicester Square), where works are sung in English.

Finding Your Feet

Dance

Dance can mean anything from classical to flamenco and jazz tap, with London playing host to top international performers throughout the year.

■ London's premier venue, the **Royal Festival Hall** (tel: 0871 663 2500. Tube: Waterloo) reopened in June 2007 after extensive refurbishment and continues to stage top-class musical events and concerts. **Sadler's Wells** (tel: 020 7863 8198. Tube: Angel) in Islington has an eclectic mix of dance programmes, although it is better known for ballet. The **Royal Ballet** is based at the Royal Opera House, Covent Garden (Tube: Covent Garden).

■ **Dance Umbrella**, an international festival of contemporary dance, is held at various venues around London between September and November (tel: 020 8741 4040 for information).

Theatre

Theatre in the capital is diverse, ranging from popular West End (Broadway-style) musicals to avant-garde productions in small independent theatres.

■ The **Royal National Theatre** (► 110) at the South Bank Centre (tel: 020 7452 3000. Tube: Waterloo) and **Barbican Centre** (► 88) produce all manner of drama. Also worth visiting is **Shakespeare's Globe** at Bankside (► 106). **The Royal Court** (► 136) and the **Old Vic** (tel: 0870 060 6628; www.oldvictheatre.com) are the most dynamic theatres promoting the works of young unknowns as well as major new plays by avant-garde writers.

■ "Off-West End" and fringe theatre has a healthy reputation. The **Almeida** (Almeida Street, Box office tel: 020 7359 4404; www.almeida.co.uk. Tube: Angel) and **Donmar Warehouse** (Earlham Street, box office: 0870 060 6624; www.donmar-warehouse.com. Tube: Covent Garden) are the major players, but theatres such as **The Gate** (11 Pembridge Road, tel: 020 7229 5387; www.gatetheatre.co.uk. Tube: Notting Hill) and **King's Head** (115 Upper Street, N1, tel: 020 7226 8561; www.kingsheadtheatre.org. Tube: Angel, Highbury and Islington) are also worth checking out.

Buying Tickets

The best way to buy a ticket for any London theatre production is to contact the venue direct (so avoiding agency commissions). However, tickets for hit plays and musicals are hard to come by, particularly at short notice, and often are only obtainable through ticket agencies. **Keith Prowse Ticketing** (tel: 0844 209 0381; www.keithprowse.com) and **TicketMaster** (tel: 0870 534 4444; www.ticketmaster.co.uk) are the most reliable. Credit card bookings made through these agencies are subject to a hefty booking fee. If you are flexible about which production you want to see, try **tkts**, a reduced-price ticket booth at Leicester Square (► 160). Expect a fairly long wait (it's open Monday to Saturday 10–7, Sunday 11–4)) and remember that tickets are limited to two pairs per person.

■ Buy your tickets directly from the concert or theatre venue, from ticket agencies or on-line. **Never buy from ticket touts (scalpers)** – the practice is illegal and you may well end up with forgeries.

■ The **lowest-price seats** are always at the top of the theatre, known as the "gods", but you will probably need binoculars.

■ **Matinées** cost less than evening shows and tickets are easier to obtain.

■ Some theatres offer **restricted-view seats** at a reduced rate.

Cinema

For movie-goers, The Odeon, Leicester Square, is recommended for the most modern and up-to-date movie experience the capital can offer.

St James's, Mayfair and Piccadilly

Getting Your Bearings

The area between Buckingham Palace and Trafalgar Square is one of London's quintessential quarters, and if you have time for only one day in the city, you should consider spending it here.

A district of considerable wealth and architectural grandeur, this area contains the leafy squares and prestigious residential buildings of Mayfair, the exclusive gentlemen's clubs of St James's, and the long-established shops and hotels of Piccadilly, one of London's great thoroughfares. Here, too, is Buckingham Palace, the monarch's official residence, which since 1993 has thrown open its doors, in part at least, to the general public during most of August and September.

The area owes its original development to St James's Palace, built by Henry VIII in the 1530s and subsequently the home of several later sovereigns, including Elizabeth I and Charles I. Charles, the current Prince of Wales, lived here, too, from 1992 to 2003, after which he moved to the adjacent Clarence House. The royal palace lent the area considerable social cachet, particularly after the 17th century, when King Charles II opened beautiful St James's Park to the public for the first time. By the 18th century, members of the aristocracy who wished to be close to court had built fine mansions in the area. In time, sumptuous arcades and exclusive Piccadilly shops sprang up to serve the area's high-spending visitors and residents. In the 19th century, Queen Victoria moved the court to Buckingham Palace, and the 20th century saw the building of the present grand ceremonial route along The Mall between Buckingham Palace and Trafalgar Square.

Today, the area's elegance and refinement make it unique in the capital. You can enjoy the parks and grand walkways, the fine old houses, the shops and galleries (notably the Royal Academy, scene of major art exhibitions), and the principal sights at either end of The Mall: Buckingham Palace, with its famous ceremonial Changing of the Guard, and Trafalgar Square, with the National Gallery, home to the country's premier art collection.

Previous page Changing of the Guard Above: Horse Guards on parade in Whitehall

★ Don't Miss

At Your Leisure

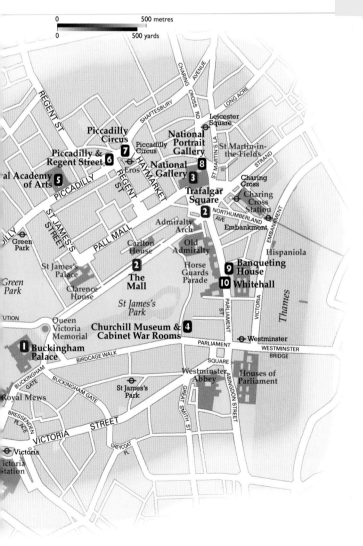

In a Day

**If you're not quite sure where to begin your travels, this itinerary
recommends a practical and enjoyable day out in St James's,
Mayfair and Piccadilly, taking in some of the best places to see
using the Getting Your Bearings map on the previous page. For more
information see the main entries.**

9:00am

Start at ❶ **Buckingham Palace** (below, ➤ 50–51) – either ogle the grand
facade through the railings or, if you are in London at the right time of
year, visit the magnificent State Rooms. To avoid waiting on the day see
Top tips (➤ 51).

10:00am

Stroll through **St James's
Park**, a tranquil oasis,
and then walk along the
broad, majestic, tree-lined
❷ **Mall** (➤ 52–53) to Horse
Guards Parade to see the
Changing of the Guard, one
of London's most famous
ceremonies. Be in place by
11 to 11:15am to find a
good vantage point.

12:15pm

The Changing of the
Guard over, walk through
to ❷ **Trafalgar Square**
(➤ 53). Since the post-
Millennium reconstruction
of the square, creating
new pedestrian areas
and crossings, a new
traffic layout, landscaping

One of the recommended highlights is the State Rooms in Buckingham
Palace (➤ 50–51), but they're open only for around six weeks every
year (August to September, dates vary) – and if you do visit them then
it's unlikely you'll be able to find a good vantage point afterwards to
watch the Changing of the Guard (or have the time to walk to Horse
Guards Parade to see it there ➤ 53). Come back another day if you
have your heart set on seeing the ceremony. You can still follow the
plan below after visiting the palace, however – you'll just be doing
everything a couple of hours later.

and new facilities, it is once again a natural and enjoyable meeting place.

1:00pm
Time for lunch. St Martin-in-the-Fields, adjacent to the National Gallery on Trafalgar Square, has an inexpensive café in its Crypt (right), and the gallery itself has a coffee bar and brasserie.

2:00pm
While away the afternoon viewing the gems of the superlative art collection at the **3 National Gallery** (below, ➤ 54–57). If you're here on a Friday, the gallery doesn't close until 9pm.

4:00pm
Drop into the **8 National Portrait Gallery** (➤ 60) for a quick look at its appealing collection of portraits of famous Brits.

Alternatively, make your way to **7 Piccadilly Circus** (➤ 60). From here it's a short stroll to some of Mayfair's squares and back lanes, or the **exclusive shops** of **6** Piccadilly (➤ 58–59). You're also just around the corner from Leicester Square, the heart of Theatreland, with sleazy, flamboyant Soho and exotic Chinatown near by (➤ 154–155).

❶ Buckingham Palace

The British sovereign's grandiose London home was built between 1701 and 1705 by the 1st Duke of Buckingham, but was redeveloped as a palace by King George IV in the 1820s, and became the official royal residence in the reign of Queen Victoria in 1837. Although it's a must-see for all visitors to London, at first glance it doesn't look terribly impressive – its stolid lines appear plain, solid and dependable rather than an exuberant celebration of majesty in stone.

While the palace is nothing special from the outside, its interior is sumptuous. The **State Rooms** were first opened to the public in 1993, a move prompted by changing attitudes within the Royal Family, and a desire to contribute funds towards the restoration of Windsor Castle (➤ 164–166). The rooms should not be missed if you're in London at the right time.

The State Rooms are where the real work of royalty goes on, providing a stage for state entertaining, investitures, receptions and official banquets. Their sheer richness and decorative theatricality are mesmerizing, from the grand marble staircase and the brightly furnished drawing rooms to the Throne Room and the elaborate red-and-gilt State Dining Room. Your feet sink softly into plush red carpets, wall coverings are almost works of art in themselves, and

The white marble Queen Victoria Memorial in front of the palace

balustrades, doors, chandeliers and windows all display spellbinding and unforgettable detail. Equally compelling are the paintings that hang in the **Picture Gallery**, including works by Canaletto, Rembrandt and Rubens, the classical sculptures and exquisite furniture. Look out in particular for the thrones and the fabulously ornamental ceilings which are some of the most elaborate imaginable. Don't expect to meet any of the Royal Family – they move elsewhere when the public come to call.

✚ 199 D4 ✉ SW1A 1AA ☎ Enquiries and credit card bookings: 020 7766 7300; www.royal.gov.uk. ◉ State Rooms: early Aug–Sep daily 9:45-3:45 (last admission 3:45). Royal Mews: Aug–Sep daily 10–5; Apr–Jul and Oct 11–4 (last admission 45 mins before closing. Closed during state visits and certain other days each year). Queen's Gallery: Oct–Jul daily 10–5:30; Aug–Sep 9:30–5:30; last admission 4:30. Closed certain days each year) ◉ Green Park, St James's Park, Victoria ◉ Piccadilly 3, 8, 9, 14, 19, 22; Victoria Street 11, 211; Grosvenor Place 2, 8, 16, 36, 38, 52, 73, 82 ◉ State Rooms: very expensive; Mews: expensive; Queen's Gallery: expensive

The Scots Guards head to Wellington Barracks after the Changing of the Guard parade

---

BUCKINGHAM PALACE: INSIDE INFO

Top tips To avoid waiting, **reserve tickets in advance** by credit card and collect them on the day. Arrangements can be made to have tickets sent out by mail. Allow seven days for United Kingdom and two to three weeks for overseas addresses.

■ You don't need to buy an **official guide** as an audio guide (available in six languages) is included in the ticket price.
■ The **Changing of the Guard** ceremony (► 53) with bands and standard bearers takes place at 11:30am in the palace forecourt and lasts 40 minutes. Try to get there by 11–11:15am to be sure of a good position – by the front railings between the gates is best.

In more detail Visit the **Royal Mews** to see the state carriages and coaches together with their horses. The collection's gem is the Gold State Coach.
■ The **Queen's Gallery** is one of the finest private collections of art in the world. Exhibitions change every six months or so. For details tel: 020 7766 7301, or visit the website (www.royal.gov.uk).

② The Mall to Trafalgar Square

The Mall is the grand, tree-lined processional avenue between Buckingham Palace and Trafalgar Square, a thoroughfare that comes into its own on ceremonial occasions such as the State Opening of Parliament in November and Trooping the Colour in June. Near the Mall are two royal parks: Green Park, which is at its best in spring when the daffodils are in flower, and St James's Park, which is a delight at any time of year.

To start your exploration, turn your back on Buckingham Palace and cross the road to the **Queen Victoria Memorial**. This white marble statue, the Mall and Admiralty Arch were laid out in the early 20th century as a memorial to Queen Victoria who died in 1901.

The Mall

These days the Mall is a busy, traffic-filled thoroughfare, albeit one whose grandeur and dignity remain majestically intact. Until the 17th century, however, it was a small country lane, its confines used by King James I to play a French game known as *palle-maille* (anglicized to pell mell). A hybrid of golf and croquet, the game has long gone out of fashion, but it is remembered in the names of the Mall and Pall Mall, one of Piccadilly's main streets. Later, King Charles II improved the area, most notably by opening St James's Park and Green Park to the public, a move that made this the fashionable spot in the capital to take a daily walk.

Looking down the Mall on the left you can see 19th-century **Clarence House**, named after its first resident, the Duke of Clarence, who became King William IV in 1830. In 1953, when Queen Elizabeth II acceded to the throne, it became the London home of the late Queen Mother. After her

The sweeping facade of Admiralty Arch

death in 2002, Prince Charles, current heir to the throne, moved here. Behind Clarence House rise the red-brick Tudor turrets of St James's Palace, built in the 1530s by Henry VIII (who died here).

From the Queen Victoria Memorial you may want to enter **St James's Park**, following shady paths towards the lake. At the bridge you have a choice: one route takes you back to the Mall, and a right turn past Carlton House Terrace, distinguished by its early 19th-century white stucco facade, leads you along the Mall to Admiralty Arch.

Nelson's Column dominates Trafalgar Square

Through to Trafalgar Square

Either way, you should take in **Horse Guards**, the huge parade ground at the park's eastern end that provides the stage for the **Changing of the Guard** (➤ Inside Info, below). Then walk through Admiralty Arch to **Trafalgar Square**, laid out in 1820 as a memorial to British naval hero Admiral Horatio Nelson, who stands three times life-size on the 52m (170-foot) column at the square's heart. Reliefs at the column's base depict four of his greatest naval victories, of which the Battle of Trafalgar against the French in 1805 – where Nelson died – was the most famous. The square's celebrated lion statues were added in the late 1860s.

The square's northern flank is dominated by the **National Gallery** (➤ 54–57), and – to its right – the fine spire of **St Martin-in-the-Fields**, a lovely church famous for its concerts and with a first-rate café and brass-rubbing centre.

TAKING A BREAK

The **Café in the Crypt** at St Martin-in-the-Fields church is a popular spot for lunch (tel: 020 7766 1158). You can enjoy a coffee, a glass of wine, a full meal or treat yourself to afternoon tea.

🕂 199 D4–F5

THE MALL TO TRAFALGAR SQUARE: INSIDE INFO

Top tips The **Changing of the Guard**, where the mounted guards change over their duties, takes place in Horse Guards Parade, off Whitehall (Mon–Sat 11am, Sun 10am). The same ceremony for foot soldiers proceeds in the forecourt of Buckingham Palace (➤ 50–51). If the weather is bad, the ceremony may be cancelled at short notice. (Daily Apr–Jul at 11:30; Aug–Dec alternate days at 11:30; tel: 020 7414 2390.)

■ **Clarence House** is normally open to the public from August to late September (tel: 020 7766 7303; www.royal.gov.uk. Admission: expensive). Visitors are given a guided tour of the ground floor.

■ In **St Martin-in-the-Fields** church free lunchtime concerts are given at 1pm on Monday, Tuesday and Friday.

❸ National Gallery

The National Gallery has one of the world's greatest collections of paintings. Covering the years from around 1250 to 1900, it presents the cream of the nation's art collection, including some 2,300 works of European art, hung in a succession of light, well-proportioned rooms. Pick a famous painter from almost any era – Botticelli, Canaletto, Cézanne, Constable, Leonardo da Vinci, Monet, Rembrandt, Renoir, Raphael, Titian, Turner, Van Gogh – and the chances are they'll be represented here.

Sainsbury Wing

The wonderfully airy Sainsbury Wing (named after the supermarket dynasty that sponsored it) was designed by architect Robert Venturi and opened in 1991. Although it is the newest part of the gallery, it displays the oldest paintings, in particular the masterpieces of the various Italian schools after about 1300. Two of its loveliest works are by **Leonardo da Vinci (Room 51)**. The unfinished *The Virgin of the Rock* (1508) depicts Mary, John the Baptist and Christ with an angel in a rocky landscape. Some of the work may be by pupils, but the sublime expression on the angel's face suggests pure Leonardo. In a specially darkened room near by, da Vinci's cartoon of *The Virgin and Child with St Anne and St John the Baptist* (*c*.1499) is an exquisite depiction of a meeting never mentioned in the Bible – Christ and his maternal grandmother.

Be certain to see **The Wilton Diptych (Room 53)**, a late 14th-century altarpiece commissioned by Richard II for his private prayers: it shows the king kneeling on the left and being presented to the Madonna and Child. Both the artist and his nationality remain a mystery. Less tantalizing but no less beautiful are two portraits – Van Eyck's *Arnolfini Portrait* (Room 56) and Giovanni Bellini's matchless *Doge Leonardo Loredan* (Room 61).

West Wing

Turn round as you cross from the Sainsbury to the West Wing for the gallery's most remarkable view – a series of receding archways designed to frame a Renaissance altarpiece on a

An allegory of motherhood – the celebrated Leonardo da Vinci cartoon (c.1499) in the National Gallery depicts the Madonna and Child with a young John the Baptist and St Anne, the mother of the Virgin Mary

The National Gallery was designed as the architectural focus of Trafalgar Square

distant wall. In the West Wing are mostly French, Italian and Dutch works from the High Renaissance. Perhaps the most memorable is Hans Holbein the Younger's *The Ambassadors* (1533) – almost life-size portraits of Jean de Dinteville and Georges de Selve (Room 4). The picture is crammed with symbol and allusion, mostly aimed at underlining the fleeting nature of earthly life. In the middle foreground of the picture is a clever *trompe l'oeil* of what appears face on to be simply a white disc; move to the right side of the painting (foot marks on the floor indicate the correct position) and it's revealed as a human skull.

North Wing

Painters who challenged the primacy of the Italians during the 16th and 17th centuries are the stars of the North Wing – Rubens, Rembrandt, Van Dyck, Velázquez, Vermeer and Claude, to name but a handful. Velázquez's *The Toilet of Venus* (also known as *The Rokeby Venus* after Rokeby Hall where it once hung) is one of the best-known paintings (Room 29). It is unusual because it shows a back view of the goddess (with an extraordinary face captured in a mirror), and because it is a nude, a genre frowned upon by the Inquisition in Spain when the work was completed in 1651.

SUGGESTED ROUTE
The gallery is divided into **four wings**, each covering a chronological period: it makes sense to visit the wings in this order:
- **Sainsbury Wing** 1250 to 1500 Rooms 51–66
- **West Wing** 1500 to 1600 Rooms 2–14
- **North Wing** 1600 to 1700 Rooms 15–32
- **East Wing** 1700 to 1900 Rooms 33–46

East Wing

The East Wing is often the busiest in the gallery, mainly because it contains some of the best-known of all British paintings. Chief among these is John Constable's *The Hay Wain* (**Room 34**), first exhibited in 1821 when the fashion was for blended brushwork and smooth painted texture: contemporary critics disapproved of what they saw as the painting's rough and unfinished nature. Today it represents an archetype of an all-but-vanished English rural landscape. More works by Constable are on display in Tate Britain (➤ 92–93) and the V&A Museum (➤ 117–120).

J M W Turner, though a contemporary of Constable, developed a radically different style. In his day he was considered madly eccentric, particularly in his later works, yet it is these mature paintings that have the most profound modern-day resonance. Two of the greatest, *The Fighting Téméraire* (1838) and *Rain, Steam and Speed* (1844), display the powerful and almost hallucinatory effects of light on air and water characteristic of the painter (Room 34). More of the same can be seen in Tate Britain's Clore Gallery (➤ 93).

Equally as popular as the Turners and Constables are the National's numerous **Impressionist masterpieces (Rooms 43 and 46)**, including a wealth of instantly recognizable paintings, such as Van Gogh's *Sunflowers* (1889) and Seurat's *The Bathers at Asnières* (1884), the latter's shimmering clarity a fitting memory to take with you back onto Trafalgar Square.

TAKING A BREAK

You can get light refreshments or a full meal at **National Dining Rooms** (➤ 63), in the Sainsbury Wing of the gallery.

Bathers at Asnières by Georges Seurat is among the best known of the National Gallery's many Impressionist masterpieces

Right: The splendid interior of the National Gallery provides a suitably grand setting for one of the greatest collections of paintings in Europe

➕ 197 F1 ✉ Trafalgar Square, WC2 ☎ 020 7747 2885; www.nationalgallery.org.uk 🕐 Sat–Thu 10–6, Fri 10–9 🍴 Restaurant and café 🚇 Charing Cross, Leicester Square 🚌 3, 6, 9, 11, 12, 13, 15, 23, 24, 29, 53, 88, 94, 139, 159, 176, 453 💷 Free; charge for special exhibitions

NATIONAL GALLERY: INSIDE INFO

Top tips The gallery displays many British artists, but many more, especially **modern British painters**, are better represented in Tate Britain's collection (► 102).

■ Two types of **audio guide** are available. You can choose one of the Themed Audio Guides, which follow themed tours, each looking at about 20 paintings, or the Gallery Audio Guide, with commentaries on more than 1,000 paintings. A highlights tour is available in 12 languages. It is nominally free (though a voluntary contribution is expected and some form of security or deposit is requested).

In more detail ArtStart in the Sainsbury Wing contains a computerized system with information on every painting and artist in the collection.

Hidden gem Most of the pictures owned by the National Gallery are on display – those not in the main galleries are in the **lower floor galleries** in the main building. Telephone before visiting to make sure that these lower galleries are open.

At Your Leisure

❹ Churchill Museum & Cabinet War Rooms

You can almost feel Churchill's presence and smell his cigar smoke and, thanks to the audio guides, you can hear his rasping voice for real as the bombs drop and the air-raid sirens sound outside. This underground warren provided secure accommodation for the War Cabinet and their military advisers during World War II and was used on more than 100 occasions. Today it is a time capsule, with the clocks stopped at 16:58 on 15 October 1940.

You can visit the Map Rooms, the Transatlantic Telephone Room, the Cabinet Room, Churchill's bedroom and a museum devoted specifically to the great British leader.

➕ 199 F4 ✉ Clive Steps, King Charles Street, SW1 ☎ 020 7930 6961 🕐 Daily 9:30–6 (last admission 5) Ⓜ Westminster, St James's Park 🚌 3,11,12, 24, 53, 77a, 88, 109, 148, 159, 211 💷 Very expensive

❺ Royal Academy of Arts

Burlington House is one of the few remaining 18th-century Piccadilly mansions. Today it houses one of London's most illustrious art galleries, the Royal Academy, which stages a variety of high-profile exhibitions. June to August sees its annual Summer Exhibition, for which every aspiring artist in the country hopes to have a piece selected. In March 2004, the Royal Academy opened its splendid 18th-century neo-Palladian suite of John Madejski Fine Rooms to provide a permanent display space for major works by Reynolds, Gainsborough, Constable, Spencer and

The Royal Academy's Summer Exhibition

Hockney, as well as the outstanding *Taddei Tondo*, one of only four marble sculptures by Michelangelo that can be seen outside Italy.

➕ 197 D1 ✉ Burlington House, Piccadilly, W1 ☎ 020 7300 8000; www.royalacademy.org.uk 🕐 Sat–Thu 10–6, Fri 10–10. Fine Rooms: Tue–Fri 1–4:30, Sat–Sun 10–6 🍴 Café and restaurant Ⓜ Piccadilly Circus, Green Park 🚌 9, 14, 22, 38 💷 Admission charge depends on the exhibition. Fine Rooms: free

[Map showing: Piccadilly Circus, Eros, Piccadilly & Regent Street ❻, Royal Academy of Arts ❺, PICCADILLY, REGENT ST, HAYMARKET, ST JAMES'S STREET, PALL MALL, Trafalgar Square ❷, Admiralty Arch, Carlton House, St James's Palace, Clarence House, The Mall ❷, Old Admiralty, Horse Guards Parade, Churchill Museum & Cabinet War Rooms ❹, WHITEHALL, PARLIAMENT ST]

❻ Piccadilly and Regent Street shopping

If you need a change from sight-seeing, visit some of London's most exclusive stores: Piccadilly, St James's and Regent Street (➤ 65–66) are home to some of London's finest.

The best of the Piccadilly shops are the old-fashioned bookstore, **Hatchards**, the high-class grocery turned department store, **Fortnum & Mason** (➤ 65), and the covered arcades of prestigious shops that lead off to left and right. **Burlington Arcade**, where top-hatted officials ensure shoppers act with due decorum (there are regulations against singing and hurrying), is the best known. Piccadilly itself was named in honour of a 17th-century tailor who made his fortune from collars known as "picadils". The mansion he built became known as Piccadilly Hall, in time lending its name to the entire street. These days much of the tailoring has moved north of Piccadilly to **Savile Row** and south to Jermyn Street (➤ 65). **Liberty** in Regent Street is a department store of class and character, with plush carpets, wood panelling and a balconied hall hung with glorious fabrics (➤ 65).

Also on Regent Street, you will find quintessential British stores, including **Burberry**; **Aquascutum**, a long-established tailors; and **Hamleys**, which features seven floors full of toys to please any child.

➕ 197 E1 ☎ www.regentstreetonline.com

Elegant Burlington Arcade

7 Piccadilly Circus

While Piccadilly Circus features large in the minds of visitors to the city (a photograph in front of the statue at its heart is almost obligatory), most Londoners dismiss it as a tacky melee of tourists, traffic and noise.

The Eros statue, which actually represents the Angel of Christian Charity not the Greek god of love, was erected in 1893 to commemorate Antony Cooper, 7th Earl of Shaftesbury (1801–85), a tireless campaigner for workers, the poor and the mentally ill. The neon advertisements were introduced in the early 20th century, and have become something of a London icon – come after dark for the best effects.

For all its faults, Piccadilly Circus is useful as a jumping-off point to other sights, heading along Shaftesbury Avenue towards Chinatown or Soho, along Coventry Street to Leicester Square, or to Regent Street and Piccadilly.

+ 197 E1

8 National Portrait Gallery

The gallery houses a fascinating and strangely beguiling collection of paintings, sculptures and photographs of eminent Britons past and present. The material dates from the early 16th century to the

modern era, and includes many of the country's most famous faces. Whatever your fields of interest, you'll almost certainly find something here to interest you.

The monarchs represented here include Richard III, Henry VII, Henry VIII, Elizabeth I (depicted several times) and many members of the present Royal Family. However, it is the portraits of non-royals that are most memorable. There is a supposed portrait of Shakespeare, a drawing of Jane Austen by her sister, a painting of the Brontë sisters by their brother Patrick and striking photographs of Oscar Wilde, Virginia Woolf and Alfred, Lord Tennyson. Among recent literary stars are Salman Rushdie and Dame Iris Murdoch.

Politicians and figures from the arts, sciences, sport and media are also well represented. Look for the portraits of British prime ministers Margaret Thatcher and Tony Blair, scientist Stephen Hawking, film director Alfred Hitchcock and soccer player David Beckham.

+ 197 F1 ✉ St Martin's Place, WC2
☎ 020 7306 0055; www.npg.org.uk
⏰ Mon–Sat 10–6 (also Thu–Fri 6–9)
Ⓠ Charing Cross, Leicester Square 🍴 Café and restaurant 🚌 3, 6, 9, 11, 12, 13, 15, 23, 24, 29, 53, 88, 91, 139, 159, 176 💷 Admission free (charge for some exhibitions)

9 Banqueting House

The Banqueting House is the only remaining part of the old Palace of Whitehall, formerly the monarch's official home, which was destroyed by fire in 1698. It was built by the great architect Inigo Jones in the early

The Contemporary Room at the National Portrait Gallery

Whitehall's elaborately decorated Banqueting House

the heart of British Government. Downing Street, a side turning blocked off by a large gate, is where the British prime minister has his (or her) official residence. Traditionally this is at No 10, while No 11 plays host to the Chancellor of the Exchequer. The only real patch of colour is provided by the mounted soldiers at Horse Guards.

At the centre of Whitehall is the Cenotaph, a memorial to the war dead and the solemn focus of the annual Remembrance Day Ceremony in November.

➕ 200 A2

17th century, and includes a painted ceiling by Flemish artist Peter Paul Rubens as its decorative centrepiece. The ceiling was commissioned in 1635 by the king, Charles I, who paid the artist £3,000, an astronomical sum at that time. This, and other paintings were all conceived as paeans to Charles's father, James I.

It was from a window of the Banqueting House that, on 30 January 1649, Charles I, tried and convicted of high treason following the defeat of Royalist forces in the English Civil War, stepped onto the scaffold and faced his executioner. As he went to his death, branded an enemy of the state, he remarked, "I have a good cause and a gracious God on my side."

➕ 200 A2 ✉ Whitehall, SW1 ☎ 0203 166 6154/5; www.hrp.org.uk ⏰ Mon–Sat 10–5; closed public hols and for functions Ⓜ Westminster, Embankment 🚌 3, 11, 12, 24, 53, 77A, 88, 159 💷 Moderate; audio guide included

🔟 Whitehall

This busy but undistinguished street lined by the bland facades of government offices takes you south from Trafalgar Square through

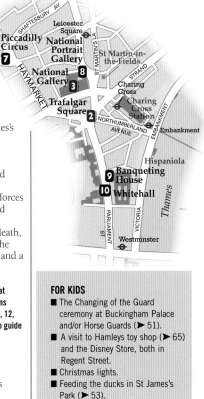

FOR KIDS

■ The Changing of the Guard ceremony at Buckingham Palace and/or Horse Guards (➤ 51).

■ A visit to Hamleys toy shop (➤ 65) and the Disney Store, both in Regent Street.

■ Christmas lights.

■ Feeding the ducks in St James's Park (➤ 53).

Where to...
Eat and Drink

Prices
Expect to pay per person for a meal excluding drinks and service:
£ under £25   ££ £25–£50   £££ over £50

Le Caprice ££

This famous restaurant, tucked neatly behind the Ritz hotel, attracts a smart celebrity crowd. Despite the stark white walls and black-and-chrome furniture, the atmosphere is far from intimidating, and the fast-paced service remains friendly at all times. The menu is a great mix of classic brasserie dishes, balanced by some more lively up-to-date ideas. Vegetarians and vegans have a good menu.

➕ 199 D5 ✉ Arlington Street, SW1
☎ 020 7629 2239; www.le-caprice.co.uk
🕑 Mon–Sat 12–3, 5.30–12, Sun 12–5, 6–11
Ⓖ Green Park

Chor Bizarre ££

This overseas branch of the New Delhi restaurant embraces its name (which means "thieves' market") with gusto, displaying a crowded and exotic collection of Indian antiques and artefacts. The menu explores the regions of India with some imagination, and provides a good choice of vegetarian dishes and tandoori favourites. Wines have been carefully chosen.

➕ 197 D1 ✉ 16 Albemarle Street, W1
☎ 020 7629 9802;
www.chorbizzarerestaurant.com
🕑 Mon–Sat 12–3, 6–11.30, Sun 12–3, 6–10.30 Ⓖ Green Park

Le Gavroche £££

Le Gavroche, London's longest-running French restaurant, is comfortable rather than opulent, with tables that are generous in size and service that is smoothly, soothingly efficient. For many years Albert Roux's classic French cooking was the solid rock on which the restaurant's seasonally changing menus were built, but now that son Michel has taken over, ideas, although firmly rooted in that same classic tradition, have moved with the times. The cooking is still confident and skilled, but with a lighter touch. The wine list is aristocratic, with prices to match.

➕ 196 B1 ✉ 43 Upper Brook Street, W1
☎ 020 7408 0881/7499 1826;
www.le-gavroche.co.uk 🕑 Mon–Fri 12–2, 6:30–11, Sat 6:30–11 Ⓖ Marble Arch

Greenhouse £££

Smart Mayfair restaurant where chef Antonin Bonnet serves exciting yet serious food using fascinating techniques from around the world. Feast on such delights as rump of Limousin veal sweetbread with wild garlic caramel and glazed leek or saddle of lamb accompanied by baby carrots, smoked cumin polenta, coffee reduction and lemon caramel. The desserts are delightful, and the restaurant has what must be one of London's most extensive wine lists. The tableside stools for ladies to put their handbags on add a nice touch.

➕ 196 C1 ✉ Hay's Mews, W1
☎ 020 7499 3331;
www.greenhouserestaurant.co.uk
🕑 Mon–Fri 12–2:30pm, Mon–Sat 6:45–11pm
Ⓖ Green Park

Inn the Park £–££

The lovely setting in the heart of Royal St James' Park, overlooking the lake, makes this stylish restaurant and self-service café a popular spot to hang out. The approach is good, simple, British seasonal fare and all dishes are freshly prepared, from tasty breakfasts and mouth-watering cakes, to sandwiches, traditional pies and Sunday roasts. In summer the place is buzzing, and there is a rooftop bar and alfresco dining area to take advantage of during milder weather. In the colder months hearty warming dishes come into their own.

➕ 199 E5 ☒ St. James's Park, SW1
☎ 020 7451 9999; www.innthepark.com
⌚ Mon–Fri 8–5, Sat, Sun 9–5; dinner daily from 5pm ⓔ St. James's Park, Green Park, Charing Cross

La Madeleine £

This truly French café lies just off Regent Street. Kick-start the day with a buttery croissant and make a light lunch of a croque-monsieur or a range of salads. At any time of the day a vast array of tarts, pastries and all sorts of cream-filled delights will be appropriate. The staff are charming, and there is limited seating on the terrace outside.

➕ 197 D1 ☒ 5 Vigo Street, W1
☎ 020 7734 8353 ⌚ Mon–Sat 8–7, Sun 11–6 ⓔ Green Park, Piccadilly

Mirabelle ££

Thanks to Marco Pierre White (▶ 39), Mirabelle is one of the most glamorous places to eat in London, serving MPW's trademark first-class classic French-style cooking. The restaurant's revamped decor matches an easier, less formal style, though tables are perhaps a little too close together. Lunch is especially good value, with the reasonably priced menu ensuring that the place is packed. Get a reservation for a patio table in fine weather.

➕ 198 C5 ☒ 56 Curzon Street, W1
☎ 020 7499 4636; ⌚ Lunch: daily 12–2:30 (also Sat–Sun 2:30–3). Dinner: Mon–Sat 6–11:30, Sun 6–10:30 ⓔ Green Park

Mitsukoshi ££

This smart, comfortable restaurant is on the lower level of a Japanese department store. The à la carte selection includes classic Japanese dishes, but choosing one of the many set meals will give an excellent introduction to the cuisine. Go for a simple *hana*, which includes an appetizer, tempura, grilled fish, miso soup and pickles, the seven-course chef's special (ordered in advance) or the sushi menu.

➕ 197 E1 ☒ Dorland House, 14–20 Lower Regent Street, SW1 ☎ 020 7930 0317; www.mitsukoshi-restaurant.co.uk ⌚ Lunch: daily 12–2. Tea daily 2–5. Dinner: daily 6–10 ⓔ Piccadilly Circus

National Dining Rooms £–££

Climb the wide, stone staircase of the National Gallery's Sainsbury Wing, take a sharp left turn, and enter this quintessentially British restaurant. The bright, modern dining room is divided into a bakery-cum-café and a lunch-only restaurant, and the menu created by head chef Jesse Dunford Wood provides classic, regional dishes. Large picture windows give fine views over Trafalgar Square.

➕ 197 F1 ☒ The National Gallery, WC2
☎ 020 7747 2525 ⌚ Daily 10–5 (Fri until 8:30) ⓔ Charing Cross

Nicole's ££

This is a fashionable place in every respect, from the chic setting in the basement of Nicole Farhi's Bond Street store to the ladies-that-lunch who come to toy with the light, ultra-modish food. The restaurant's less figure-conscious clientele will be equally satisfied – an earthier approach can be discerned with such rustic fare as duck confit appearing on the menu. Breakfast is served from 8 to 11:30.

➕ 196 C2 ☒ 158 New Bond Street, W1
☎ 020 7499 8408; www.nicolefarhi.com
⌚ Daily 8–5:30 ⓔ Green Park, Bond Street

Nobu £££

Nobuyuki Matsuhisa brings the full force of his pan-American experience (which ranges from restaurants in the United States to travels in South America) to bear on the first floor of the seriously chic Metropolitan Hotel. This is the ultimate place to see-and-be-seen. The combination of the ultra-modern interior and the trendy clientele add up to an irresistible package, especially when New York-style service and spiced-up Japanese cooking are thrown into the equation. Reservations essential.

198 C5 ⊠ **Metropolitan Hotel, 19 Old Park Lane, W1** ☎ **020 7447 4747; www.noburestaurants.com** Ⓛ Lunch: Mon–Fri 12–2:15, Sat–Sun 12:30–2:30. Dinner: Mon–Fri 6–10:15, Sat 6–11, Sun 6–9:30 Ⓤ **Hyde Park Corner, Green Park**

Quaglino's ££

Make an entrance down the sweeping staircase, feel the buzz and experience a bit of Hollywood glitz. This is the most glamorous of the Conran mega-restaurants and it's a slick experience. You can just go for a drink in the bar or try out a menu that has a strong French bistro feel. If you prefer, traditional English classics such as fish and chips with tartare sauce are on offer. The crustacea bar is a major feature.

199 D5 ⊠ **16 Bury Street,**

St James's, SW1 ☎ **020 7930 6767; www.quaglinos.co.uk** Ⓛ Lunch: daily 12–3. Dinner: Mon–Thu 5:30–10:30, Fri–Sat 5:30–12 Ⓤ **Green Park**

Rasa W1 £–££

Das Sreedharan opened this lavish, spacious restaurant after the huge success of his first restaurant in East London. His exquisite vegetarian food from the Kerala region is considered to be some of the best Indian cooking in town, and meat dishes drawing upon the influences found in the north of Kerala are also available. The menu offers a wide range of poppadums, stuffed pastries, curries, dosas, lentil patties and some excellent breads. Several of the curries feature banana – as more than 250 varieties are grown in Kerala. Fish lovers shouldn't miss the *kappayum menum*, a spicy dish with king fish, chillies and ginger.

196 C2 ⊠ **6 Dering Street, W1** ☎ **020 7629 1346; www.rasarestaurants.com** Ⓛ Mon–Sat 12–3, 6–11 Ⓤ **Oxford Circus**

Sotheby's Café ££

One of Bond Street's best-kept secrets is tucked away in the lobby of Sotheby's auction house. Join the café's cosmopolitan clientele for stylish lunches and afternoon tea.

196 C2 ⊠ **34 Bond Street, W1** ☎ **020 7293 5077** Ⓛ Mon–Fri 9:30–11:30, 12–4:45 Ⓤ **Bond Street**

The Square £££

Nigel Platts-Martin's exceptional restaurant combines the allure of chic, spacious premises with a prestigious setting – just a short distance from Berkeley Square. His highly regarded chef and partner, Philip Howard, offers imaginative, yet classically based, Modern French cooking. Dishes are prepared with great attention to detail and champion free-range and organic produce.

196 C1 ⊠ **6 Bruton Street, W1** ☎ **020 7495 7100; www.squarerestaurant.com** Ⓛ Lunch: Mon–Fri 12–2:30. Dinner: Mon–Sat 6:30–10, Sun 6:30–9:30 Ⓤ **Bond Street**

Tamarind ££

This prestigious Indian restaurant serves an imaginative interpretation of Indian regional cooking in its discreetly designed basement dining room. Dishes are prepared with imported herbs and spices to create some truly memorable flavours.

198 C5 ⊠ **20 Queen Street, W1** ☎ **020 7629 3561; www.tamarindrestaurant.com** Ⓛ Lunch: Mon–Fri, Sun 12–2:45. Dinner: Mon–Sat 5:30–11, Sun 6–10:30 Ⓤ **Green Park**

The Wolseley £–££

The award-winning Wolseley is housed in an opulent art deco building, once home to a bank, resplendent with chandeliers and marble pillars. Despite its grandeur it is friendly, serves excellent Modern British café-style food throughout the day and is perfect for breakfast or afternoon tea.

199 D5 ⊠ **160 Piccadilly, W1** ☎ **020 7499 6996; www.thewolseley.com** Ⓛ Mon–Fri 7am–midnight, Sat 8am–midnight, Sun 8am–11pm Ⓤ **Green Park**

Where to...
Shop

SAVILE ROW AND JERMYN STREET

Savile Row (Tube: Piccadilly Circus) is synonymous with top-quality men's clothes made to order. There are several long-established tailors here: try either **Henry Poole** (15 Savile Row, W1, tel: 020 7734 5985), founded in 1806, or **Kilgour, French & Stanbury** (8 Savile Row, W1, tel: 020 7734 6905), dating from 1882.

Jermyn Street (Tube: Piccadilly Circus) has the monopoly on men's shirt makers. Try **Turnbull & Asser** (71–72 Jermyn Street, W1, tel: 020 7808 3000), **Harvie & Hudson** (77 Jermyn Street, W1, tel: 020 7930 3949), and **Hilditch & Key** (73 Jermyn Street, W1, tel: 020 7930 5336).

REGENT STREET

Regent Street (Tube: Piccadilly Circus) is home to stores on a grand scale. **Aquascutum** (100 Regent Street, W1, tel: 020 7675 8200) is *the* place to buy the classic English raincoat and tailored, tweedy jackets for both men and women, **Burberry** (157–167 Regent Street, W1, tel: 020 7968 0000) is the home of the distinctive English trenchcoat, and **Austin Reed** (103–113 Regent Street, W1, tel: 020 7734 6789) is good for Savile Row-style clothes at lower prices. At the Oxford Circus end of Regent Street is the famed store **Liberty** (210–220 Regent Street, W1, tel: 020 7734 1234. Tube: Oxford Circus). Even the facade, a mock-Tudor extravaganza, exudes great character. Within, the shop is a treasure trove of antique oriental carpets, furnishings, fabrics and leather goods, as well as cutting-edge fashion, luxury cosmetics and wonderful accessories.

Hamleys (188–196 Regent Street, W1, tel: 0870 333 2455. Tube: Piccadilly Circus) is one of the world's largest toy stores. Prices are higher than elsewhere and at weekends it's packed, but there are magic tricks and demonstrations.

PICCADILLY

Fortnum & Mason is a London institution (181 Piccadilly, W1, tel: 020 7734 8040. Tube: Piccadilly Circus). Its renowned food emporium sells everything from own-brand marmalades, teas and condiments to hams, pâtes, cheeses, bread and fruit. It is less well known as an excellent department store with up-to-date women's designer fashions and a splendid stationery and gift section.

The Piccadilly branch of **Waterstones** (203–206 Piccadilly, tel: 020 7851 2400. Tube: Piccadilly Circus), is where to go if you are looking for a good holiday read.

BOND STREET

Bond Street is a showcase for fast-paced, high-fashion, major international designers and their innovative stores, none more so than **Donna Karan** (46 Conduit Street, W1, tel: 020 7479 7900. Tube: Bond Street), **Gucci** (34 Old Bond Street, W1, tel: 020 7629 2716. Tube: Piccadilly Circus) and **Emporio Armani** (51–52 New Bond Street, W1, tel: 020 7491 8080. Tube: Bond Street).

Formerly a jeweller, **Asprey** (167 New Bond Street, W1, tel: 020 7493 6767. Tube: Bond Street) relaunched itself in 2004 as a luxury lifestyle emporium. Also setting out their wares are jewellers such as **Tiffany & Co** (25 Old Bond Street, W1, tel: 020 7409

Where to...
Be Entertained

CINEMA

The **Curzon Mayfair** (38 Curzon Street, W1, tel: 0871 7033 989. Tube: Green Park) shows art-house, foreign and some mainstream movies. **The Institute of Contemporary Arts (ICA)** (Nash House, The Mall, W1, tel: 020 7930 3647. Tube: Charing Cross) has a small cinema and hosts groupings of films linked by director, style or theme. It is known for its unusual and sometimes challenging films. **Prince Charles Cinema** (7 Leicester Place, WC2, tel: 0870 811 2559. Tube: Leicester Square, Piccadilly Circus) is an independent cinema offering low prices and a wide programme, including contemporary films, sing-along shows and classics.

CLUBS

100 Club (100 Oxford Street, W1, tel: 020 7636 0933. Tube: Oxford Circus), where The Rolling Stones, The Kinks, The Sex Pistols and The Clash have all played, follows an eclectic booking policy that also takes in traditional jazz, blues, jive and many other styles.

COMEDY

If you enjoy hard-hitting stand-up comedy, head for **The Comedy Store** (1a Oxendon Street, W1, recorded information tel: 0844 847 1728. Tube: Piccadilly Circus). Shows start at 8pm (Tue–Sun), but for the best seats get to the venue when the doors open at 6:30pm.

OXFORD STREET

Here you'll find big department stores. **John Lewis** (278–306 Oxford Street, W1, tel: 020 7629 7711. Tube: Oxford Circus) sells everything from fabrics to computers, **Marks & Spencer**, at both Marble Arch (458 Oxford Street, W1, tel: 020 7935 7954. Tube: Marble Arch) and north of Oxford Circus (173 Oxford Street, W1, tel: 020 7437 7722. Tube: Bond Street) is good for wardrobe staples. **Selfridges** (400 Oxford Street, W1, tel: 0800 123 400. Tube: Bond Street) has cosmetics, fashions, and a food hall with various cafés. In 2009 **Topshop** opened the largest fashion store in the world (36–38 Great Castle Street, tel: 0844 848 7487. Tube: Oxford Circus).

SOUTH MOLTON STREET

On South Molton Street there are smaller, quirkier boutiques, among them **Browns** (24–27 South Molton Street, W1, tel: 020 7514 0016. Tube: Bond Street) – a series of interconnected little shops at the knife-edge of fashion.

2790. Tube: Piccadilly Circus) and **Cartier** (175 New Bond Street, W1, tel: 020 7408 5700. Tube: Bond Street), two great auction houses, **Sotheby's** (34–35 New Bond Street, W1, tel: 020 7293 5000. Tube: Bond Street) and **Bonhams** (101 New Bond Street, W1, tel: 020 7447 7447. Tube: Bond Street), and representatives of the art- and antiques-dealing world, notably the **Fine Art Society** (148 New Bond Street, W1, tel: 020 7629 5116. Tube: Bond Street). Here, too, is **Fenwick** (63 New Bond Street, W1, tel: 020 7629 9161. Tube: Bond Street), a fashion-orientated department store.

Gray's Antique Market (1–7 Davies Mews, W1, tel: 020 7629 7034. Tube: Bond Street) is noted for jewellery and oriental artefacts.

The City

Getting Your Bearings

The City of London, the commercial heart of the capital, is one of the busiest financial centres in the world, with banks, corporate headquarters and insurance companies occupying dramatic showcases of modern architecture. Yet alongside the glass-and-steel office buildings, you find beautiful 17th-century churches, cobbled alleyways, historic markets and even fragments of the original Roman city wall.

The modern City stands on the site of the Roman settlement of Londinium, and has long been a centre of finance and government. Historically, it had an identity separate to that of the rest of the capital. When Edward the Confessor moved his palace from the City of London to Westminster in 1042, the area retained some of its ancient privileges, and later in the 14th century secured charters granting it the right to elect its own mayor and council. Even the

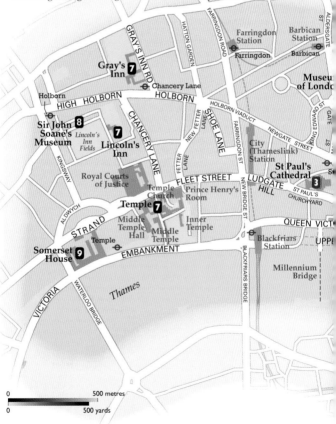

sovereign could not enter the City without formal permission. Today, the legacy of these privileges still survives. The Corporation of London, the successor to the original council, which is overseen by the Lord Mayor, administers the City through council meetings held in the Guildhall.

Much of the medieval City was destroyed by the Great Fire of 1666 (➤ 12), although the Tower of London survived. In the construction boom that followed, architect Sir Christopher Wren was commissioned to build more than 50 churches, the most prominent and well-known of which is St Paul's Cathedral. Many of the lesser-known Wren churches survived the severe bombing of World War II, and remain tucked away in quiet streets.

The City is also home to the modern Barbican Centre, a performing arts complex, as well as the acclaimed Museum of London, where the story of the capital is brought to life. On the western boundary of the City lie the historic Inns of Court, the heart of legal London. Next to Lincoln's Inn is Sir John Soane's Museum, a 19th-century time capsule, while back on the river, Somerset House is home to the Courtauld Gallery, a collection of paintings, ranging from the Gothic to the 20th century, sculpture and decorative arts.

★ Don't Miss

1. Tower of London ➤ 72
2. Tower Bridge ➤ 76
3. St Paul's Cathedral ➤ 78

At Your Leisure

4. Leadenhall Market ➤ 80
5. Bank of England Museum ➤ 80
6. Museum of London ➤ 80
7. Inns of Court ➤ 81
8. Sir John Soane's Museum ➤ 82
9. Somerset House ➤ 83

Page 67: Detail of St Paul's Cathedral

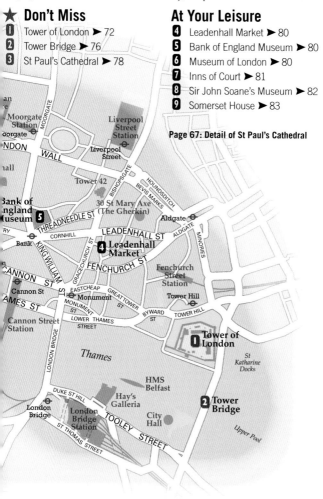

In a Day

If you're not quite sure where to begin your travels, this itinerary recommends a practical and enjoyable day out in the City, taking in some of the best places to see using the Getting Your Bearings map on the previous page. For more information see the main entries.

9:00am

Try to be at the **1** Tower of London (left, ➤ 72–75) as it opens (at 10am on Sunday and Monday) to beat the worst of the crowds, even if this means you may get caught up in the morning rush hour. The rewards are the Crown Jewels, ravens, Beefeaters and an insight into the long and often bloody history of London from the perspective of its famous fortress. You can buy your entrance ticket in advance from any Underground station.

11:30am

Walk up on to nearby **2** Tower Bridge (below, ➤ 76–77) and visit the Tower Bridge Exhibition for

an excellent history of the structure. Stunning views of the River Thames make the climb to the top worthwhile.

1:00pm
Take a break for lunch. For top-quality fare head across to the south bank of the river to Cantina del Ponte (➤ 108). Reservations are recommended.

2:15pm
Walk back across the bridge and catch the No 15 bus from Tower Hill, the main road to the north of the Tower, which will deliver you outside St Paul's Cathedral.

3:00pm
Climb up to the galleries at the top of the dome of **3 St Paul's Cathedral** (above, ➤ 78–79) for magnificent views of the city. Stop for a coffee in the café in the crypt, then soak up the magnificence of the architecture and artefacts around you.

5:00pm
If possible, stay on in St Paul's for evensong – the times of services are posted inside and outside the cathedral (or visit their website).

To move on from St Paul's, catch the No 15 bus back to Trafalgar Square or use St Paul's Underground station, which is just beside the cathedral.

❶ Tower of London

The Tower of London has always fascinated visitors – even 300 years ago it was a popular attraction – and today it is one of the country's top tourist sights. Begun by William the Conqueror shortly after the 1066 conquest, it has survived for more than 900 years as a palace, prison, place of execution, arsenal, royal mint and jewel house. Throughout this time it has remained woven into the fabric of London and its history, while maintaining its essential character as a fortress and self-contained world within the defensive walls.

The Crown Jewels

Begin your exploration of the Tower by visiting the Jewel House, where the Crown Jewels are on display. You may have a long wait to see the collection, one of the richest in the world, but there is archive footage of the Coronation of Queen Elizabeth II to put you in the mood while you wait, providing a prelude to and preview of the exhibition. The most dazzling piece in the collection is the **Imperial State Crown**, used by the monarch at the State Opening of Parliament in October or November, and crusted with 2,868 diamonds, 273 pearls, 17 sapphires, 11 emeralds and 5 rubies. Among the collection's other treasures is the **Sovereign's Sceptre**, which contains the world's largest cut diamond, Cullinan I. Also worth a look is the crown of the late Queen Elizabeth the Queen Mother. It contains the fabulous Koh-i-Noor diamond, which is only

ever used in a woman's crown as it is believed to bring bad luck to men.

For fascinating background on the Crown Jewels, visit the "Crowns and Diamonds" display in the Martin Tower, accessed via the Salt Tower, whose walls bear graffiti carved by prisoners.

Tower Green

This benign-looking spot was the place of execution of seven high-ranking prisoners, the most notable of whom were Anne Boleyn

Left: The Tower of London was begun in 1066, its position affording clear views of any enemy forces that might approach up the Thames

Above: The Royal Room in the White Tower

and Catherine Howard, Henry VIII's second and fifth wives (both beheaded following charges of adultery and treason). Execution here was an option reserved for the illustrious – less socially elevated prisoners met a much slower, more painful end on nearby Tower Hill. The executioner's axe and block are on display in the White Tower.

The White Tower

The Tower's oldest and most striking feature is the White Tower, begun around 1078, its basic form having remained unchanged for more than 900 years. Today its highlight is a superlative collection of armour, a display that manages to be awe-inspiring and strangely beautiful at the same time. Henry VIII's personal armour is the main attraction, but smaller pieces, such as the suits crafted for young boys, are equally interesting. Be sure to see the evocative St John's Chapel on the first floor, one of England's earliest remaining church interiors, and also take a peep into some of the tower's "garderobes" – 11th-century lavatories.

The Bloody Tower

Not all prisoners in the Tower lived – and died – in terrible conditions. Some passed their time in more humane lodgings. One such prisoner was Sir Walter Raleigh, explorer, philosopher and scientist, who was held in the Bloody Tower from 1603 to 1616, accused of plotting against James I. The Tower's most notorious incumbents, partly the reason for its

THE TOWER RAVENS

Ravens have been associated with the Tower throughout its history. Legend tells how King Charles II wanted to get rid of the birds, but was told that if they ever left the White Tower the kingdom would fall and disaster would strike. No chances are taken these days – one wing of each raven is clipped.

name, were the "Princes in the Tower". Following the death of King Edward IV in 1483, the princes – the King's sons Edward (the heir to the throne) and his younger brother Richard – were put in the Tower under the "protection" of their uncle, Richard, Duke of Gloucester. However, the boys mysteriously vanished and, in their absence, their uncle was crowned King Richard III. The skeletons of two boys, presumed to be those of the princes, were found hidden in the White Tower 200 years later. Richard's involvement, or otherwise, in the boys' death has been much debated since, but never proved one way or the other.

The Medieval Palace

The entrance to the Medieval Palace lies just beside the infamous Traitors' Gate, the river entrance to the Tower

Above: The Tower seen across the River Thames

Right: Traitor's Gate was the entrance to the Tower from the river

Below: The forbidding walls of the Tower

BEEFEATERS

The tower's guards, or Yeoman Warders, are commonly known as Beefeaters – believed to be due to them being able to eat as much beef as they liked from the King's table. About 35 in number, they all have a military background, and perform ceremonial duties around the Tower – they'll also answer your questions and give you directions.

through which many prisoners arrived for their execution. The palace is laid out as it would have been in Edward I's reign (1272–1307), and staffed by costumed guides.

From the palace you should stroll along the Wall Walk on the Tower's south side, a route that offers fine views of Tower Bridge (➤ 76–77). This route also takes you through the Wakefield Tower, in whose upper chamber Edward I's throne room has been dramatically reconstructed.

TAKING A BREAK

The cafés of nearby **Leadenhall Market** (➤ 80) are a great place to stop for a coffee or a light lunch. Alternatively, the Tower has its own restaurant and café.

🚩 202 C3 ✉ Tower Hill, EC3 ☎ 0870 756 6060; www.hrp.org.uk 🕐 Mar–Oct Tue–Sat 9–5:30, Sun–Mon 10–5:30; Nov–Feb Tue–Sat 9–4:30, Sun–Mon 10–4:30. Last admission 30 min before closing 🍴 Café and restaurant 🚇 Tower Hill 🚌 15, 25, 42, 78, 100, RV1 💷 Very expensive

---

TOWER OF LONDON: INSIDE INFO

Top tips Come **early** in the morning to avoid the crowds.
- Buy admission tickets at one of the nearby Tube stations to **avoid a long wait** at the main ticket office.
- On arrival, head straight for the Jewel House and visit the **Crown Jewels** – this is the Tower's most popular attraction and soon becomes crowded.
- Be **flexible** in your approach to what you visit and when: if one part of the Tower is busy, give it a miss and return later.
- If you have time, the Yeoman Warders (Beefeaters) lead free, hour-long **guided tours**, departing every 30 mins (until 3:30 in summer, 2:30 in winter), throughout the day. Most of the guides are great characters and bring the history of the Tower wonderfully alive.

❷ Tower Bridge

Tower Bridge is one of London's most familiar landmarks and the views from its upper walkway are some of the city's best, yet it has occupied its prominent place on the capital's skyline for only a little over 100 years.

By the late 1800s, crossing the River Thames had become a major problem. London Bridge was then the city's most easterly crossing, but more than a third of the population lived even further east. Building a new bridge, however, posed a dilemma for architects and planners. Any construction had to allow tall-masted ships to reach the Upper Pool, one of the busiest stretches of river in the world, handling ships and goods from all corners of the British Empire. It also needed to be strong and adaptable enough to allow for the passage

Opened in 1894, Tower Bridge is one of the most recognizable bridges in the world

TOWER BRIDGE: INSIDE INFO

Top tips Try to see the **bridge lifting**; tel: 020 7940 3984 or visit the website for times.

■ Make a return visit to see the bridge at **night-time** – it looks fabulous when spot-lit.

■ Even if you choose not to visit the exhibition, don't miss the magnificent view from either of the **bridge's piers**.

of motor and horse-drawn vehicles. Though designs had been submitted to Parliament since the 1850s (more than 50 were rejected), it wasn't until 1886 that one was finally approved. The plan for a remarkable lifting roadway (known as a "bascule" bridge after the French word for see-saw), was the brainchild of architect Horace Jones and engineer John Wolfe Barry.

Access to the bridge's towers and walkways is via the **Tower Bridge Exhibition**, a display of film, artefacts and photographs explaining the history, construction and operation of the bridge. You also get to visit the original Victorian engine rooms, which were used to power the bridge right up until 1976.

The highlight of your visit, however, is the view from the upper walkway, where there are also some fascinating archive photographs, as well as interactive computers which offer more detail on Tower Bridge and the surrounding area.

TAKING A BREAK

If you fancy a treat, head across to the south bank of the river for lunch at **Cantina del Ponte** (► 108). The food is great, as are views of the bridge.

➕ 202 C3 ☎ 020 7403 3761, www.towerbridge.org.uk
🕐 Apr–Sep daily 10–6:30; Oct–Mar 9:30–6. Last entry 1 hour before closing time 🚇 Tower Hill, London Bridge 🚌 15, 25, 40, 42, 47, 78, 100, RV1 💷 Expensive

VITAL STATISTICS

■ The bridge took eight years to build.

■ Its structure is brick and steel, but it is clad in Portland stone and granite to complement the nearby Tower of London.

■ Tower Bridge is made up of more than 27,000 tonnes of bricks, enough to build around 350 detached homes.

■ Each moving bascule weighs 1,200 tonnes.

■ The height from the road to the upper walkways is 33m (108 feet).

❸ St Paul's Cathedral

The towering dome of St Paul's Cathedral has stood sentinel over London for around 300 years, a lasting testament to the revolutionary genius of its architect, Sir Christopher Wren. Innovative and controversial, the cathedral rose from the ashes of the Great Fire of London in the 17th century, making it a positive youngster when compared with the medieval cathedrals of most European countries. Centuries later it became a symbol of London's unbeatable spirit, standing proud throughout the wartime Blitz of 1940–41. Later again it was the scene of national events, such as the wedding of Prince Charles to the late Diana, Princess of Wales (then Lady Diana Spencer) in 1981.

VITAL STATISTICS
- The cathedral's largest bell, Great Paul, which weighs 17 tonnes, is rung at 1pm every day for 5 minutes.
- The distance from ground level to the very top of the cross on the cathedral's roof measures just short of 112m (368 feet).
- The clock, Big Tom, on the right-hand tower on the cathedral's West Front, is 5m (16 feet) in diameter and the minute hand 3m (10 feet) in length.

ST PAUL'S CATHEDRAL: INSIDE INFO

Top tip Guided tours (90 mins; additional charge) run at 10:45, 11:15, 1:30 and 2. Audio tours in eight languages are also available from 9 to 3:30.

Hidden gem The choir, one of the finest in the world, sing on Sunday at 11:30am (Eucharist) and 3:15pm (evensong). **Evensong** on weekdays is usually at 5pm, but check on the lists posted at the cathedral or the website.

Looking up at the dome of St Paul's Cathedral

On first entering the cathedral, via the **West Front** between the towers, take a few moments to just soak up the building's grandeur. Soaring arches lead the eye towards the huge space below the main dome, and on to a series of smaller, decorated domes that rise above the choir and distant high altar.

Move to the centre of the nave, marked by an intricate black-and-white compass pattern and a memorial to Wren, which includes the line "Reader, if you seek his monument, look around you". Looking up into the **dome** from here you can admire the Whispering Gallery, the monochrome frescoes by 18th-century architectural painter Sir James Thornhill (1716–19) of the life of St Paul, and the windows in the upper lantern. The ceiling's shimmering mosaics, completed in the 1890s, are made from around 30 million pieces of glass.

Then take in the area around the **altar**, a part of the cathedral filled with exquisite works of art. Master woodcarver Grinling Gibbons designed the limewood choir stalls, and Jean Tijou, a Huguenot refugee, created the intricate ironwork gates (both were completed in 1720). The canopy, based on a bronze canopy in St Peter's, Rome, is made of English oak and dates from as recently as 1958.

The Galleries and Crypt

The dome's three galleries are open to the public and are all unmissable if you've the time, energy and a head for heights. The best interior views come from the **Whispering Gallery** (259 steps). The gallery's name describes the strange acoustic effect that allows something said on one side of the gallery to be heard on the other. For panoramas of London you'll need to climb to the top two galleries, the **Stone Gallery** (378 steps) and the **Golden Gallery** (a further 152 steps).

Downstairs is the **crypt**, a peaceful, atmospheric space, with around 200 graves and memorials, the grandest of which belong to heroes such as Admiral Lord Nelson and the Duke of Wellington, who defeated Napoleon at Waterloo in 1815.

TAKING A BREAK

St Paul's offers two options: the **Refectory** self-service restaurant (open Mon–Sun 12–3); and the **Crypt Café** (Mon–Sat 9–5 Sun 12–4), ideal for a light lunch or afternoon tea.

➕ 201 E4 ☎ 020 7236 4128; www.stpauls.co.uk ✉ Ludgate Hill, EC4 🕐 Mon–Sat 8:30–4:30 (last admission 4) 🍴 Café and restaurant 🚇 St Paul's 🚌 4, 11, 15, 17, 23, 25, 26, 100, 172 💷 Very expensive; free for Sun service

At Your Leisure

4 Leadenhall Market

This iron-and-glass Victorian food hall, built on the site of an ancient medieval market, now caters for the needs of City workers, with plenty of eating places, tailors, shoe shops, bookshops, chemists and grocers. The huge glass roof and finely renovated and painted ironwork, plus the bustle of the crowds, make this one of the best places in the City to browse, grab a snack or linger over lunch.

🖪 202 B4 ✉ Whittington Avenue, EC3 ⏰ Mon–Fri 7–4 🚇 Monument 🚌 25, 40

5 Bank of England Museum

You won't see mountains of gold, but the material that is on display is surprisingly interesting – and is helped along by an excellent audio guide. There are a couple of gold ingots on show, which always draw a big crowd, but more fascinating are the displays explaining how bank notes are printed and the complex security devices employed to beat counterfeiters. If you fancy yourself as a financial whizz-kid, there are interactive computer programs that allow you to simulate trading on the foreign exchange markets – after a few minutes trying to get to grips with the processes you can see how real City superstars begin to justify their huge salaries.

🖪 202 A4 ✉ Bartholomew Lane, EC2 ☎ 020 7601 5545; www.bankofengland.co.uk ⓘ The lower galleries are due to re-open in spring 2010, following a major redevelopment 🚇 Bank 🚌 4, 8, 17, 21, 25, 26, 43, 48, 76, 133, 141, 149, 172, 242 💷 Free

6 Museum of London

This fascinating museum details the story of London from prehistoric times to the present day, its magnificent array of exhibits laid out chronologically to present a cogent and colourful account of the city's evolution.

The Roman Gallery is particularly well illustrated, and includes excellent reconstructions of Roman-era rooms. Look also for the panelled 17th-century interior of a prosperous merchant's home, complete with appropriate music, and the streets of Victorian shops, with the requisite fittings and goods.

On a smaller scale, the working model of the Great Fire of London, accompanied by the words of contemporary diarist Samuel Pepys, is an excellent illustration of the drama of this cataclysmic event (► 12–14). Perhaps the most gorgeous exhibit, however, is the Lord Mayor's

The Barbican

Barbican Centre

Moorgate Station

Museum of London 6

LONDON WALL

MOORGATE

Guildhall

Tower 42

BISHOPSGATE

HOUNDSDITCH

BEVIS MARKS

NEWGATE STREET

KING EDWARD ST

ALDERS. GATE

ST MARTIN'S LE GRAND

Bank of England Museum 5

POULTRY

Bank

THREADNEEDLE ST

CORNHILL

30 St Mary Axe (The Gherkin)

LEADENHALL ST

Leadenhall Market 4

GRACECHURCH ST

FENCHURCH ST

Leadenhall Market is one of London's popular venues for fresh produce, shops and eateries

Coach, commissioned in 1757. A confection of colour and ornament, it is covered in magnificent carvings and sculptures and has panels by the Florentine artist Cipriani decorating its sides. The coach is still used during the annual Lord Mayor's Parade in November, and the coronation of a new sovereign.

🔁 201 F5 ⊠ London Wall, EC2 ☎ 020 7001 9844; www.museumoflondon.org.uk ⏰ Daily 10–6; last admission 5:30 🍴 Café 🚇 St Paul's, Barbican 🚌 4, 8, 25, 56, 100, 172, 242, 521 💷 Free

⑦ Inns of Court

Entered through narrow, easy-to-miss gateways, the four Inns of Court are a world away from the busy city outside. Their ancient buildings, well-kept gardens and hushed atmosphere create an aura of quiet industry. Home to London's legal profession, the Inns began life in the 14th century as hostels where lawyers stayed. Until the 19th century, the only way to obtain legal qualifications was to serve an apprenticeship at the Inns, and even today barristers must be members of an Inn.

While most of the buildings are private, some are open to the public; even if you don't see inside any of the august institutions it is enough simply to wander the small lanes and cobbled alleyways, stumbling upon unexpected courtyards and gardens and breathing the rarefied legal air.

FOR KIDS
- Tower of London (▶ 72–75)
- St Paul's Cathedral galleries (▶ 79)
- Museum of London (▶ 80)

The way to see the Inns is to start at the Temple and then walk to Lincoln's Inn and Gray's Inn.

Inner and Middle Temple

Temple Church, consecrated in 1185, originally had links with the Knights Templar, a confraternity of soldier monks established to protect pilgrims travelling to the Holy Land. This may account for the building's unusual circular plan, which mirrors that of the Church of the Holy Sepulchre in Jerusalem. The floor of the church has ancient effigies of the Knights' patrons, though date from after the 13th century as the Knights fell out of favour and the Order was abolished in 1312. The church is a quiet oasis in a busy part of the city.

The imposing **Middle Temple Hall**, where it is said Queen Elizabeth I attended the first performance of Shakespeare's *Twelfth Night*, retains its 16th-century oak-panelled interior.

🔁 200 C4 ⊠ Access from Fleet Street, just opposite end of Chancery Lane, EC4

ST OLAVE'S CHURCH RECITALS
This tiny, medieval church had a lucky escape when it was spared the ravages of the Great Fire of London in 1666 (▶ 12–14) by a sudden change of wind direction. The church was restored after wartime bombing, it has been restored. It is the burial place of famed diary-keeper Samuel Pepys, who used to worship at the church. Every Wednesday and Thursday lunchtime (except August) at 1:05pm there are free classical music recitals, a tradition of more than 50 years. A donation is welcomed though.

🔁 202 B3 ⊠ Hart Street, EC3 ⏰ Mon–Fri 10–5, recitals: Wed–Thu 1:05 🚇 Aldgate, Tower Hill

🌐 Middle Temple Hall: usually Mon–Fri 10–12, 3–4, but it can be closed if there is a function taking place 🚇 Temple

Lincoln's Inn

Lincoln's Inn is large, well maintained and spacious, and its red-brick buildings are constructed on a grand scale, particularly the four-storey mansions, New Hall and library of New Square (begun in 1680). Many illustrious British politicians studied here, among them Pitt the Younger, Walpole, Disraeli, Gladstone and Asquith. Other former students include William Penn, founder of Pennsylvania, and 17th-century poet John Donne. Make a special point of seeing the Inn's chapel, built above a beautiful undercroft with massive pillars and dramatic vaulting.

✚ 200 C5 ✉ Entrances off Chancery Lane and Lincoln's Inn Fields, WC2 🌐 Chapel: Mon–Fri 12–2:30 🚇 Holborn

Gray's Inn

This Inn dates from the 14th century, but was much restored after damage during World War II. Famous names to have passed through its portals include the writer Charles Dickens, who was a clerk here between 1827 and 1828. Its highlights are the extensive gardens or "Walks" as they are commonly known (Mon–Fri 12– 2:30), once the setting for some infamous duels and where diarist

Samuel Pepys used to admire the ladies promenading. The chapel is also open to the public, but lacks the charm of its Lincoln's Inn equivalent (left).

✚ 200 C5 🚇 High Holborn, WC1 🌐 Walks and chapel Mon–Fri 12–2:30 🚇 Holborn

❽ Sir John Soane's Museum

When 19th-century gentleman, architect and art collector Sir John Soane died in 1837, he left his home and its contents to the nation. The only condition of his bequest, the terms of which were enshrined in a special Act of Parliament, was that nothing in his home was altered. The resulting museum, a charming artistic and social showcase, has remained unchanged for 150 years.

Soane's passion was for collecting; a passion that seems to have been more or less unchecked or unguided – he simply bought whatever caught his eye. As a result, the house is packed with a miscellany of beautiful but eclectic objects, with ceramics, books, paintings, statues and even a skeleton jostling for space. One of the collection's highlights is the ancient Egyptian sarcophagus of Pharaoh Seti I, carved from a single block of limestone and engraved with scenes from the afterlife to guide the soul of the deceased. When the sarcophagus was delivered, Soane, totally enraptured with his new treasure,

greeted its arrival with a three-day reception party.

For many years this jewel of a museum was known only to the well-informed few. Now that the secret is out, you can expect more people; come early or late on weekdays to avoid the worst crowds in the small rooms and stairways.

➕ 200 B5 ✉ 13 Lincoln's Inn Fields, WC2 ☎ 020 7405 2107; www.soane.org 🕐 Tue–Sat 10–5 (also first Tue of month 6–9spm with some rooms candlelit). Groups of six or more must book in advance 🚇 Holborn 🚌 1, 8, 25, 68, 91, 168, 171, 188, 242, 521 💷 Free (donation)

9 Somerset House

Once the repository of birth, marriage and death records, this majestic riverside building is now home to a superb art collection.

The famous, long-established Courtauld Institute Gallery's reputation rests largely on its collection of Impressionist and post-Impressionist paintings, which includes works by Cézanne, Seurat, Gauguin, Renoir, Monet, Manet (*Bar at the Folies-Bergère*), Toulouse-Lautrec and Van Gogh (including his famous 1889 work, *Self-Portrait with a Bandaged Ear*). Rooms on the lower floors contain earlier paintings, many

The Courtauld Gallery in Somerset House holds many treasures, including paintings and ceramics

of them religious works. The 15th-century *Triptych* by the Master of Flemalle (Room 1) and *Adam and Eve* by Lucas Cranach the Elder (1526) are among the highlights.

There is also a schedule of visiting art and photographic exhibitions and a Contemporary Ceramics gallery (open 10:30–6), where you can browse and buy from one of the largest modern ceramic collections in the country. Somerset House also hosts music gigs, with big-name performers, such as Lily Allen, having played there. In winter, from around November, you can enjoy or participate in the spectacle of skaters swishing around an ice rink, specially constructed in the grounds, while summer sees a season of open-air films at the Film4 Summer Screen.

➕ 200 B4 ✉ Strand WC2 ☎ 020 7845 I4600 (recorded information); www.somerset-house.org.uk 🕐 Daily 10–6 🍴 Café, Admiralty restaurant 🚇 Temple (closed Sun), Embankment or Covent Garden 🚌 1, 4, 6, 9, 11, 13, 15, 23, 77a, 91, 176 💷 Courtauld Institute Gallery: moderate, free to under 18s, free Mon 10–2

Where to...
Eat and Drink

Prices
Expect to pay per person for a meal excluding drinks and service:
£ under £25   ££ £25–£50   £££ over £50

Alba £

This smart, modern Italian restaurant, just a short walk from the Barbican Centre, provides excellent value for money and is deservedly popular. It is filled with business people at lunchtime and theatregoers in the evening. The menu is short, encouraging some serious cooking. Dishes such as fried sea bass or lamb rump with pumpkin purée, and classics like *risotto primavera* are prepared with first-rate ingredients. The annotated wine list gives an impressive selection of wines from the best Italian vineyards.

➕ Off map 201 F5 🍽 107 Whitecross Street, EC1 ☎ 020 7588 1798; www.albarestaurant.com 🕐 Mon–Fri 12–3, 6–11; closed 10 days Christmas, bank holidays 🚇 Barbican

Club Gascon ££

Pascal Aussignac, from Toulouse in southwest France, has rapidly established a name for himself in this gastronomically evolving part of London. He offers top-class Gascon cooking with the emphasis on *foie gras* and duck, which are supplied direct by French farmers and producers in Gascony. Although traditionally prepared dishes are Aussignac's specialities, he is not afraid to experiment. Tables may be cramped, but the atmosphere at Club Gascon is vibrant. Highly recommended. Booking is essential.

➕ 201 E5 🍽 57 West Smithfield, EC1 ☎ 020 7796 0600; www.clubgascon.com 🕐 Lunch: Mon–Fri 12–2. Dinner: Mon–Sat 7–10.30 🚇 Farringdon

The Eagle £

The Eagle was one of the pioneers of converted pubs specializing in very good food and still leads the field. Choose from a short, but mouth-watering selection of Asian- and Mediterranean-influenced dishes; all are great value for money. Reservations are not taken as this establishment is lively and often crowded, you need to arrive early to secure a table and have the best choice from the blackboard. You order and pay for your food and drink at the bar.

➕ Off map 201 D5 🍽 159 Farringdon Road, EC1 ☎ 020 7837 1353 🕐 Daily 12–11 (Sun until 5) 🚇 Farringdon

Haz Premier Place ££

The noisy buzz adds to the enjoyment at this lively restaurant, popular with business types and visitors alike. Good fresh and tasty Turkish cuisine is served at large tables in slick style. It's perfect for both carnivores and vegetarians – the main menu is extensive and set meals are particularly good value.

A great discovery in the heart of the City, especially as the restaurant is open all weekend, which is unusual in this neck of the woods.

➕ 202 B5 🍽 9 Cutler Street, E1 ☎ 020 7929 7923; www.hazrestaurant.co.uk 🕐 Daily 11:30–11:30 🚇 Liverpool Street

MPW Steakhouse & Grill ££

Set in the heart of the city, this elegant and lively steakhouse and grill is now under the guidance of Marco Pierre White and James Robertson, founder of Lanes (formerly on this site). Alongside the exquisite steaks, you will find some classic English dishes, such as Lancashire hotpot and shepherd's

pie, all served up with style. Daily desserts are English classics or sample a choice of English cheeses.
✚ 202 C5 ⊠ East India House, 109–117 Middlesex Street, E1 ☎ 020 7247 5050; www.mpwsteakhouseandgrill.com ❻ Lunch: Mon–Sat 12–3; dinner: Mon–Fri 5:30–10, Sat 6–10 Ⓤ Liverpool Street

Medcalf £–££

Housed in a former butcher's shop in buzzing Exmouth Market in trendy Clerkenwell, Medcalf serves the best of Modern British cooking into the early evening and is a popular bar later on, with DJs on Friday and Saturday nights. The cooking draws from a seasonal and often organic menu, featuring classic British dishes such as oxtail, scallops and oysters, but the chic young crowd that is drawn here is anything but traditional.
✚ Off map 201 D5 ⊠ 40 Exmouth Market, EC1 ☎ 020 7833 3533 ❻ Lunch: Mon–Fri 12–3, Sat–Sun 12–4. Dinner: Mon–Wed 6–9:45, Thu–Sat 5:30–10:15. Bar: Mon–Sat 12–11 (Fri to 1am), Sun 12–6 Ⓤ Farringdon

Moro ££

The standard of cooking at this busy, critically acclaimed Spanish/North African restaurant is consistently excellent, with good raw materials simply cooked in a wood-burning oven or chargrilled. The minimalist decor, with a long zinc bar down one wall, an open-plan kitchen along another and plain, close-packed wooden tables, creates an informal setting. Make reservations well in advance.
✚ Off map 201 D5 ⊠ 34–36 Exmouth Market, EC1 ☎ 020 7833 8336; www.moro.co.uk ❻ Lunch: Mon–Sat 12:30–2:30. Dinner: Mon–Sat 7–10:30 Ⓤ Farringdon

Quality Chop House £–££

Much of the original character of this former Victorian chop house has been preserved, including high-backed mahogany booths. The food is a fashionable mix of updated traditional English dishes and French brasserie classics, with eggs, bacon and french fries, fish soup

with *rouille*, confit of duck, and Toulouse sausage with mash and onion gravy never off the menu.
✚ Off map 201 D5 ⊠ 94 Farringdon Road, EC1 ☎ 020 7837 5093; www.qualitychophouse.co.uk ❻ Lunch: Mon–Fri 12–3. Dinner: Mon–Sat 6–11:30, Sun 12–10:30 Ⓤ Farringdon, King's Cross

St John ££

Back-to-basics eating is the principle behind this Clerkenwell hotspot near Smithfield. The decor of the former smokehouse is starkly white and minimalist, and an open-plan kitchen adds to the informality. Traditional old English recipes are reworked – offal (organ meats) is greatly favoured – and sit happily alongside modern Mediterranean dishes on the short menu. The kitchen adopts a simple approach, using prime fresh produce.
✚ Off map 201 E5 ⊠ 26 St John Street, EC1 ☎ 020 7251 0848; www.stjohnrestaurant.co.uk ❻ Lunch: Mon–Fri 12–3. Dinner: Mon–Sat 6–11, Sun 1–3 Ⓤ Farringdon

BARS

Cicada £

At this stylish bar/restaurant, drinkers outnumber those eating in the evening. The young clientele creates a lively atmosphere. The food, should you wish to eat here, is oriental in style, backed up by excellent, inexpensive wines from a list that includes chilled sake.
✚ Off map 201 E5 ⊠ 132–136 St John Street, EC1 ☎ 020 7608 1550; www.rickerrestaurants.com ❻ Mon–Fri 12–11, Sat 12s–late Ⓤ Farringdon

Dirty Dicks £

This classic London pub was established in 1745. Across the road from Liverpool Street Station, it features gnarled, wooden beams, and used barrels as casual tables. Avoid the vaults, where dead rats and cats are bizarrely displayed!
✚ 202 B5 ⊠ 202 Bishopsgate, EC2 ☎ 020 7283 5888; www.dirtydicks.co.uk ❻ Mon–Thu 11am–midnight, Fri–Sat 11am–1am, Sun 11–10:30 Ⓤ Liverpool Street

Where to...
Shop

The City of London is not a significant shopping area. Shops here are largely geared to the needs of office workers, and sandwich bars, wine bars and pubs dominate, with a few tourist gift shops near the City sights. However, the few **markets** that remain here have strong historic and social roots and make an enjoyable outing.

Columbia Road Flower Market (Columbia Road, E2, open Sun 8–2. Tube: Old Street) is where many Londoners stock up with plants for their patios and window boxes and flowers for their homes. Even if you don't want to buy anything, it's worth a visit.

Petticoat Lane Market (Middlesex Street and beyond, E1, open Mon–Fri 10–2:30, Sun 9–2. Tube: Aldgate) is an institution.

It's good for inexpensive clothes and shoes. However, busloads of tourists on Sunday make browsing difficult. The end of the market by Aldgate East Underground station is devoted to leather jackets. Offer cash for the best deal.

The giant Victorian covered **Spitalfields Market** (Commercial Street between Lamb Street and Brushfield Street, E1, open market stalls: Tue–Fri 10–4, Sun 9–5; restaurants: Mon–Fri 8am–11pm, Sat–Sun 9am–11pm; shops: usually daily 10–7. Tube: Liverpool Street) is filled with crafts and has many food outlets selling comestibles from crêpes to sushi and tandoori. The market has a good fine-food market, which operates every Thu, Fri and Sun 10–5 in Crispin Place. Antiques stalls feature on Thursday.

Where to...
Be Entertained

Much of the City remains quiet in the evenings. The Barbican Centre and Broadgate Centre are the area's focal points.

When the **Barbican Centre** (Silk Street, EC2. Box Office tel: 020 7638 8891; general information tel: 020 7638 4141) first opened, journalists wrote critical reviews about how difficult it was for concert-goers to find their way around this behemoth in a featureless part of the City. Music- and theatre-lovers crowd in, however, lured by the centre's proximity to Clerkenwell, London's latest culinary hotspot, as well as by the cultural programme.

The Barbican is the home of the London Symphony Orchestra, which offers about 85 concerts a year with performances by some of the world's top musicians. In addition, there are two theatres and three cinema screens, where you can see the latest movies.

It's well worth dropping by the Barbican, especially at weekends when a variety of free entertainment is on offer. There are also various cafes on the different levels.

The Barbican is best reached by Underground. Barbican and Moorgate stations are the closest, and have the bonus of clearly marked directions to the complex.

At the **Broadgate Centre** (Broadgate Circus, Eldon Street, EC2. Tube: Moorgate), tiers of shops and restaurants line an impressive amphitheatre, where you can ice-skate in winter and enjoy open-air entertainment in summer, or sit and enjoy a sandwich.

Westminster and
the South Bank

Getting Your Bearings

Stand on one of the bridges or embankments and as you gaze at the slowly flowing River Thames you can't help but notice the contrast between the water's stately progress and the noise and drama of the surrounding city.

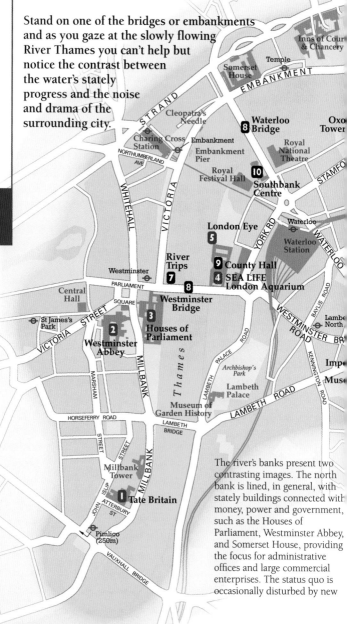

The river's banks present two contrasting images. The north bank is lined, in general, with stately buildings connected with money, power and government, such as the Houses of Parliament, Westminster Abbey, and Somerset House, providing the focus for administrative offices and large commercial enterprises. The status quo is occasionally disturbed by new buildings – Charing Cross railway station is a notable example – but generally the river's north side is stable and established, retaining the political, historical and religious significance it has enjoyed for centuries.

The South Bank has a very different flavour. In Shakespeare's time it was the place to which actors, considered a bad influence, were banished and where early theatre flourished. The reborn Globe is turning the clock back 400 years.

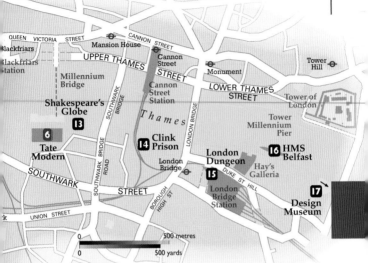

By the early 20th century the area was a mixture of wasteland and heavy industry, but after World War II, the Southbank Centre, and the Royal Festival Hall in particular, marked the start of a makeover. Continuing the shift, as London entered the new millennium, the old Bankside Power Station was transformed from industrial behemoth to cultural superstar in the shape of the Tate Modern gallery. Yet even Tate Modern has been eclipsed in popularity and profile by the surprise success of the London Eye. This elegant, slow-moving observation wheel has rapidly become London's hottest ticket and is the perfect vantage point for planning your day.

Page 87: Detail of Westminster Abbey

★ Don't Miss

At Your Leisure

In a Day

If you're not quite sure where to begin your travels, this itinerary recommends a practical and enjoyable day out exploring Westminster and the South Bank, taking in some of the best places to see using the Getting Your Bearings map on the previous page. For more information see the main entries.

9:30am
Allow 2 hours to enjoy the grandeur of **2 Westminster Abbey** (➤ 94–96), seeking out the numerous memorials to royal and literary figures among breathtaking architecture, particularly the Royal Chapels.

11:30am
Admire the **3 Houses of Parliament** and Big Ben (above, ➤ 97), cross **8 Westminster Bridge** (➤ 103) and turn left, towards the landmark **5 London Eye** (opposite, ➤ 99). Here you are spoiled for choice, with the Eye, the **4 SEA LIFE London Aquarium** (➤ 99) and the attractions of **9 County Hall** (➤ 103–104). Note: trips on the London Eye should be reserved in advance.

1:30pm

Stroll along the river to the
⑪ Oxo Tower (➤ 104–105),
take a lift (elevator) to the top
for a wonderful view over the
Thames, and have lunch in
their brasserie (➤ 109).

2:30pm

After lunch, browse in the
tower's designer workshops,
then make your way to ⑥ Tate
Modern (right, ➤ 100–101),
London's striking modern
art gallery, set in the former
Bankside Power Station.
Choose a couple of galleries
and take an audio tour rather
than trying to see the whole
collection. If you have any
energy left, ⑱ Shakespeare's
Globe (➤ 104), a faithful
reconstruction of the original
Globe Theatre, is just a short
walk away.

❶Tate Britain

Until 2000, this Millbank gallery housed the Tate's entire collection, though limited space meant that only a fraction of the works were on display at any one time. The solution was simple: divide the collection between two sites. Since the creation of Tate Modern (➤ 100–101), the gallery space has been refurbished and expanded. Both critics and general public seem delighted with the results.

Gallery Highlights

Tate Britain covers five centuries of British art, from *A Man in a Black Cap* by John Bettes (1545), to work by latter-day painters Sir Matthew Smith, Francis Bacon and Gilbert & George and sculptures by Henry Moore and Bernard Meadows. All the paintings at Tate Britain are periodically rehung and sometimes disappear into storage for lack of space – though since the split this is much less of a problem. During any visit, however, you can count on seeing great works by Hogarth, Reynolds, Gainsborough, Constable and, of course,

Large, well-lit galleries display Tate Britain's extensive collection

Opposite: Imposing steps up to the gallery

J M W Turner. Turner is regarded as the greatest homegrown talent and has his own wing, the **Clore Gallery**. A couple of his paintings not to miss are the action-packed *The Battle of Trafalgar, as Seen from the Mizen Starboard Shrouds of the Victory* and *Snow Storm: Hannibal and his Army Crossing the Alps*.

For many visitors the favourites are still the impossibly romantic works of the late 19th-century **Pre-Raphaelites** – principally John Everett Millais, William Holman Hunt and, in particular, Dante Gabriel Rossetti, who founded this avant garde brotherhood of artists. There are many outstanding paintings on display from this group, but, in particular, look for Millais' powerful *Ophelia* – which depicts the character from *Hamlet* singing as she drowns in a beautiful, flower-lined river – Rossetti's radical *Ecce Ancilla Domini! (The Annunciation)* and *The Haunted Manor* by William Holman Hunt.

Equine lovers will want to head for the works of **George Stubbs**, who portrays horses in exquisite and uncannily accurate detail – partly inspired by his scientific research.

The Turner Prize

Tate Britain hosts the annual and controversial Turner Prize, which celebrates the cutting edge of contemporary art. Eligible artists must be under 50 years old and have completed an outstanding work or exhibition in the year leading up to the nominations. Only four artists are nominated and their work is exhibited at Tate Britain from October to January. The winner is announced in December. In 2009 the prize was £25,000.

TAKING A BREAK

The **Rex Whistler restaurant**, on the lower floor in the gallery, is a relaxing place to dine, serving modern British dishes. There is also a café opposite the restaurant.

🕂 199 F2 ✉ Millbank, SW1 ☎ 020 7887 8888; www.tate.org.uk ⊕ Daily 10–5:50 (also 1st Fri in month 6–10) 🍴 Café, Rex Whistler restaurant 🚇 Westminster, Vauxhall 🚌 2, 3, 36, 87, 88, 159, 185, 436, 507, C10 🎟 Free

❷ Westminster Abbey

Britain's greatest religious building is a church, a national shrine, the setting for coronations and a burial place for some of the most celebrated figures from almost a thousand years of British history. Most of the country's sovereigns, from William the Conqueror in 1066 to Queen Elizabeth II in 1953, have been crowned at Westminster, while in 1997 it was the setting for the funeral of Diana, Princess of Wales. The building has ancient roots, but construction of the present structure, a masterpiece of medieval architecture, began in the 13th century. Since then the building has grown and evolved, a process that continues to the present day as ever more modern memorials are erected.

Westminster Abbey is a top tourist destination, drawing huge crowds. It's impossible to appreciate all the abbey's riches in one visit, so concentrate on the highlights below.

The Visitors Route

Visitors follow a set route around the abbey. From the entrance through the North Door you head first along the ambulatory, the passageway leading to the far end of the abbey. At the top of the steps, the chapel on the left contains the **tomb of Elizabeth I** (1533–1603) and her older half-sister, **Mary Tudor** (1516–58), daughters of the much-married Henry VIII. Although they lie close in death, there was little love lost beween them in life – Mary was a Catholic, Elizabeth a Protestant at a time when religious beliefs divided the country and religious persecution was rife.

Next comes the sublime **Henry VII Chapel**, built in 1512, possibly to ease Henry's troubled conscience: his route to the throne was a violent one. The abbey's most gorgeous chapel, it was described by one commentator as *orbis miraculum,* or a wonder of the world. The brilliantly detailed and gilded fan vaulting of the roof is particularly fine, as are the vivid banners of the Knights of the Order of the Bath (an order of chivalry bestowed by the monarch) above the oak choir stalls. Behind the altar are the magnificent tombs and gilded effigies of Henry VII and his wife, Elizabeth, created to a design by Henry himself.

As you leave this area, a side chapel holds the tomb of Mary, Queen of Scots (1542–87). Mary, a rival to Elizabeth I's throne, was imprisoned for 19 years before finally being executed in 1587. Mary's son, James VI of Scotland,

POETS' CORNER

Notables buried here:
- Alfred, Lord Tennyson
- Dylan Thomas
- Henry James
- T S Eliot
- George Eliot
- William Wordsworth
- Jane Austen
- The Brontë sisters

became James I of England when the unmarried, childless Elizabeth died. He had his mother's body exhumed and brought to the abbey 25 years after her death and erected the monuments to both Elizabeth I and Mary – but his mother's is much the grander.

As you go back down the stairs don't miss the unassuming chair facing you. This is the **Coronation Chair**, dating from 1296, and has been used at the coronation of most British monarchs. For several centuries anyone could sit on it: many who did left their mark in the form of graffiti.

Next comes **Poets' Corner**, packed with the graves and memorials of literary superstars. You'll spot Geoffrey Chaucer, author of *The Canterbury Tales*; Shakespeare, commemorated by a memorial (he is buried in Stratford-upon-Avon); and Charles Dickens, buried here against his wishes on the orders of Queen Victoria. Thomas Hardy's ashes are here, but his heart was buried in Dorset, the setting for many of his novels.

From Poets' Corner, walk towards the centre of the abbey and the highly decorated **altar and choir stalls**. One of the loveliest views in the abbey opens up from the steps leading to

The stunning view along the choir stalls towards the altar

DOWDING   BAR   PORTAL

the altar, looking along the length of the nave to the window above the West Door. For a restful interlude head into the 13th-century **cloisters**, a covered passageway around a small garden once used for reflection by monks. Contemplation is also the effect created by the simple black slab memorial at the western end of the abbey – the **Tomb of the Unknown Soldier**, an elegant testimony to the dead of war.

The Battle of Britain window contains the badges of the 65 fighter squadrons that took part in that World War II battle

🕂 199 F4 ✉ Broad Sanctuary, SW1 ☎ 020 7654 4900; www.westminster-abbey.org 🕓 Thu–Tue 9:30–4:30, Wed 9:30–7. Last admission 1 hour before closing. Sun open for worship only. College Garden: Apr–Sep Tue–Thu 10–6; Oct–Mar 10–4. Chapter House daily 10:30–3:30 (natural light permitting), Abbey Museum and Pyx Chamber: daily 10:30–4 🍴 Coffee counter in cloisters and Broad Sanctuary 🚇 Westminster, St James's Park 🚌 3, 11, 24, 53, 159, 211 💷 Expensive

WESTMINSTER ABBEY: INSIDE INFO

Top tips Attend a **choral service** to see the abbey at its best. Evensong is at 5pm on weekdays, except Wednesday, 3pm Saturday and Sunday. Times of other services are displayed, otherwise ring for details.
■ **Guided tours** led by abbey vergers leave several times daily (90 min, additional charge). Book at the information desk. There is also an **audio guide**, available in several languages, which provides good additional background (charge).

In more detail Off the cloisters, explore the beautiful 13th-century **Chapter House**, the **Pyx Chamber**, also a survivor of the original fabric, and the **Abbey Museum** with its fascinating wax effigies of royalty.

Hidden gems The **College Garden** (Open Apr–Sep Tue–Thu 10–6; Oct–Mar 10–4) is a haven of tranquillity. On Wednesdays in July and August there are brass band concerts. Access to the garden is from the cloisters, via the delightful Little Cloister.
■ Look for the **statues above the West Door** celebrating modern Christian martyrs.

❸ Houses of Parliament

Spectacularly located at the edge of the River Thames, beside Westminster Bridge, the Houses of Parliament is the most iconic of all London sights. It is home to the House of Commons and the House of Lords. Don't miss it.

The Houses of Parliament and Big Ben Tower at night

Much of the parliament building was rebuilt in the 19th century following a fire, but Westminster Hall, part of the original palace, dates from 1097. The Victoria Tower (102m/335 feet) stands at the southern end and the **Big Ben clock tower** (98m/322 feet) at the other (Big Ben is the bell).

During the elaborate **State Opening of Parliament ceremony**, which usually occurs in November or December, the Queen presides over the non-elected peers of the House of Lords, before the junior members of the process, the elected Members of Parliament (MPs) from the House of Commons, are allowed in. They then slam the door of the Commons chamber in the face of Black Rod, the Queens representative, to confirm their independence from the Lords.

Parliament is open to everyone from the UK, and overseas visitors, although non-UK residents can only tour Parliament during the **Summer Opening** (dates vary each year), when it is in recess. Outside of Summer Opening, UK-residents can request a tour via their local MP. Otherwise, throughout the year, everyone can freely attend debates, committees and judicial hearings, and visit the Archive.

TAKING A BREAK

There are some restaurants near by, including **Quirinale**, a good Italian restaurant, on Great Peter Street.

✚ 200 A1

④ SEA LIFE London Aquarium

Having undergone a £5 million revamp in early 2009, this aquarium is now even more of a must see, especially for those visitors with young children. Among the new inspiring features are the mesmerizing blue whale skeleton glass tunnel walkway, a giant ray lagoon and the slightly nerve-wracking Shark Walk.

Located alongside the London Eye, the aquarium is set out in themed zones over three floors. At the core is the mightily impressive **Pacific Zone shark tank**. The new Shark Walk greets you with the dare "if you are brave enough". The Perspex walkway, which floats above the water, takes you to within touching distance of the sharks gliding menacingly below. The new 25m (82-foot) long glass tunnel walkway has been ingeniously crafted to mimic a blue whale skeleton. It gives amazing views of the fish, rays and sharks swimming all around you. There are regular scheduled feed times around the various displays.

Sharks glide close to visitors in the Pacific Zone shark tank

TAKING A BREAK

There is strictly no eating and drinking allowed inside the aquarium. The **Dalí Café** is near by, at Dalí Universe (► 103–104). There are many other eateries in the area.

➕ 200 B2 ✉ County Hall, Westminster Bridge Road, SE1 ☎ 020 7967 8002; www.londonaquarium.co.uk ⊕ Daily 10–6 🍴 Options in County Hall 🚇 Westminster, Waterloo 🚌 12, 53, 76, 148, 171A, 211, P11 💰 Very expensive

5 London Eye

Dominating the city skyline for miles around, the multi-award-winning London Eye is the country's most successful Millennium project. At 135m (443 feet) in diameter, it is the biggest wheel of its kind in the world. The 32 glass capsules are fixed on the outside (rather than hung from it), so you can enjoy totally unobstructed 360-degree views over the city.

The Eye is one of the most popular attractions in the capital

The London Eye is in constant motion, rotating just a couple of centimetres per second at the hub of the wheel, and takes 30 minutes for a full revolution. Each capsule represents one of the boroughs of London, and on a clear day you can see many of them as **the view** extends for around 40km (25 miles), to beyond the city limits.

Around 3.5 million visitors a year take this ultimate aerial ride, with up to 800 people on the wheel at any one time. July and August are the busiest months and generally most days are busy between 11am and 3pm, so it is essential to make a reservation by telephone or in person. Even then, you may wait 30 minutes or so before boarding, unless you buy a Fast Track ticket, which allows you to turn up just 15 minutes before your flight time

TAKING A BREAK

Options, include cafés and restaurants, in and around County Hall. **The Zen Café** is nearest.

➕ 200 B2 ✉ County Hall Riverside Buildings , SE1 ☎ Ticket hotline: 0870 500 0600 (small booking charge); www.londoneye. com 🕐 May, Jun, Sep daily 10–9, Jul–Aug 10–9:30; Oct–Apr 10–8 🍴 Cafés 🚇 Westminster, Waterloo 🚌 1, 4, 26, 59, 68, 76, 77,168, 171, 172, 176, 188, 211, 243, 341, 381, 507, 521, X68, RV1 💷 Very expensive

6 Tate Modern

Although a relative newcomer as an art museum, Tate Modern is a world-class gallery and one of London's top attractions. The gallery encompasses the spectrum of modern art movements from 19th-century Impressionism to the challenging work of young British artists of the late 20th and early 21st centuries.

Once inside the strikingly converted power station, many visitors find the scale of the Turbine Hall, which occupies the bulk of the building, amazing: it resembles a vast cathedral, measuring 160m (525 feet) in length and 35m (115 feet) in height. This space is partly filled by works especially commissioned for the venue.

Above: *The Gardener Vallier* (*c.*1906) by Paul Cézanne is among the gallery's collection

Permanent Collection

The collection is exhibited on Levels 3 and 5. Each level is divided into two: the east end of **Level 3**, devoted to **"Material Gestures"**, is the place to begin. It opens with Francis Bacon's *Seated Figure,* before moving into mixed sculpture and painting, featuring Giacometti's bronze figures, work by Mattisse and Picasso's intriguing monochrome *Goat's Skull, Bottle and Candle*. A highlight here is Claude Monet's evocative *Water-Lilies*. The west side of Level 3 is allotted to "Poetry and Dream", with a whole room devoted to Surrealism, featuring Picasso's *Weeping Woman* and Pollock's powerful *Naked Man with Knife*.

The eastern half of **Level 5** is entitled **"Energy and Process"**. It starts with Dider Roth's evocative *Self-Portrait as a Drowning Man* and rounds off with Pistoletto's intriguing *Venus*

Left: Sculpture at the gallery includes *The Kiss* by Rodin (1901–04)

TATE MODERN: INSIDE INFO

Top tips To avoid the crush, visit on weekday mornings, or take advantage of the late opening on Fridays and Saturdays – by 8:30pm the crowds thin out.

■ **Self-guided audio tours**, with special interest tours on architecture and for children, are available.

■ **Photography** is allowed only in the Turbine Hall.

■ The **Millennium Bridge**, which links St Paul's Cathedral to Tate Modern, is the best way to approach the gallery, taking visitors across the Thames and straight into its heart.

of the Rags. To the west, "States of Flux" celebrates Cubism, Futurism and Vorticism, with works by Pablo Picasso, Henri Matisse and George Segal.

Breathtaking Views

For many visitors, the views of London from the upper floors of the gallery are as exciting as the art. From the East Room of **Level 7**, there is a superb panorama north, over the Millennium Bridge to St Paul's Cathedral. The view from the east window looks down upon Shakespeare's Globe (➤ 106) and spreads across towards Docklands. From the south window, you can look across to the London Eye (➤ 99).

TAKING A BREAK

The **Globe Café** (➤ 108) serves light lunch dishes. The museum's top-floor restaurant is also good.

Galleries within Tate Modern are open and uncluttered

➕ 201 E3 ✉ Bankside, SE1 ☎ 020 7887 8008; www.tate.org.uk
🕐 Daily 10–6 (Fri–Sat also 6–10pm), last admission 45 min before closing
Ⓢ Southwark Ⓡ Waterloo (East), Blackfriars, London Bridge 🚌 45, 63, 100, 344, 381, RV1 💷 Free; admission charge for special exhibitions on Level 4

At Your Leisure

A cruise boat heads along the Thames near County Hall and the London Eye

DuckTours

London's most novel river ride is aboard a yellow amphibious ex-World War II DUKW vehicle. It begins on dry land (from behind the London Eye), tours various central London landmarks, then returns to Vauxhall to splash down into the Thames and cruise the river for 30 to 35 minutes. Reservations essential, tel: 020 7928 3132; www.londonducktours. co.uk.

From Westminster Millennium Pier

Upriver to Kew (1.5 hours), Richmond (3 hours) and Hampton Court (4.5 hours) tel: 020 7930 2062; www.wpsa.co.uk.

Downriver to Tower Millennium Pier (35–45 min) and Greenwich (65–75 min) tel: 020 7740 0400; www.citycruises.com.
✚ 200 B2

From Embankment Pier

Downriver to Greenwich (1 hour) www.thamesclippers.com
✚ 200 B3

From Tower Millennium Pier

Upriver to Embankment (25 min) www.thamesclippers.com
Downriver to Greenwich (30–40 min) www.thamesclippers.com
Evening cruises On a dinner and cabaret cruise (3 hours) you can sightsee while wining, dining and dancing aboard the *London Showboat*. The cruise operates Wed–Sun, tel: 020 7740 0400.
✚ 200 B3

🄻 River Trips

A trip along the Thames is a tremendous way to see the city, away from the Underground and traffic-clogged streets. Piers in central London from where you can take trips are Embankment, Bankside, Festival, Tower Millennium, Waterloo Millennium and Westminster Millennium. Services east to Greenwich (with connections to the Thames Barrier) pass through urban and industrial landscape, but offer views of Greenwich (➤ 176–179). Services upstream to Hampton Court via Kew (➤ 162–163), Putney, Richmond and on to Kingston are more rural, the river meandering through parks and alongside some of London's more village-like residential enclaves. An evening cruise is also a lovely way to see the city, the river banks enlivened by the twinkling and gleaming of a million lights. Note that timetables vary from month to month, so be sure to go to the piers or telephone for latest details.

Westminster and Waterloo Bridges

Westminster Bridge (built in 1862) is one of over 30 across the Thames, but in 1750 the original bridge on this site was only the second crossing, built after London Bridge. Near Westminster Bridge stop at

The *Space Elephant* sculpture by Salvador Dalí outside the Dalí Universe in County Hall

Westminster Pier to check on the times, prices and destinations of the river trips (opposite) available.

From Waterloo Bridge you will have one of the finest views of London. Looking east, the dominant landmarks are St Paul's Cathedral (➤ 78– 79), St Bride's Church spire, Tower 42 (formerly the NatWest Tower), Lloyd's Building (➤ 173) and – in the far distance – Canary Wharf. In the near distance, on the right, stands the Oxo Tower (➤ 104–105).

As you walk to the north side of the bridge, the grand building to the right is Somerset House (➤ 83), the only remaining example of the 18th-century mansions that once lined the Strand. It now houses the Courtauld Institute Gallery's permanent collection.

Westminster Bridge ✚ 200 B2
Waterloo Bridge ✚ 200 B3

County Hall

The former London County Council headquarters now house a range of attractions, galleries, function rooms and two hotels.

As you wander into the surreal **Dalí Universe** and read on the walls such epigrams as "To be a real Dalinian one must first be a real masochist" and "There is less madness to my method than there is method to my madness", you begin to get some idea of what is in store. The most notable of the 500-plus exhibits are the sculptures. Many of these are eye-popping, such as the disturbingly dislocated *Space Venus*. Look out too for the Mae West red lips sofa and beautiful glass sculptures of Dalí's trademark soft watches.

For film buffs, the interactive **The Movieum**, a museum of the British film industry is an unforgettable experience. From *Star Wars* to *Superman*, and *Alien* to *Gladiator*, the displays and action zones give an enthralling insight into how the films were made – including iconic sets where you can have your photo taken – how scripts are put together and some of the famous people who work behind the camera. You can even have a go at making your own 30-second movie trailer in the green screen area.

Opposite: Inside the Imperial War Museum
Below: The Oxo Tower

Namco Station's vast games and entertainment centre is an ideal place to keep childlike minds (young and old) occupied for hours. It features pool tables, dodgems, video arcade games and ten-pin bowling.
✚ 200 B2 ✉ County Hall, Riverside Buildings SE1 🍴 Café 🚇 Westminster, Waterloo 🚌 12, 24, 26, 76, 77, 148, 176, 243, 341, 381, 507, 521, X68

Dalí Universe
☎ 0870 744 7485; www.daliuniverse.com
🕐 Daily 9:30–6 (last admission 5) 💷 Very expensive

The Movieum
☎ 0207 202 7040; www.themovieum.com
🕐 Mon–Fri 10–5, Sat–Sun 10–6 💷 Very expensive

Namco Station
☎ 020 7967 1066; www.namcoexperience.com
🕐 Daily 10am–midnight

🔟 Southbank Centre

The vibrant South Bank arts complex houses the Royal National Theatre and Hayward Theatre. In addition, concert halls include the wonderful Royal Festival Hall, cinemas, bars, a gallery and restaurants. Though architecturally austere, on a warm summer's day it can still be a pleasant spot in which to relax. There is a genuine buzz, thanks to the crowds of people drawn to the complex's restaurants and cafés, and the (often free) concerts and exhibitions held in the major lobbies. For more information, ▶ 110. An on-going programme of redevelopment is set to give the complex a makeover.
✚ 200 C3 ☎ 0871 663 2501; www.southbankcentre.co.uk 🚇 Waterloo
🚌 Waterloo Bridge 1, 4, 26, 59, 68, 76, 77, 168, 171, 172, 176, 188, 211, 243, 341, 381, 501, 507, 521, X68, RV1

⓫ Oxo Tower

This landmark building contains a mixture of private and public housing, bars and restaurants (▶ 109) and designer workshops. The tower's windows are cleverly placed to spell out the word "OXO"

oral descriptions recorded by ordinary people whose lives were deeply affected by their wartime experiences. If you have never experienced war, this museum will deepen your understanding.

Although beyond the actual South Bank, the museum is just one Tube stop from Waterloo station.

➕ Off map 200 C1
✉ Lambeth Road, SE1 ☎ 020 7416 5000; www.iwm.org.uk
🕐 Daily 10–6 🍴 Café 🚇 Lambeth North, Elephant and Castle, Waterloo 🚌 1, 12, 45, 53, 63, 68, 168, 171, 172, 176, 188, 344, C10
🎟 Free

(a brand of stock cube), a ploy by the architect to evade rules against riverside advertising. Visit the observation area for superb views.

➕ 201 D3 ✉ Barge House Street, SE1 ☎ 020 7021 1686; www.oxotower. co.uk 🕐 Observation area, Level 8: daily 11–10; studios and shops Tue–Sun 11–6
🚇 Blackfriars, Waterloo 🚌 45, 63, 100, 381
🎟 Free all areas

12 Imperial War Museum

This fascinating but sobering museum is much more than a display of military might or a glorification of war – despite the name, the monstrous guns in the forecourt and the militaristic slant of the vehicles on display in the main hall.

The museum's real emphasis and strengths are the way in which it focuses on the effects of war in the 20th century on the lives of soldiers and civilians alike. This is achieved through a comprehensive collection of artefacts, documents, photographs, works of art, and sound and film archive footage. The most moving testimonies come from

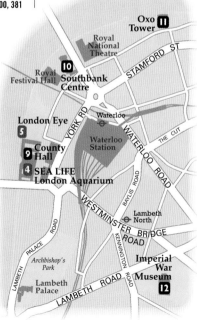

The Globe is a faithful recreation of the original Elizabethan theatre

13 Shakespeare's Globe

This is a reconstruction of the Globe Theatre (whose original site lay some 300m away/330 yards) in which Shakespeare was an actor and shareholder, and in which many of his plays were first performed. The project was the brainchild of Sam Wanamaker, the American film actor and director, who died before its completion. His legacy is an extraordinary achievement, not least because the theatre itself is a wonderfully intimate and atmospheric space. It is built of unseasoned oak held together with 9,500 oak pegs, topped by the first thatched roof completed in the city since the Great Fire of London in 1666. It is also partly open to the elements, as was the original Globe, with standing room in front of the stage where theatregoers can heckle the actors in true Elizabethan fashion.

A visit to the exhibition and a tour of the theatre (or nearby site of the contemporary Rose theatre) is highly worthwhile and will certainly whet your appetite for a performance. The tours cover the project, future plans and costumes from past productions.

🚇 201 F3 ✉ 21 New Globe Walk, Bankside, SE1 ☎ 020 7902 1400; box office 020 7401 9919; www.shakespeares-globe.org
🕐 Exhibition and tours: times vary, but generally Mar–Apr daily 9–5; May–Oct Mon–Sat 9–12:30 (Globe), 1–5 (Rose), Sun 9–11:30 (Globe), noon–5 (Rose). No access to theatre during matinees 🍴 Coffee bar, café and restaurant 🚇 Mansion House, London Bridge, Cannon Street 🚌 Blackfriars Bridge 45, 63, 100; Southwark Street 344, 381 💰 Very expensive

14 Clink Prison

The museum is built on the same site as the notorious Clink Prison, which dated back to Tudor times and gave rise to the popular phrase "in the clink" for being imprisoned. Life behind bars then was a desperate experience: the jailers used every trick to make money from the impoverished inmates, including renting out candles and charging for lighter leg chains. The museum features sobering, often gloomily lit, displays of torture instruments and the techniques used for restraint. It is a fascinating and moving reminder of the grim lives of the prisoners, but is possibly not a great choice for nervous children.

🚇 201 F3 ✉ 1 Clink Street, SE1 ☎ 020 7403 0900; www.clink.co.uk 🕐 Mon–Fri 10–6, Sat–Sun 10–9 🚇 London Bridge 🚌 H17, 21, 35, 40, 43, 47, 48, 133, 141, 149, 344 💰 Moderate

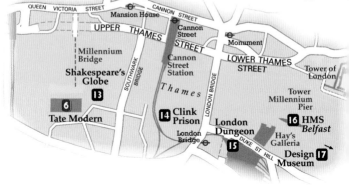

15 London Dungeon

For the ultimate in spooky, adrenaline-filled adventures, the London Dungeon experience takes you deep below the streets of London into the murky and grisly world of torture and pain. It is fun, though, as long as you don't mind a bit of gore and facing some innate fears! The rather startling line-up of attractions include: Boat Ride to Hell, which plunges you into a total darkness filled with scary characters; encounters with Jack the Ripper, London's notorious 19th-century murderer and Sweeney Todd, the city's murderous barber; an all too real look into what it felt like to be running for your life during the Great Fire of London; and the Tooley Street surgery, where you encounter the blood-spattered butcher surgeon. The tour takes 90 minutes.

🚇 202 B3 ✉ 28–34 Tooley Street, SE1
☎ 020 7403 7221; www.thedungeons.com
🕐 Times vary month to month, but generally open daily1 0–5:30 (longer in school holidays)
Ⓜ London Bridge 🚌 21, 35, 40, 43, 47, 48, 78, 133, 149, 381 💷 Very expensive

16 HMS *Belfast*

This World War II vessel, the biggest cruiser ever built by the Royal Navy, took part in the Normandy landings, and remained in service until 1965. Preserved in the state it enjoyed during active service, the ship is now moored between Tower Bridge and London Bridge on the south side of the Thames. It houses displays connected with recent Royal Navy history, but it is the ship itself that is the true attraction. You can explore from the bridge to the engine and boiler rooms nine decks below, taking in the cramped quarters of the officers and crew, the galleys, punishment cells and sick bays, as well as the gun turrets, magazines and shell rooms.

🚇 202 B3 ✉ Moored off Morgans Lane, Tooley Street, SE1 ☎ 020 7940 6300; www.iwm.org.uk 🕐 Mar–Oct daily 10–6 (last admission 5); Nov–Feb 10–5 (last admission 4)
🍴 Many near by Ⓜ London Bridge, Tower Hill, Monument 🚌 42, 47, 78, 381, RV1 💷 Very expensive; children 15 or under free

17 Design Museum

Near Tower Bridge, this relatively new museum – it opened in 1989 – contains a fascinating and eclectic collection of modern design, ranging from industrial and graphic to fashion and furniture, and beyond. What the museum lacks in size (it is set over just two floors), it makes up for with plenty of quirky and iconic items, including Clive Sinclair's C5 personal electric vehicle, which famously wowed the media but not the buying public, motorway road signs and some of the early personal computers. The museum also hosts several temporary and touring exhibitions, current details of which can be found on the website. There is a regular lecture series, featuring some of the leading names in the design world.

🚇 202 C2 ✉ 28 Shad Thames, SE1 ☎ 020 7403 6933, www.designmuseum.org 🕐 Daily 10–5:45 (last entry 5:15) Ⓜ London Bridge
🚌 42, 47, 78, 188, 381 💷 Expensive

HMS *Belfast* is moored on the Thames near Tower Bridge

FOR KIDS
■ SEA LIFE London Aquarium (➤ 98)
■ Boat trip downriver or on the Duck Tour (➤ 102)
■ London Eye (➤ 99)
■ HMS *Belfast* (➤ left)

Where to...
Eat and Drink

Prices

Expect to pay per person for a meal, excluding drinks and service:
£ under £25   ££ £25–£50   £££ over £50

Anchor & Hope £

Probably the best time to go to this popular gastropub is for a late lunch or pre-theatre meal, as they have a no-booking policy and you will need to be patient if you want a table in the evening. The good hearty British cuisine is all very well cooked and includes some imaginative choices such as earthy pigeon and foie gras terrine and rich shin of beef in red wine, infused with rosemary and juniper. There is a good choice of wines.

🚇 201 D2 ☒ 36 The Cut, SE1 ☎ 020 7928 9898 ⏰ Mon 5pm–11, Tue–Sat 11–11, Sun 12:30–5 🚇 Southwark, Waterloo

Bengal Clipper £

A former spice warehouse at Butler's Wharf makes a particularly fitting setting for this respected Indian restaurant. The spacious dining room is dominated by a central grand piano, the surroundings have a strong sense of style and comfort, and the service is elegant. The menu specializes in mainly Bengali and Goan dishes. Special menus offer very good value.

🚇 202 C2 ☒ Butler's Wharf, SE1 ☎ 020 7357 9001; www.bengalclipper. co.uk ⏰ Lunch: daily 12–2:30 (also Sun 12–4). Dinner: Mon–Sat 6–11:30, Sun 6–11 🚇 London Bridge, Tower Hill

Caffè Vergnano 1882 £

This Italian-style coffee bar and restaurant opened its second London branch in 2007 at the Southbank Centre. Credited to serve the best espresso in town, the 124-year-old Italian blend is certainly unique. The refined, sleek interior tempts you to sit back and relax while you enjoy a cup of aromatic and full-bodied espresso with a beautiful "crema" dispensed from a gleaming machine. Your cappuccino is served with 1882 stencilled on the creamy foam in chocolate powder.

🚇 200 C3 ☒ Festival Terrace, SE1 ☎ 020 7921 9339; www.caffevergnano1882.co.uk ⏰ Mon–Fri 8am–10pm, Sat 9am–10pm, Sun 10–10 🚇 Waterloo

Cantina del Ponte £–££

This simple Italian-style eatery, set on the wharf by Tower Bridge, has fabulous views back over the City. It is the least expensive of the Conran Gastrodome restaurants and the mainly Italian-inspired menu brings a simple choice of grilled or roasted meats and fish. In summer, ask for a table on the terrace.

🚇 202 C2 ☒ Butler's Wharf Building, 36c Shad Thames, SE1 ☎ 020 7403 5403; www.cantina.co.uk ⏰ Lunch: daily 12–3. Dinner Mon–Sat 6–11, Sun 6–10 🚇 London Bridge, Tower Hill

Globe Café £

Enjoy stunning river views from the Georgian building that forms part of the Globe theatre complex on the South Bank (► 106). This airy, bright café serves light lunch and supper dishes such as pasta and salads, as well as cakes and sandwiches. The grill/restaurant on the first floor has the same river views, and offers an à la carte menu, as well as good-value pre- and post-theatre menus.

🚇 201 F3 ☒ 21 New Globe Walk, Bankside, SE1 ☎ 020 7902 1576; www.shakespeares-globe.org ⏰ Café: daily 9–5; brasserie: Mon–Sat 12–2:30, 5:30–10, Sun 11–5 🚇 Cannon Street, London Bridge, Mansion House

Livebait £

The menu at this informal and slightly cramped seafood restaurant incorporates traditional dishes such as rock and native oysters, Cornish mackerel fillets, and langoustines with mayonnaise. Added to this is a selection of interesting dishes that reflects Asian, oriental and Mediterranean influences (often on the same plate). Close to the Old Vic and South Bank Centre.

➕ 201 D2 ⊠ 43 The Cut, SE1
☎ 020 7928 7211; www.livebaitrestaurants.co.uk ⏰ Mon–Sat 12–11, Sun 12:30–9
Ⓜ Waterloo

Lovage £

The Lovage is one of a collection of fashionable eateries to be found at Butler's Wharf. The unusual layout features a balconied mezzanine, with a bar on the lower floor (where informal snacks are available). There's a definite buzz, and the kitchen copes well with the mix of Indian styles. All the dishes are reasonably priced and the lunch menu offers a good choice and exceptional value.

➕ 202 C2 ⊠ 13–15 Queen Elizabeth Street, SE1 ☎ 0845 226 9411;
www.lovagerestaurant.com ⏰ Lunch: daily 12–2:30. Dinner: daily 6–11:30 (Fri–Sat until 12) Ⓜ London Bridge, Tower Hill

Oxo Tower ££–£££

The Oxo Tower may be a Thames-side landmark, but it can be hard to find the entrance to it. However, the eighth-floor restaurant brings ample reward in stunning river vistas, taking in St Paul's and the Houses of Parliament. Window tables are not essential, as the view dominates the entire ultra-chic space. Dishes are drawn from a global melting pot of influences, but on the evening menu there are more classic interpretations of European cooking.

➕ 201 D3 ⊠ 8th Floor, OXO Tower Wharf, Barge House Street, SE1 ☎ 020 7803 3888;
www.oxotower.co.uk ⏰ Lunch: Mon–Sat 12–2:30, Sun 12–3. Dinner: Mon–Sat 6–11, Sun 6:30–10 Ⓜ Blackfriars

RSJ ££

The name RSJ refers to the rolled steel joist that crosses the ceiling of this long-established, family-owned restaurant. Among its numerous charms are a comfortably warm but contemporary interior, good, modern Anglo-French cooking strong on seasonal ingredients, great vegetarian dishes and a much applauded wine list. The fixed-price lunch is excellent value should you be heading for a matinee at the Royal National Theatre. Highly recommended.

➕ 201 D3 ⊠ 33 Coin Street, SE1
☎ 020 7928 4554; www.rsj.uk.com
⏰ Lunch: Mon–Fri 12–2:30.
Dinner: Mon–Sat 5:30–11 Ⓜ Waterloo

Tas Restaurant £

In a street full of places to eat, Tas offers something different with its Turkish food and choice of *meze*. The restaurant is large and brightly lit, with pale wooden tables and flooring and an open kitchen at the back; the chatter and hubbub create a definite buzz. Main courses are served in generous portions and represent excellent value for money, as do the set menus.

➕ 201 D2 ⊠ 33 The Cut, SE1 ☎ 020 7928 1444; www.tasrestaurant.co.uk ⏰ Mon–Sat 12–11:30, Sun 12–10:30 Ⓜ Waterloo

BARS

Gordon's Wine Bar £

Dating from 1890 and claiming to be the oldest established wine bar in town, this dark, cobwebby place is a gem. Descend the stone steps to rub shoulders with commuters, wine lovers and inquisitive visitors who come not only to drink in the atmosphere but to sample an excellent range of wines, plus traditional ports and madeiras. A healthy buffet salad bar, hot meals and a traditional roast on Sunday are served.

➕ 200 A3 ⊠ 47 Villiers Street, WC2
☎ 020 7930 1408; www.gordonswinebar.com ⏰ Mon–Sat 11–11, Sun 12–10
Ⓜ Embankment

Where to...
Shop

Borough Market (open Thu 11–5, Fri 12–6, Sat 9–4. Tube: London Bridge), at the junction of Borough High Street and Southwark Street, is the capital's best for fine food shopping and attracts London's more discerning shoppers and celebrity chefs too. It's worth a visit also to glimpse one of the few truly Dickensian areas left in London.

Hay's Galleria, opening on to the River Walk by the Thames (Tube: London Bridge), was one of the first warehouse developments. An impressive Victorian-style iron-and-glass roof covers a huge atrium that is surrounded by a mixture of offices, shops and cafés. The Galleria is noted for some quirky shops, but during the week the shops and eateries tend to cater for the needs of office workers.

Gabriel's Wharf (Upper Ground, SE1. Tube: Waterloo), by Waterloo Bridge, close to the Southbank Centre, is a great place to buy unusual gifts. The lively complex contains design and craft workshops, where silversmiths and ceramicists sell their work, as well as several cafés. In summer a number of open-air events create a lively atmosphere.

The **Riverside Walk Market**, which sells second-hand books, is set up on the wide, paved space by the Thames under Waterloo Bridge every weekend from noon to 7pm, and irregularly on weekdays. The stalls stock mostly old paperbacks, but there are a few gems, including children's books, plays, poetry, science fiction and old map prints, to be found if you persevere.

Where to...
Be Entertained

FILM AND THEATRE

The **Southbank Centre** (▲ 104. Tube: Waterloo) is London's major performing arts complex incorporating the **Royal Festival Hall**, the **Queen Elizabeth Hall** and the **Purcell Room**, all venues for music and dance. A major restoration project is under way. **The Royal National Theatre** (tel: 020 7452 3000; www. nationaltheatre.org.uk) comprises the Lyttelton, Olivier and Cottesloe theatres, and the **BFI South Bank** (tel: 020 7928 3232; ww.bfi.org.uk) shows both subtitled foreign films and mainstream releases.

Retrospectives and exhibitions of contemporary art, painting, sculpture and photography at the **Hayward Gallery** (Belvedere Road, SE1, tel: 0871 663 2519; www.haywardgallery.org.uk. Tube: Waterloo) are a must for art lovers.

The **British Film Institute London IMAX Cinema** (1 Charlie Chaplin Walk, SE1, tel: 0870 787 2525; www.bfi.org.uk. Tube: Waterloo) screens 2D and 3D films on the UKs largest screen.

CLUBS

Try the cutting-edge **Ministry of Sound** (103 Gaunt Street, SE1, tel: 0870 060 0010. Tube: Elephant and Castle). MoS plays different music on different nights (with dress codes in operation), so check listings magazines (▲ 43) or visit the website (www. ministryofsound.com). An evening here won't be cheap.

Knightsbridge, Kensington and Chelsea

Getting Your Bearings

These premier residential districts were once leafy villages, favoured by the wealthy for their healthy distance from the dirt and pollution of early London. Today they still retain an ambience of exclusivity: their houses are grand, the streets still leafy, and the area has attracted many consulates and embassies to its genteel environs.

Ladbroke Grove (800m)

9 **Portobello Road Market**

Bayswater

Queensway

BAYSWATER ROAD

Notting Hill Gate

NOTTING HILL GATE

8 **Kensington Gardens**

Round Pond

Kensington Palace **5**

High Street Kensington

KENSINGTON ROAD

KENSINGTON HIGH ST

Kensington first gained its fashionable reputation in the late 17th century when royalty moved to Kensington Palace. The palace remains a royal home – though parts are open to the public – and the gardens are among London's prettiest. Kensington Gardens occupy the western swathe of Hyde Park, which extends all the way to Marble Arch, affording a magnificent green space at the very heart of the city. In the middle is the Serpentine, an artificial lake.

Much of Kensington is scattered with monuments to Queen Victoria's husband, Prince Albert, who died prematurely in 1861. The Albert Memorial on the edge of Kensington Gardens is the principal example, but more subtle reminders of the royal consort survive elsewhere. It was the Prince's idea that profits from the Great Exhibition (held in Hyde Park in 1851) should be used to establish an education centre in the area. The colleges and institutions of South Kensington were the result, among them three of the capital's foremost museums: the V&A Museum, the Science Museum and the Natural History Museum.

Knightsbridge is Kensington's neighbour to the east and, if anything, is even more exclusive as a residential address. It also has a smart commercial aspect, including the department store Harrods. More affluent residents use the shop as a local store, but most Londoners and tourists are content with a voyeuristic look at the richness and variety of its stock, its lavish interiors and the tempting food halls.

Previous page: The Albert Memorial

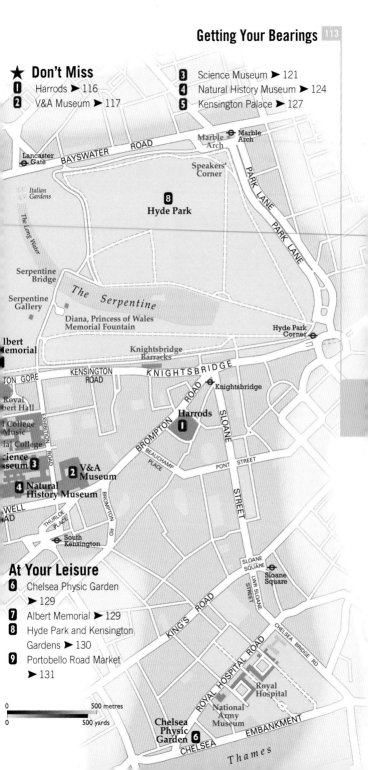

★ **Don't Miss**

1 Harrods ➤ 116
2 V&A Museum ➤ 117
3 Science Museum ➤ 121
4 Natural History Museum ➤ 124
5 Kensington Palace ➤ 127

Lancaster Gate
BAYSWATER ROAD
Marble Arch
Marble Arch
Speakers' Corner
PARK LANE
PARK LANE
Italian Gardens
8 Hyde Park
The Long Water
Serpentine Bridge
Serpentine Gallery
The Serpentine
Diana, Princess of Wales Memorial Fountain
Hyde Park Corner
Albert Memorial
Knightsbridge Barracks
KENSINGTON ROAD
TON GORE
KNIGHTSBRIDGE
Knightsbridge
Royal Albert Hall
College Music
al College
cience seum 3
EXHIBITION ROAD
Harrods 1
BROMPTON ROAD
SLOANE STREET
4 Natural History Museum
2 V&A Museum
BEAUCHAMP PLACE
PONT STREET
WELL AD
THURLOE PLACE
BROMPTON RD
South Kensington
SLOANE SQUARE
Sloane Square
LWR SLOANE STREET

At Your Leisure

6 Chelsea Physic Garden ➤ 129
7 Albert Memorial ➤ 129
8 Hyde Park and Kensington Gardens ➤ 130
9 Portobello Road Market ➤ 131

KING'S ROAD
CHELSEA BRIDGE RD
ROYAL HOSPITAL ROAD
Royal Hospital
National Army Museum

0 ———— 500 metres
0 ———— 500 yards

Chelsea Physic Garden 6
CHELSEA EMBANKMENT
Thames

In a Day

If you're not quite sure where to begin your travels, this itinerary recommends a practical and enjoyable day out exploring Knightsbridge, Kensington and Chelsea, taking in some of the best places to see using the Getting Your Bearings map on the previous page. For more information see the main entries.

10:00am

❶ Harrods (left, ➤ 116) is essential viewing even if you don't want to spend any money. Don't miss the food halls, the pet department, the exotic Egyptian Hall and the splendid Egyptian escalators. Have a coffee in one of the many in-store cafés.

11:30am

Wander along Brompton Road, lined with exclusive shops, to the Victoria and Albert Museum. Alternatively, if you don't fancy the 800m (half-mile) walk, catch a No C1, 14 or 74 bus, any of which will drop you near the museum. The other museums are across the road. The **❷ Victoria and Albert Museum** (➤ 117–120), the national museum of art and design, is filled with all manner of beautiful objects; the **❹ Natural History Museum** (➤ 124–126) covers the earth's flora, fauna and geology; and the **❸** Science Museum (opposite top, ➤ 121–123) investigates every imaginable aspect of science. The best approach is to choose one museum and give it a couple of hours – don't try to tackle too much in one go.

1:30pm

Have a leisurely lunch in the area at one of the museum cafés or in a patisserie or pub in nearby Brompton Road.

2:45pm

Walk north up Exhibition Road, turn left into Kensington Gore to the Royal Albert Hall and admire the **❼ Albert Memorial** opposite (➤ 129–130). If the weather is fine, head into Kensington Gardens and across to the Round Pond and Kensington Palace. Otherwise, buses No 9, 10 or 52 run towards Kensington High Street along Kensington Gore; get off at

he Broad Walk (it's just a couple of stops along) and walk straight into
ne gardens near the palace. (Note that in winter the last admission to
Kensington Palace is at 4pm.)

3:30pm

Look around 5 **Kensington Palace** (➤ 127–128), which is less grand than
Buckingham Palace, but the sort of place where you can imagine people
actually living. The palace's royal dress collection is especially good.

5:00pm

Have a break in the Orangery (➤ 133) and then enjoy an evening walk
through 8 **Kensington Gardens** and into 8 **Hyde Park** (below, ➤ 130–131).
You might even take a rowing boat out on the Serpentine as a peaceful
finale to the day.

❶ Harrods

Harrods is a London institution. It began when Henry Charles Harrod, a grocer and tea merchant, opened a small shop in 1849. Today it contains more than 300 departments spread across seven floors, still striving to fulfil its motto *Omnia Omnibus Ubique* – all things, for all people, everywhere.

Harrods works hard to maintain its reputation as London's premier department store. Liveried commissionaires (known as Green Men) patrol the doors and if you are deemed to be dressed inappropriately you'll be refused entry. Rucksacks, leggings, shorts or revealing clothing are to be avoided.

The store's most popular departments are the cavernous ground-floor **food halls**, resplendent with decorative tiles and vaulted ceilings, where cornucopian displays of fish, fruit and myriad other foodstuffs tempt shoppers. Handsomely packaged teas and coffees, and jars bearing the distinctive Harrods logo are available: good for gifts or souvenirs, and an inexpensive way to acquire the trademark carrier bag!

Also worth a special look are the **Egyptian Hall**, complete with sphinxes (also on the ground floor) and the **Egyptian Escalator** that carries you to the store's upper floors. One perennial favourite is the **pet department** (on the fourth floor), whose most publicized sale was a baby elephant in 1967; the shop keeps smaller livestock these days.

During your visit, keep an ear open for the distinctive sound of The Harrods' bagpipers who perform occasionally, usually in the late morning on the ground floor (telephone for details).

The Harrods experience isn't complete unless you come back after dark when the vast exterior is brilliantly illuminated with thousands of lights.

Stop in the ground-floor food halls at the **Harrods Famous Deli** for delicious salt beef bagels or smoked salmon on rye.

Harrods' food halls are the most famous of the store's 300 or more departments

---

🕂 198 A4 ✉ 87–135 Brompton Road, SW1 ☎ 020 7730 1234; www.harrods.com 🕐 Mon–Sat 10–8, Sun 12–6 🍴 Bars and restaurants, including a deli, pizzeria, rotisserie and a pub (serving Harrods' own beer) Ⓤ Knightsbridge 🚌 C1, 9, 10, 14, 19, 22, 52, 74, 137, 414

2 V&A Museum

The V&A (also known as the Victoria and Albert Museum), the national museum of art and design, was founded in 1852 with the aim of making art accessible, educating working people and inspiring designers and manufacturers. One of Europe's great museums, its 10km (6 miles) of galleries are crammed with exquisite exhibits.

This is the sort of place where you want to take everything home: some Meissen, perhaps, a few Persian carpets, an Indian throne, or the Heneage Jewel once owned by Queen Elizabeth I. The range of objects is staggering – sculpture, ceramics, glass, furniture, metalwork, textiles, paintings, photography, prints, drawings, jewellery, costume and musical instruments. In addition to the wealth of beautiful works of art, the V&A also has the most peaceful atmosphere and most interesting shop of all the major London museums.

A major renovation project continues, with new ceramics galleries opening in 2010. Due to changes, some galleries may be closed at short notice – check on the website.

The ornate exterior of the museum

Medieval Treasury

One of many highlights in the treasury is the Limoges enamel Becket Casket, dating from 1180. It is covered with images depicting the death of St Thomas Becket at the hands of four knights loyal to King Henry II, whom Becket had angered by refusing to let Church authority be compromised by the Crown. The casket reputedly contained a bloodstained scrap of fabric from the clothes St Thomas was wearing at his death. Look also for the early church vestments, especially the Butler-Bowden Cope, embellished with fine embroidery.

Nehru Gallery of Indian Art

The gallery features a fine display of textiles and paintings, together with a variety of other interesting artefacts, such as a white jade wine cup and thumb ring belonging to Shah Jehan (a 17th-century Mogul emperor of India and the builder of the Taj Mahal). One of the museum's most idiosyncratic items is also here – *Tipu's Tiger* (*c*.1790), a life-size wooden automaton from Mysore depicting a tiger eating a man. A musical box inside the tiger's body can reproduce the growls of the tiger and screams of the victim.

Raphael Cartoons

The V&A's Raphael Cartoons were commissioned by Pope Leo X in 1515 as designs for tapestries to hang in the Sistine Chapel in the Vatican. The word cartoon properly refers to

The revamped jewellery gallery shows pieces to superb effect

Casts and copies from the Italian Renaissance in the Dorothy and Michael Hintze Gallery

a full-size preparatory drawing for works in other media. Important works of art, they depict scenes from the lives of St Peter and St Paul.

Dress Collection

This collection traces the development of men's, women's and children's clothing through the ages. One of the museum's most popular sections, it gives you a chance to smirk at the fashions of your forebears, admire the often sumptuous dresses of centuries past, or marvel at historical oddities such as the 1.5m (5-foot) wide mantua, a formal dress worn by 18th-century women for ceremonial occasions. Clothes from Dior, Issey Miyake, Versace and Chanel represent modern fashion. Check the website for temporary exhibitions.

Art and Design

The **Morris, Gamble and Poynter rooms** are named after and decorated in the styles of three leading 19th-century artists and designers: the hugely influential William Morris (1834–96), who designed furniture and textiles, among much else; James Gamble (1835–1919), who worked as part of the museum's design team and produced stained glass and ceramics for his room; and the artist Edward Poynter (1836–1919). They retain their original function as public refreshment rooms, the V&A having been the first museum in the world to provide its patrons with such facilities. Their painted tiles, friezes, columns, quotations and glass windows provide plenty to admire as you sip your coffee. Look in particular for some of the quotations that form part of the decorative scheme.

Photographic Gallery

A selection of the museum's 300,000 photographic works is displayed here, alongside changing displays. This is one of the few spaces devoted to photography in a major London museum.

Cast Rooms

These contain some of the museum's largest exhibits. In the 19th century, art students were less able to travel to study masterpieces at first hand and to aid them reproductions (often casts) were made of famous sculptures. The rooms are packed with statues, windows, pulpits and altars: size was clearly of no concern – parts of Trajan's Column in Rome and the Portico de la Gloria from Santiago de Compostela in Spain are reproduced.

Silver Gallery

This gallery traces the history of silver from the 14th century, with examples of every size, shape and provenance. Exhibits range from the dramatic 18th-century **Macclesfield Wine Service**, testimony to an era of grand living, to the silver snuff box that King Charles II gave to Nell Gwynn.

Glass Gallery

The sparkling Glass Gallery tells the story of glass from 2500BC to the present day. Make a special point of seeing *The Luck of Edenhall*, a 13th-century Syrian vessel probably brought home by a crusader, but said by legend to have been created by fairies.

Jameel Gallery

The V&A is undergoing a major transformation, which saw the opening of the Jameel Gallery in 2006, displaying the Islamic art collection of more than 40 items.

TAKING A BREAK

Stop at **Emporio Armani Caffè** (191 Brompton Road, SW3, tel: 020 7823 8818, closed Sun), an elegant first-floor café where Armani-clad waiters serve delicious Italian food.

✚ 195 E1 ✉ Cromwell Road, SW7 ☎ 020 7942 2000 (recorded information); www.vam.ac.uk ⏰ Sat–Thu 10–5:45; Fri 10–10 Ⓔ South Kensington 🚌 C1, 14, 74 🎟 Free

---

V&A MUSEUM: INSIDE INFO

Top tips Late viewing takes place on Friday, with certain galleries remaining open until 10pm. There is a **Friday night lecture programme**, from 7–8 in the Lecture Theatre, with prominent designers and artists speaking. Admission to the galleries is free, though some events may carry a separate charge.

Hidden gems Take time to see the office of Pittsburgh department store proprietor Edgar J Kaufmann, designed by American architect Frank Lloyd Wright (1867–1959). It is the only example of Wright's work in Europe.
■ The **John Constable Collection** is the world's largest collection of works by this leading 19th-century British landscape artist (1776–1837).

③ Science Museum

Technophobes needn't be afraid of this museum: the science here is presented in a simple and user-friendly way, with plenty of child-pleasing, hands-on displays and clever devices to make sense of complex and everyday items alike. The museum embraces all branches of pure and applied science, from their beginnings to modern times, covering the ground with enormous visual panache and a real desire to communicate the excitement and vibrancy of science.

who am I?

1

The museum's popular Who Am I? exhibit

Be warned before you start, you can easily spend the whole day here and still not see everything. With the addition in 2000 of the stunning Wellcome Wing, and its attendant IMAX cinema and space simulator ride, the Science Museum, always one of London's biggest and best museums, took on an even larger dimension. It is best to concentrate on just a couple of themed galleries, interspersing these with fun areas such as the cinema and rides. If you have children, let them off the leash in the museum's many acclaimed hands-on areas.

Ground Floor

The best way to start your visit is by strolling through **Making the Modern World**. This dramatic gallery displays many icons and "firsts" of the modern age; from Stephenson's record-breaking 1829 locomotive, the *Rocket*, to the scorched and battered Apollo 10 Command Module that orbited the moon in May 1969 as a precursor to the lunar landings (for a full history of space flight head to the adjacent Space Gallery).

Many peoples' favourites, however, are the huge, hypnotically rotating mill engines that powered the Industrial Revolution and are still steamed for museum visitors.

Wellcome Wing
To enter the deep-neon-blue world of the Wellcome Wing, its three upper floors suspended almost magically in mid-air, is truly to walk into the future. Many of the exhibits in this part of the museum deal with cutting-edge technology, and just-breaking scientific stories are monitored here in real time.

Rides and Films
If the latest advances in medicine and nuclear physics sounds a bit too much like hard work, take a ride across the galaxy on a virtual voyage simulator, or for an even more exciting show, head to the top floor where the IMAX cinema will astound you with images as tall as five double-decker buses, and suck you right into the screen. Films portray themes such as the universe and Earth as you have never seen them before, but for eye-popping, state-of-the-art, cinematic special effects take the kids to *Cyberworld 3D*.

Just Explore
There are so many other diverse galleries to visit – Food, Gas, Computers, Time, Chemical Industry, Marine Engineering, Photography, Health, Geophysics and Oceanography, to name just a few – that it is difficult to know where to head for next. Try to make time, however, for **Flight**, a fascinating display chronicling the history of manned flight from the Montgolfiers' balloons to supersonic engines. Historic aircraft duck and dive, slung from every available piece of ceiling, and high-level walkways get you right up into the air alongside these beautiful gleaming machines.

TAKING A BREAK
Despite its name, the **Deep Blue Café** is a high-quality, waiter-service restaurant serving suitably up-to-the-minute meals in an open-plan setting from which you can gape at the £40 million Wellcome Wing. The Revolution

Splitting the atom

The Splitting the Atom exhibition

FOR KIDS
The museum is committed to involving children and the four specialist galleries for them are all staffed by informative "Explainers".

■ **The Garden** (basement): aimed at 3- to 6-year-olds.

■ **Flight Lab** (third floor): explains the mysteries of flight.

■ **Launch Pad** (basement): a range of scientific principles explained in a fun, hands-on environment.

At weekends and holidays access to these areas may be restricted and timed ticketing may operate. If this is the case, tickets are allocated at the entrance to each gallery. Pick up a Children's Trail guide from the bookshop.

The central atrium, seen from the second floor walkway

Café on the ground floor sits right next to a splendid mill engine behemoth of the Industrial Revolution.

🗺 195 E1 ✉ Exhibition Road, SW7 ☎ 0870 870 4868;
www.sciencemuseum.org.uk 🕐 Daily 10–6 🍴 Restaurant and cafés
🚇 South Kensington 🚌 C1, 9, 10, 14, 49, 52, 70, 345, 360, 414 💷 Free.
IMAX Cinema: expensive; simulators: inexpensive

SCIENCE MUSEUM: INSIDE INFO

Top tips The **Launch Pad** (► For Kids panel, opposite) is particularly popular. To avoid the worst of the crowds, visit it either early or late in the day.

In more detail The **Science and Art of Medicine** (fifth floor) provides a fascinating and detailed history of medicine. It also looks at how different cultures interpret and treat illnesses. The range of items on display is remarkable, and includes old medical instruments, skulls, costumes, anatomical models and even shrunken heads.

■ The **Secret Life of the Home** (in the basement) houses a fun collection illustrating how the everyday household items we take for granted have evolved and operate. There's also a set of household objects that never caught on – visitors are invited to guess their function.

4 Natural History Museum

The Natural History Museum has a staggering 69 million specimens, many (but not all) of which are on display. They cover life forms and the Earth's building blocks from the most distant past to the modern day. Everything in, under or on the Earth is here, the flora and fauna – from dinosaurs and whales to butterflies, humming birds and human beings – in the Green Zone and Blue Zone galleries, and the geological material in the Red Zone. Displays in these galleries are entertaining and interactive; be warned, you could easily spend a whole day here.

Before you go in, take a look at the museum building, designed in the late 19th century in the style of a cathedral. Measuring some 200m (220 yards), it was the first building in Britain to be entirely faced in terracotta.

The suggested route below will take about two hours, or pick up the free museum plan, which has a useful breakdown of the museum's highlights.

The Natural History Museum is home to more than 69 million objects

Green Zone

The Central Hall (Green Zone). This remarkable gallery is the entrance hall to the Life Galleries and contains a variety of breathtaking exhibits. The 26m (85-foot) long cast of the fossilized skeleton of a Diplodocus dinosaur holds centre stage, but the alcoves around the hall display remarkable items, such as the fossilized egg of the Madagascan elephant bird (which is as big as a football). Follow the stairs to the third floor to see the section of a giant sequoia tree from San Francisco (giant sequoias are the largest living things on the planet) and notice how the dates of major historical events have been marked on the tree's growth rings.

Special raised walkways bring you face to face with the likes of Tyrannosaurus rex in the Dinosaur Gallery

Ecology. This is one of the most visually impressive areas in the museum, with a striking mirrored video display of the Water Cycle, and a walk-in leaf to illustrate just how vital plants are to the life of the planet. It does a good job of explaining often complex ecological issues and the need for responsibility with regard to the environment.

Creepy Crawlies. In this gallery devoted to bugs and beasties, you'll learn more than you ever wanted to know about insects, spiders, crustaceans and centipedes. It will leave you wondering just what lurks in your home; not for the squeamish.

Blue Zone

Dinosaurs. The dramatic and popular displays here examine
many aspects of most species of dinosaur, including some of
the many theories as to why they became extinct. A raised
walkway enables visitors to get close to the exhibits, and the
exhibition includes a robotics display of dinosaurs in action.

Mammals. Some of the material in these galleries consists
of stuffed animals behind glass, and has been part of the
museum for decades. This said, the straightforward displays
are almost a relief after the overwhelming variety of exhibits
in other galleries: the model of the blue whale (28m/92-feet-
long), in particular, is a perennial favourite.

Red Zone

Visions of Earth. An escalator transports visitors away from
the Earth Galleries' impressive entrance hall through a huge
hollow earth sculpture into the upper galleries. It's a stunning
introduction to this part of the museum, but before you go
up examine the displays behind the tiny portholes in the
walls: many of the specimens on show here are beautifully
shaped and have almost impossibly brilliant colours. Look, in
particular, for the piece of moon rock and the ancient fossils
that were once believed to have been the devil's toenail and
the weapons of Zeus.

The Power Within. This highly visual gallery seeks to
explain volcanoes and earthquakes; its memorable centrepiece
is a mock-up of a supermarket which simulates the 1995
Kobe earthquake in Japan that killed 6,000 people.

Earth's Treasury. Such is the beauty and variety of the
items on show, it takes a while to realize that what is on
display is simply specimens of gems, rocks and minerals.
Exhibits range from priceless diamonds, emeralds and
sapphires to grains of sand: you'll never look at a humble
rock in quite the same way again.

TAKING A BREAK

Stop for lunch at either **Emporio Armani Caffè** (➤ 120),
on the Brompton Road, or in one of the museum's cafés or its
restaurant (all are child-friendly).

🕂 195 D1 ✉ Cromwell Road, SW7 ☎ 020 7942 5000; www.nhm.ac.uk
🕐 Daily 10–5:50 (last admission 5:30) 🍴 Cafés, restaurant, snack bar
and fast-food restaurant 🚇 South Kensington 🚌 C1, 14, 49, 70, 74, 345,
360, 414 🎟 Free

NATURAL HISTORY MUSEUM: INSIDE INFO

Top tips The main museum entrance on Cromwell Road leads into the Green
Zone: during busy periods use the entrance in Exhibition Road, which takes
you to the Earth Galleries. The two are joined by **Gallery 50**.
■ The museum is **quietest** early or late on weekdays, but all periods during
   school holidays are busy.
■ **Look out for** the exciting new Darwin Centre.

5 Kensington Palace

Kensington Palace has been the home of various members of royalty for many centuries, and came most recently to public notice when the late Diana, Princess of Wales moved here. This is an attractive and historic palace, well worth a visit for its setting, art treasures, State Apartments, fine furnishings and Royal Ceremonial Dress Collection.

The south front of Kensington Palace was designed in 1695 by Nicholas Hawksmoor

The mansion began life as a country house in 1605, but was converted into a palace by Sir Christopher Wren for King William III and Queen Mary II following their accession to the throne in 1689 and their decision to move from damp, riverside Whitehall. Later resident monarchs included Queen Anne, George I and George II, while Queen Victoria was born, baptized and grew up in the palace. It was also here that she was woken one morning in June 1837 to be told that her uncle (William IV) had died and that she was Queen. Today, several members of the royal family have private apartments in the palace.

Visiting the Palace

Begin downstairs with the **Royal Ceremonial Dress Collection** and then move upstairs to the **State Apartments**. In the former, you can see the sumptuous clothes that would have been worn by those being presented at court at the turn of the 19th century. For many visitors, the most interesting part of the exhibition are the dresses belonging to the late Diana, Princess of Wales.

Upstairs, the apartments of King William III and (less grand) rooms of his wife, Queen Mary II, have been restored to their 18th-century appearance. Their most impressive corner is the Cupola Room, decorated in the style of ancient Rome with an excess of gilded statues and classical painting: it was here that Queen Victoria's baptism took place in 1819. The room's centrepiece is an 18th-century clock called *The Temple of the Four Grand Monarchies of the World*, whose intricate decoration far outshines the tiny clockface itself.

The palace has seen its share of tragedy. Mary II succumbed to smallpox here at the age of 32 in 1694, and when Queen Anne's beloved husband, Prince George, died in 1708, she did not return to the palace for many months. Like Mary, she also died here six years later, at 49 years of age, a sad figure who, despite 18 pregnancies, saw none of her children live beyond the age of 11. King George II ended his days here too – while on the lavatory.

The King's Gallery holds the famous Van Dyck portrait of Charles I

TAKING A BREAK

Enjoy a classic English afternoon tea in pleasant surroundings in the **Orangery** (➤ 133).

✚ 194 B3 ✉ The Broad Walk, Kensington Gardens, W8
☎ 020 7937 9561; www.hrp.org.uk 🕐 Mar–Oct daily 10–6 (last entry 5pm); Nov–Feb daily 10–5 (last entry 4pm) 🍴 Restaurant in the Orangery (➤ 133) serving light meals, snacks and afternoon tea 🚇 High Street Kensington, Queensway, Notting Hill 🚌 C1, 9, 10, 27, 28, 49, 52, 70, 94, 328 💷 Very expensive

---

KENSINGTON PALACE: INSIDE INFO

Top tips Access to the palace is from the back of the building, from The Broad Walk in Kensington Gardens.

■ There is no official monument here to Diana, Princess of Wales, but in Kensington Gardens is a **Memorial Playground** and in Hyde Park is a **fountain** (➤ 130–131).

■ Be sure to visit the **Orangery** (➤ 133), built for Queen Anne and now a restaurant, and don't miss the pretty **Sunken Garden**.

At Your Leisure

⑥ Chelsea Physic Garden

This small garden is a quiet corner of pretty, rural tranquillity in the heart of the city, with more than 5,000 species of plants growing in attractive profusion. Established in 1673, it was founded by the Royal Society of Apothecaries to study medicinal plants, making it the oldest botanical garden in England after Oxford's. It also retains the country's oldest rockery (1773) and the first cedars in England were planted here in 1683. After green-seeded cotton plants from the West Indies were nurtured in the garden, seed was sent to Georgia in the American colonies in 1732 and contributed to what would later develop into the huge cotton plantations of the South.

🔁 198 A1 ✉ Swan Walk, 66 Royal Hospital Road, SW3 ☎ 020 7352 5646; www.chelseaphysicgarden.co.uk ⑥ Apr–Oct Wed–Fri 12–5, Sun 12–6 Ⓤ Sloane Square 🚍 239 💷 Expensive

⑦ Albert Memorial

This gleaming memorial is the most florid and exuberant of all London's monumental statues. It was

FOR KIDS
■ Science Museum (➤ 121–123)
■ Natural History Museum (➤ 124–126)
■ Boating on the Serpentine or feeding the ducks in Kensington Gardens and Hyde Park (➤ 130–131)
■ Harrods' toy department (➤ 116)

completed in 1872 by Sir George Gilbert Scott, winner of a competition to design a national memorial to Prince Albert of Saxe-Coburg-Gotha (1819–61), Queen Victoria's husband, though it was not unveiled until four years later. Victoria and Albert married in 1840, but Albert died of typhoid aged just 41 years, a blow from which Victoria never quite recovered.

What Albert – who didn't want a memorial – would have made of the neo-Gothic pile is hard to imagine: his spectacularly gilded statue is some

Chelsea Physic Garden is one of the country's oldest botanical gardens

three times life size, and the edifice as a whole rises 55m (180 feet), its apex crowned by the figures of Faith, Hope and Charity. The figures around the edges portray subjects such as astronomy, poetry and sculpture, plus enterprises close to Albert's heart, including agriculture, manufacturing and commerce. The 169 sculptures around the statue's base are figures from history – there's not one woman among them – while those set slightly apart are allegories of the continents of Europe, Africa, America and Asia. ✚ 195 D2 ✉ South Carriage Drive, Kensington Gardens, SW7 ☎ 020 7495 0916 for guided tours 🚇 High Street Kensington, Knightsbridge 🚌 9, 10, 52

🟦 Hyde Park and Kensington Gardens

Most of the large swathe of green southwest of Marble Arch is

near Marble Arch, is the place to air your views – anyone is entitled to stand up here and (within certain parameters) speak their mind: Sunday afternoons draw the most orators. Further west stretches the **Serpentine**, an artificial lake created in 1730 by Caroline, wife of George II, for boating and bathing. It's now a good a place to while away an hour on the water – rowing boats and pedaloes are available for a fee on the northern bank. You can also swim at certain times in a designated area off the south shore. Close by is the **Diana, Princess of Wales Memorial Fountain**, an 80m (88-yard) oval ring of Cornish granite in which water flows at different speeds.

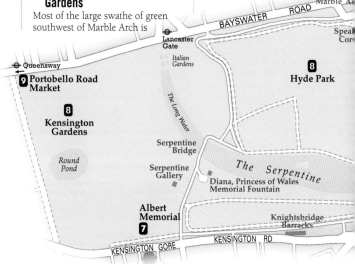

Hyde Park, but Kensington Gardens, which were formerly the grounds of Kensington Palace (➤ 127–128), occupies an area to the west of the Serpentine lake.

Originally a hunting ground for Henry VIII, **Hyde Park** was opened to the public in the early 17th century, and today provides a magnificent and peaceful area in which to escape the city. **Speakers' Corner**, at its northeastern edge

The **Serpentine Gallery** shows a changing programme of often controversial modern art throughout the year.

Other art in the park includes a variety of statues, most famously that of **Peter Pan** (1912), which was paid for by the story's author, J M Barrie, who lived near by. It's just off a walkway on the Serpentine's west bank, near the lake's northern limit.

The red building "Alice's" on the corner of Portobello Road Market

Hyde Park
195 F3 Daily 5am–midnight
Hyde Park Corner, Knightsbridge, Lancaster Gate, Marble Arch

Kensington Gardens
195 D3 Daily 5am–midnight
High Street Kensington, Bayswater, Queensway, Lancaster Gate

Serpentine Gallery
195 D3 020 7402 6075; www.serpentinegallery.org
Daily 10–6 during exhibitions
Lancaster Gate Free

9 Portobello Road Market
Portobello is London's largest market, the long street and its environs hosting a wide variety of food, modern clothing, crafts and junk markets, as well as the specialist small shops and antiques shops (and stalls) that first made it famous. On Saturday it is the scene of what is reputedly the world's largest antiques market, with more than 1,500 traders, the majority of whom are located at the street's southern end

after the intersection with Westbourne Grove. Fruit stalls dominate beyond Elgin Crescent, while junk, second-hand clothes and more off-beat shops and stalls take over beyond the "Westway" elevated section of road.

The range and quality of antiques and other goods is enormous. At the top end, prices are as high as any in London, but bargains and one-offs can still be found; it's great fun to browse and people-watch even if you don't want to buy anything.

Note that on fine summer days the market is often extremely crowded (and you should beware of pickpockets).

194 A4 General: Mon–Sat 8–6:30 (Thu closes 1pm). Antiques: Sat; Clothes/bric-a-brac: Fri, Sat, Sun Notting Hill Gate, Ladbroke Grove 7, 23, 27, 28, 31, 52, 70, 328

Diana Memorial Fountain, Hyde Park

Where to...
Eat and Drink

Prices
Expect to pay per person for a meal excluding drinks and service:

£ under £25 £££ £25–£50 £££ over £50

The Ark £–££

The clever use of mirrors has given depth to the narrow room at this revamped Kensington favourite. The menu includes a mixture of classic, modern and regional Italian dishes. Expect good al dente pasta and rustic meat dishes served with polenta. An attractively priced lunch menu has proved immensely popular, and in the evening the menu expands and gains some specials.

🖶 194 B3 🖾 122 Palace Gardens Terrace, W8 ☎ 020 7229 4024; www.ark-restaurant. com ⓦ Lunch: Tue–Sat 12–3. Dinner: Mon–Sat 6–11 Ⓜ Notting Hill Gate

Bibendum ££

Sir Terence Conran opened his flagship restaurant in the acclaimed Michelin building in 1987. It is relaxed and highly professional, and the magnificent dining room is a great setting. The wide range of classic European dishes on the menu is given a modern twist, and the depth of the wine list is a real talking point. There is a daily-changing lunch menu.

🖶 Off map 195 E1 🖾 Michelin House, 81 Fulham Road, SW3 ☎ 020 7581 5817; www.bibendum.co.uk ⓦ Lunch: Mon–Fri 12–2:30, Sat–Sun 12:30–3. Dinner: Mon–Sat 7–11, Sun 7–10:30 Ⓜ South Kensington

Bluebird ££

A flower shop, café, bar and epicerie are all part of the experience at Terence Conran's Bluebird/Gastrodome. There is a great buzz from the smart restaurant. The menu is simply conceived and includes an eclectic range of modern European dishes. There is a strong seafood selection and more rustic choices such as chicken and mushroom pie. They have a special Sunday lunch menu.

🖶 Off map 198 A2 🖾 350 King's Road, SW3 ☎ 020 7559 1000; www.bluebird-restaurant. com ⓦ Mon–Fri 12–2:30, 6–10:30, Sat–Sun 12–3:30, 6–10:30 (Sun 9:30) Ⓜ Sloane Square

Cambio de Tercio ££

Acclaimed as one of the best Spanish restaurants outside the Iberian Peninsula, this friendly restaurant serves up exquisite Modern Spanish cooking. Dishes veer from the innovative – skate wing with pig's ear – to the classic, such as baby lamb chops, oxtail or grilled tuna, albeit with a modern twist. Desserts are superb; make sure to leave room for the home-made ice cream. If you want a less expensive or lighter but equally authentic Spanish meal, just cross the road to their tapas bar offshoot, Tendido Cero.

🖶 Off map 195 E1 🖾 163 Old Brompton Road, SW3 ☎ 020 7244 8970; www.cambiodetercio.co.uk ⓦ Lunch: Mon–Fri 12–2:30, Sat–Sun 12–3:30. Dinner: Mon–Sat 7–11:30, Sun 7–11. Tendido de Cero Lunch: Mon–Fri 12–2:30, Sat–Sun 12–3. Dinner: daily 6:30–11 Ⓜ Gloucester Road, South Kensington

Fifth Floor at Harvey Nichols ££

The Fifth Floor restaurant, on the top floor of the designer-label Harvey Nichols department store (▶ 134), forms part of a food lover's paradise that takes in a food hall, café and bar, and Yo! Sushi. The dining room is chic and the food slick, using British produce in an innovative way. Afternoon tea is a shopper's treat. Both the restaurant and bar can become crowded at peak times. Reservations are essential.

➕ 198 A4 ⊠ Harvey Nichols, Knightsbridge, SW1 ☎ 020 7235 5250; www.harveynichols.com ⓦ Lunch: Mon–Thu 12–3, Fri–Sun 12–4. Dinner: Mon–Sat 6–11:30 ⓠ Knightsbridge

The Orangery £

The elegant, white, light Orangery provides a pleasant, informal setting for English afternoon tea. Four set teas are offered, one including champagne, or you could just plump for a selection of delicious cakes and a pot of tea. Light lunches are available between noon and 3pm.

➕ 194 B3 ⊠ Kensington Palace, Kensington Gardens, W8 ☎ 020 7938 1406; www.hrp.org.uk ⓦ Mar–Oct daily 10–6; Nov–Feb 10–5. Afternoon tea: 3–6 (Nov–Feb 2:30–5) ⓠ High Street Kensington

Racine ££

Only in France does it get any more French than in this popular Knightsbridge brasserie, just opposite the South Kensington museums. There's an authentic bustle and a rather masculine decor of dark wood and deep brown leather. This is just the place for hearty bourgeois fare such as rabbit in mustard sauce, steak and *frites*, or perhaps langoustines, and for dessert, *pot au chocolat*. Even the simple dishes have big flavours.

➕ 195 E1 ⊠ 239 Brompton Road, SW3 ☎ 020 7584 4477 ⓦ Mon–Fri noon–3, 6–10:30, Sat–Sun 12–3:30, 6–10 ⓠ South Kensington

Restaurant Gordon Ramsay £££

One of the country's most acclaimed chefs, Michelin-starred Gordon Ramsay learned his skills in the best kitchens in France and in London, where he worked under Marco Pierre White and Albert Roux. Ramsay installed at the former La Tante Claire (discreetly restyled), Gordon Ramsay enthrals customers with a rich, yet light style of haute cuisine. The best value – and the best way to sample the Ramsay style – is the set three-course lunch. Reserving well in advance is essential.

➕ 198 A1 ⊠ 68–69 Royal Hospital Road, SW3 ☎ 020 7352 4441; www.gordonramsay.com ⓦ Mon–Fri 12–2:30, 6:30–11 ⓠ Sloane Square

Zafferano £££

In an understated room, the plain walls, terracotta floor, comfortable chairs and closely set tables all contribute to an air of classy informality. Star chef Giorgio Locatelli established Zafferano as London's leading Italian restaurant and, although he has now gone, the cooking is still excellent. Food is presented with an understanding and flair that many more pretentious establishments have difficultly matching. Uncluttered and simply conceived dishes based on the finest ingredients, exact technique and clear flavours are the driving force behind both the lunch and dinner menus. Expect classics with a twist such as veal shin ravioli with saffron. For a romantic setting, book a table in the first room.

➕ 198 B3 ⊠ 15 Lowndes Street, SW1 ☎ 020 7235 5800; www.zafferanorestaurant.com ⓦ Lunch: Mon–Fri 12–2:30, Sat–Sun 12:30–3. Dinner: Mon–Sat 7–11, Sun 7–10:30 ⓠ Knightsbridge

BARS

Boisdale of Belgravia ££

An astonishing range of 170 single malt whiskies is available at London's premier whisky bar. Furnishings offer the odd spot of tartan to emphasize the Scottish theme. Despite the presence of a cigar bar, this is not in any way a male preserve. Indeed, it's a pleasant place, with an attractive courtyard, a cosy, dark, atmospheric bar and an adjoining restaurant that specializes in Scottish dishes. Live jazz is performed nightly.

➕ 198 C3 ⊠ 15 Eccleston Street, SW1 ☎ 020 7730 6922; www.boisdale.co.uk ⓦ Mon–Fri 12–1am, Sat 7pm–1am ⓠ Victoria

Where to...
Shop

Many shops in this area don't open until 10am, often closing at 6pm. On a Sunday this generally becomes noon to 5pm. Late-night shopping is Wednesday (Kensington High Street, Thursday), with shops generally adding an extra hour on to their usual closing times.

KNIGHTSBRIDGE

Harvey Nichols (109–125 Knightsbridge, SW1, tel: 020 7235 5000; www.harveynichols. com. Open: Mon–Sat 10–8, Sun 12–6. Tube: Knightsbridge). Fashion addicts can indulge themselves on three floors of designer womenswear, two floors of menswear and a ground floor given over to up-to-the-minute accessories such as hosiery, Dolce e Gabbana sunglasses and all manner of scarves, perfumes and cosmetics. Minimalist surroundings house an industrial steel-and-glass fifth-floor food emporium, consisting of an opulent food hall, a sushi bar, a café, a bar and a restaurant.

Harrods is a must on most tourist itineraries (▶ 116). The store is renowned for food, but is also strong on fashion.

SLOANE STREET

Sloane Street, bounded at its northern end by Knightsbridge Underground station and on its southern end by Sloane Square, is a serious showcase for international designers. Italy is represented by the romantic designs of **Alberta Ferretti** (205–206 Sloane Street, SW1, tel: 020 7235 2349. Tube: Knightsbridge) – gauzes and shimmering silks in a chandeliered setting; by that master of understated neutrality, **Armani** (37 Sloane Street, SW1, tel: 020 7235 6232; www.giorgioarmani. com. Tube: Knightsbridge); and by the funky uniformity of **Prada** (43–45 Sloane Street, SW1, tel: 020 7235 0008. Tube: Knightsbridge). Just around the corner, **Agent Provocateur** (16 Pont Street, SW1, tel: 020 7235 0229; www.agentprovocateur.com. Tube: Knightsbridge) sells top-quality saucy lingerie.

If all the choice of high fashion sends you into a wardrobe (or wallet) crisis, slip into the old-established stationery sanctuary of **Smythson's** (135 Sloane Street, SW1, tel: 020 7730 5520; www. smythson.com. Tube: Sloane Square) to scoop up leather-bound diaries and notebooks, bags and wallets, plus perfect engraved paper and envelopes at reasonable prices.

KENSINGTON HIGH STREET AND KENSINGTON CHURCH STREET

Kensington High Street might be less slick, but it is very long and has lots of useful shops clustered around the High Street Kensington Underground station. Here you will find most familiar high-street names such as Laura Ashley, Zara and Gap, plus a major branch of Marks & Spencer. The Whole Food Market, which sells only natural and organic food, opened here in 2007 and is the largest food retailer in London.

Running north, opposite Barkers Arcade, is Kensington Church Street (Tube: Kensington High Street), an antiques lover's dream, with a fabulous concentration of dealers. Works by important 19th- and early 20th-century designers such as William Morris and Pugin are for sale at **Haslam & Whiteway** (105 Kensington Church Street, W8, tel: 020 7229 1145; www. haslamandwhiteway.com). Cornish ware, Midwinter and Poole potteries are the speciality at **Richard Dennis** (144 Kensington Church Street, W8, tel: 020 7727 2061, open by appointment only). Richard Dennis can organize shipping, as can **John Jesse** (160 Kensington Church Street, W8, tel: 020 7229 0312), who stocks 20th-century design, including art nouveau prints.

Wherever you buy, don't forget to thoroughly inspect the goods, haggle and request a receipt with an accurate description of the item.

SOUTH KENSINGTON

Individual shops at the Natural History Museum (▶ 124–126), the Science Museum (▶ 121–123) and the V&A Museum (▶ 117–120) stock all the educational lines that you might expect: pocket-money toys, dinosaurs and pretty minerals at the Natural History Museum; rockets and robots at the Science Museum.

The museum shops, however, are also a good hunting ground for top-quality gifts for discerning grown-ups.

The **V&A shop** is a real Aladdin's cave. A Crafts Council section sells contemporary works by British artists – one-off gifts and future collectables – while the main section is filled with clever reproductions of 18th-century ceramics, antique dolls and teddy bears, a vast selection of William Morris memorabilia and lavish coffee-table art books. At the Science Museum, adults will find an unusual range of gadgetry and scientific instruments.

KING'S ROAD

The young and young at heart flock to this Chelsea thoroughfare for its boutiques and other interesting shops. A promenade can start at Sloane Square (Tube: Sloane Square) and take in the entire length of the long road, or just a fraction; either way there is a crop of coffee bars, from the chains such as Starbucks to independent cafés, at which to fuel your progress.

Peter Jones department store (Sloane Square, SW1, tel: 020 7730 3434; www.peterjones.co.uk) is on Sloane Square itself. Ted Baker, Monsoon and Jigsaw begin a roll-call of mid-price fashion names as you begin to wander down the King's Road. Further along, the vintage clothes shop **Steinberg & Tolkien** (193 King's Road, SW3, tel: 020 7376 3660) has a dazzling array of garments, including Pucci shirts, 1970s kaftans and cases of old jewellery and wacky accessories. Teenagers love dressing up at **Ad Hoc** (153 King's Road, SW3, tel 020 7376 8829; www.adhoclondon.co.uk) full of hats, costume jewellery, wigs, hosiery and all sorts of unsuitable garments! Downwind of **Lush** (123 King's Road, SW3, tel: 020 7376 8348; www.lush.co.uk), you can smell in advance the fragrant natural cosmetics: soaps sliced from huge blocks to order, fizzing bath bombs and gooey hand-mixed face packs, plus fun packaging and labelling.

Heal's (234 King's Road, SW3, tel: 020 7349 8411; www.heals.co.uk) has things for the home, from furniture to photo frames, as does the fashionable **Designers' Guild** (267–271 & 275–277 King's Road, SW3, tel: 020 7351 5775), towards the World's End of the King's Road (Tube: West Brompton, Earl's Court).

Food fans might enjoy trekking this far along to discover the **Bluebird** (▶ 132) with its café, bar, restaurant and food market. Check out the bakery's lovely fresh breads such as rosemary or spinach, the delicatessen counters and unusual dry goods. Opposite, the sweet-toothed can indulge at **Rococo** chocolates (321 King's Road, SW3, tel: 020 7352 5857; www.rococochocolates.com) with its bars of dark and milk artisan chocolate flavoured with ingredients like Earl Grey tea, chilli, nutmeg, cardamom and wild mint.

Where to...
Be Entertained

CINEMA

Commercial choice is between the **two multi-screen Cineworld cinemas**, showing recent releases (279 King's Road, SW3 and 142 Fulham Road, SW10, tel: 0871 200 2000; www.cineworld.co.uk. Tube: South Kensington).

The **Chelsea Cinema** (206 King's Road, SW3, tel: 020 7351 3742; www.curzoncinemas.com. Tube: Earl's Court) shows similar films, with the bonus of the most comfortable cinema seats in town. It also has a small bar.

At the **Gate Picturehouse** (Notting Hill Gate, W11, tel: 0871 704 2058. Tube: Notting Hill Gate), both trendy art-house films and mainstream blockbusters are screened.

CLASSICAL MUSIC

The **Proms**, as the Henry Wood Promenade Concerts are known, is one of the world's greatest music festivals. Concerts are held nightly at the **Royal Albert Hall** (Kensington Gore, tel: 0845 401 5045; www.royal alberthall.com. Tube: South Kensington) for a seven-week period every summer, beginning in mid-July.

Visiting international orchestras, soloists and conductors join the BBC Symphony Orchestra to perform a wide range of music. If you are prepared to wait, you can buy inexpensive standing-only tickets. Those with less stamina (but deeper pockets) can choose from a range of more expensive seats or even boxes.

NIGHTLIFE

Nightclubs are not found in abundance in this part of the city. Try **Bar Cuba** (11–13 Kensington High Street, W8, tel: 020 7938 4137. Tube: Kensington High Street), a chic place with a smart clientele. It offers a broad spectrum of Latin music, with occasional live bands.

If you like jazz, try the **606 Club** (90 Lots Road, SW10, tel: 020 7352 5953; www.606club.co.uk. Tube: Fulham Broadway), where groups such as the bluesy, modern jazz Julian Siegel Quartet play. It is open to non-members.

At the sophisticated **Pizza on the Park** (11–13 Knightsbridge, SW1, tel: 020 7235 7825; www.pizzaonthepark.co.uk. Tube: Hyde Park Corner), you can listen to live music every night, provided by resident company American Songbook in London. Book ahead for concerts by leading cabaret artists (check the website).

THEATRE

Whether shocking, disturbing or just plain brilliant, the **Royal Court** (Sloane Square, SW1, tel: 020 7565 5000. Tube: Sloane Square), home of the English Stage Company, has nurtured some of Britain's best modern playwrights, and is the place for modern theatre at its very best. A multimillion-pound refurbishment has uplifted the experience for theatregoers, replacing cramped conditions in the two theatres with superb facilities.

The **Holland Park Theatre** (Holland Park, W8, tel: 0845 230 9769. Tube: Holland Park) is a popular open-air venue that operates only in the summer months. With the ruins of the 17th-century Holland House as a backdrop, and occasional accompaniment from the peacocks wandering freely through the park, the theatre plays host to the Royal Ballet, as well as offering a well-regarded opera season.

Covent Garden, Bloomsbury and Soho

Getting Your Bearings

Exploration of these districts underlines London's amazing variety: within the space of a few streets an area's character can change from classy to run down, from retail to residential, and from busy and exciting to genteel and refined.

ZSL **7**
London Zoo

6 Regent's Park

Open Air Theatre

Queen Mary's Garden

Boating Lake

PRINCE ALBERT ROAD

Grand Union Canal (Regent's Canal)

PARK ROAD

London Central Mosque

Madame Tussauds **3**

Baker St

MARYLEBONE ROAD

University of Westminster

PADDINGTON ST

BAKER STREET

MARYLEBONE HIGH STREET

THAYER ST

Regent's Park

PARK CRES

Wallace Collection **8**

WIGMORE STREET

JAMES ST

OXFORD STREET

Bond Street

★ **Don't Miss**

1 British Museum ➤ 142
2 British Library ➤ 146
3 Madame Tussauds ➤ 148
4 Covent Garden ➤ 150

At Your Leisure

5 Camden Markets ➤ 152
6 Regent's Park ➤ 152
7 ZSL London Zoo ➤ 153
8 Wallace Collection ➤ 154
9 Chinatown ➤ 154
10 Cartoon Museum ➤ 155
11 London Transport Museum ➤ 155

Up until the 1970s Covent Garden was the site of London's wholesale fruit and vegetable market, but when this moved out, the market building was transformed into a small shopping centre and craft market. Gentrification has since spread, and the market and surrounding area have become a vibrant shopping and entertainment district.

Previous page: The Great Court, British Museum

West of Covent Garden lie Chinatown and Soho, crammed with restaurants, bars and clubs. Soho has a reputation as London's gay village and red-light district, and neon lights and advertisements for strip joints and sex shops lend a seedy air.

Travel just a few minutes north of Covent Garden, however, and you find yourself in sedate Bloomsbury. The district gave its name to a group of early 20th-century writers and artists who lived in the area. Its houses are handsome, and its streets and squares chic: a fitting home for the British Museum. On its northern edge Bloomsbury merges into King's Cross, the site for the British Library, one of the capital's most costly public buildings. West of Bloomsbury lie the elegant streets and squares of Marylebone and one of London's most visited attractions, Madame Tussauds. If this is not to your taste, consider the Wallace Collection, a treasury of art and artefacts housed in an 18th-century town house.

Map labels:

1 km
½ mile

Primrose Hill

Camden Markets **5**

7 ZSL London Zoo

Regent's Park

KENTISH TOWN ROAD
CAMDEN ROAD
YORK WAY
COLLEGE PL
CAMDEN ST
CAMDEN HIGH ST
HAMPSTEAD RD
ALBANY ST
PRINCE ALBERT RD

Camden Markets **5**

King's Cross Station

St Pancras International Station

British Library **2**

King's Cross St Pancras

EVERSHOLT STREET

Euston Station

Euston

HAMPSTEAD ROAD

UPPER WOBURN PL
TAVISTOCK SQUARE
WOBURN PL

EUSTON ROAD

Euston Square

University College

Warren Street

GOWER STREET

Russell Square

TOTTENHAM COURT ROAD

University of London

SOUTHAMPTON ROW

British Telecom Tower

CHENIES ST

Goodge Street

GOODGE ST

RUSSELL SQUARE

BEDFORD SQUARE
MONTAGUE PL

MER STREET

1
British Museum

10 Cartoon Museum

GREAT RUSSELL STREET
BLOOMSBURY WAY

Holborn

Tottenham Court Road

NEW OXFORD STREET

HIGH HOLBORN

KINGSWAY

OXFORD STREET

CHARING CROSS ROAD

ENDELL ST

Royal Opera House

MONMOUTH ST

LONG ACRE

Covent Garden

SHAFTESBURY AVENUE

9 Chinatown

Leicester Square

Jubilee Market

Covent Garden **4** **11** **London Transport Museum**

0 500 metres
0 500 yards

In a Day

If you're not quite sure where to begin your travels, this itinerary recommends a practical and enjoyable day out exploring Covent Garden, Bloomsbury and Soho, taking in some of the best places to see using the Getting Your Bearings map on the previous page. For more information see the main entries.

9:00am

Arrive at the ❶ **British Museum** (above, ➤ 142–145) for when the Great Court opens at 9am. Spend some time admiring this splendid new concourse, before exploring the museum itself, full of beautiful pieces from bygone civilizations, including the Elgin Marbles.

12:00 noon

Take lunch in one of the many cafés and pubs near the museum or bring along a picnic to eat in leafy Russell Square.

1:00pm

From Russell Square catch a No 91 bus or take a 30-minute walk through Bloomsbury to the ❷ **British Library** (➤ 146–147). Look at the outside of the building from the spacious piazza then admire some of the world's loveliest old books and manuscripts. Stop for a coffee in the café here.

2:30pm

The No 30 bus takes you along Euston Road to Marylebone Road and ❸ **Madame Tussauds** (opposite top, ➤ 148–149). The waxworks are popular

year-round and you will probably have a wait in the long queue to get in, so try to buy your ticket in advance.

4:30pm

Take the Underground from Baker Street to **4 Covent Garden** (Neal's Yard, below, ➤ 150–151). The market, shops, street entertainers and the area's great choice of restaurants, pubs and bars make this a lively place to spend the early evening. It's a short walk from here to many West End theatres (➤ 160).

❶ British Museum

The British Museum houses one of the world's foremost collections, containing a wealth of antiquities illuminating the history of civilizations and cultures from across the globe. Founded in 1753 around the private collection of Sir Hans Sloane, it now possesses more than 6 million artefacts arranged in a magnificent building with several miles of galleries. The exhibits on display include ancient sculpture, sublime paintings, exquisite jewellery and a host of other treasures.

The British Museum is vast, with more than enough beautiful exhibits to sustain several lengthy visits, so for those with only a short amount of time, the key is not to try to see it all in one visit. Be ruthlessly selective and try not to get too distracted.

The colonnaded main building of the British Museum was built in 1844 to replace the earlier Montagu House, which had become too small to house the museum's growing collection

Great Court

Start by visiting the (**Queen Elizabeth II**) **Great Court.** This spectacular concourse area, created by glassing over the museum's central courtyard, is part of an on-going programme of redevelopment. At its heart lies the beautiful 19th-century Reading Room, which formerly housed the British Library (▶ 146–147), but is now open to the general public. Marx, Lenin, George Bernard Shaw and hundreds of other luminaries studied here. The Great Court serves as the museum's central information area: pick up a museum plan before starting your exploration of the galleries.

Egyptian Galleries

These galleries, which house one of the best collections of Egyptian antiquities outside Egypt, are among the museum's highlights. Funerary art and artefacts dominate, with exquisitely decorated coffins, mummies, sarcophagi, jewellery,

The museum's Great Court

models and scrolls. The gilded inner coffin of Henutmehyt (c.1290BC) is particularly impressive. Also look for the case containing "Ginger", the 5,000-year-old mummified body of an Egyptian, whose leathery remains always draw a crowd. He still has a few tufts of red hair, but is missing his left index finger (it was "collected" by an early visitor to the museum).

The most important exhibit in these galleries, and perhaps the entire museum, is the **Rosetta Stone** (196BC). Its significance lies in the three languages of its inscriptions: Greek at the bottom, Egyptian hieroglyphs at the top, a cursive form of the Egyptian between the two. Discovered accidentally in 1799, the stone enabled Egyptian hieroglyphs to be deciphered, allowing much

SUGGESTED ROUTE
Follow this route to cover some of the museum's highlights with minimum fuss.

Ground floor:
■ Room 4 Egyptian Sculpture Gallery
■ Rooms 6–10 Assyrian Galleries
■ Room 18 The Sculptures of the Parthenon
First floor:
■ Room 41 Early Medieval (Sutton Hoo)
■ Room 49 Weston Gallery of Roman Britain (Mildenhall Treasure)
■ Rooms 61–66 Egyptian Galleries

of Egyptian civilization to be
understood. Less important, but
more visually arresting, is the **head
of Rameses II**: it was carved for the
ruler's memorial temple in Thebes
in the 13th century BC.

Elgin Marbles

The museum's most controversial
sculptures are the Elgin Marbles,
named after Lord Elgin, a British
diplomat who brought them to
England in 1816. Most are from a
5th-century BC frieze removed from
the Parthenon, the most important
temple in ancient Athens, and
they probably depict a festival in
honour of Athena. Modern Greece
believes the Marbles should be
returned, claiming it is wrong that
a foreign museum should possess such important national
cultural relics.

Winged,
human-headed
bull sculptures
from Assyria
(865–860BC)

Assyrian Displays

The Assyrians, who lived in what is now northern Iraq,
are represented by, among other things, the entrance of
Khorsabad, Palace of Sargon (721–705BC), a glorious
example of the massive carvings of winged bulls with human
heads that guarded their palaces. Equally beguiling are the
reliefs of King Ashurbanipal, the last great Assyrian king; they
depict a lion hunt, and once adorned his palace in Ninevah.

British Exhibits

British artefacts are also celebrated. The 7th-century Anglo-
Saxon **Sutton Hoo Ship Burial exhibits** – weapons and
helmets in particular – provide a valuable insight into the
Dark Ages, a period of British and European history about
which relatively little is known. The treasures were found in
1939 during excavations of burial mounds close to the River

A parthenon
from ancient
Greece

Mummies are among the most popular exhibits in the museum

Deben near Woodbridge in Suffolk, a site which, before the construction of sea walls, lay just 185m (200 yards) from the high-water level. The **Mildenhall Treasure**, a collection of 4th-century Roman silverware, was found at Mildenhall, in Suffolk, just a few years later. Mystery still surrounds the discovery of the treasure, which was not immediately declared to the authorities. Its centrepiece is the 8kg (18-pound) Great Dish, decorated with images of Neptune, the sea god.

TAKING A BREAK

The **Coffee Gallery** (23 Museum Street, WC1, tel: 020 7436 0455) is a good place to stop for a light lunch.

🞢 197 F3 ✉ Great Russell Street, WC1 ☎ 020 7323 8000; www.britishmuseum.org 🕐 Main galleries: Sat–Wed 10–5:30, Thu–Fri 10–8:30. Great Court: Sun–Wed 9–6, Thu–Sat 9am–11pm 🍴 Cafés and restaurants 🚇 Holborn, Tottenham Court Road, Russell Square 🚌 Tottenham Court Road, northbound, and Gower Street, southbound 10, 24, 29, 73, 134; Southampton Row 68, 91, 188; New Oxford Street 7, 8, 19, 25, 38, 55, 98 💷 Free

---

BRITISH MUSEUM: INSIDE INFO

Top tips The museum has two entrances: the main one on **Great Russell Street** and a quieter one on **Montague Place**.
■ Video and still photography is **generally allowed**.
■ **Guided tours** of the museum's highlights (10:30, 1, 3; 90 mins; charge) or individual galleries (30–40 mins; free) are available. For further information, or to sign up, ask at information points in the Great Court. Audio guides are also available.

In more detail The **Mexican Gallery (Room 27)** contains several impressive displays, the loveliest of which are the turquoise mosaic statues from the Mixtec–Aztec era (1400–1521).
■ If you have time, admire the craftsmanship of the gold and silver **Oxus Treasure (Room 51)**, Persian artefacts dating from the 5th or 4th century BC.

One to miss The famous **Portland Vase**, a piece of Roman blown glass, is rather small and unimpressive. Repairs to it are all too clearly visible.

② British Library

The British Library ranks alongside the National Library of Congress in Washington and the Bibliothèque Nationale in Paris as one of the three greatest libraries in the world. Its contents include some of the world's most incredible printed treasures. Exhibits span almost three millennia, from the Buddhist Diamond Sutra of AD868, the world's oldest printed book, up to the modern manuscripts of Paul McCartney and John Lennon. Along the way they take in Shakespeare's First Folio, the Gutenberg Bible, the Magna Carta and the notebooks of Leonardo da Vinci. The purpose-built, modern library buildings, grouped around an attractive central plaza, provide an airy, attractive, user-friendly space in which to enjoy the collection.

John Ritblat Gallery: Treasures of the British Library

This contains the library's most valuable items, including maps, religious texts, letters and literary and musical manuscripts. The gallery is remarkable for the fame, age, breadth and quality of its collection. The light is kept low to protect the material and the atmosphere is almost hallowed – as indeed it should be in the presence of the Lindisfarne Gospels and Bedford Hours, two of the loveliest early English illuminated manuscripts.

The binding of the Lindisfarne Gospels (*c.*AD698)

Among the other treasures on display are original manuscripts by Jane Austen and Charlotte Brontë, scores by Mozart and Handel, including the *Messiah*, letters from Gandhi, and Lord Nelson's last (unfinished) love letter to Lady Hamilton.

For an interactive experience head for **Turning the Pages**, a unique computer-based system (just off the John Ritblat Gallery) that allows visitors to "browse" through some of the treasures a page at a time; it is also available online.

Other Galleries

The library's two other galleries offer a more practical look at books.

BRITISH LIBRARY: INSIDE INFO

Top tip Visit the **café or restaurant**, as from here you can enjoy some of the best views of the central glass tower that houses the 65,000 leather-bound volumes of King George III's library.

In more detail Guided tours provide an introduction to the history and workings of the library (1 hour, moderate charge, Mon, Wed and Fri at 3pm, Sat 10:30am and 3pm. Tours on Sun at 11:30am and 3pm include a visit to a reading room. For reservations tel: 01937 546 546).

The **Pearson Gallery** interprets and enlivens the library's great collections and is the location for special exhibitions, while the **Workshop of Words, Sounds and Images** investigates the technology of book production, printing and sound recording. It offers an interactive, computer-based chance to design a book page. There are demonstrations of calligraphy, book-making and printing on Saturdays.

TAKING A BREAK

Visit the library's café or restaurant (► Inside Info, above). Alternatively, try **Patisserie Deux Amis** (63 Judd Street, WC1, tel: 020 7383 7029), a simple café serving filled baguettes and delicious cakes.

🟦 197 F5 🖂 96 Euston Road, NW1 ☎ 0870 444 1500; www.bl.uk 🕙 Mon–Fri 9:30–6 (also Tue 6–8), Sat 9:30–5, Sun and public hols 11–5 🍴 Restaurant, coffee shop and café 🚇 King's Cross 🚌 10, 30, 73, 91 💷 Free

Counting money and paying wages, from the *Treatise on the Vices* (Italian School, 14th century)

VITAL STATISTICS

- The library basement is equivalent to more than five storeys and holds 621km (388 miles) of shelving.
- Some 14 million books are stored in the basement, but the library's total collection numbers more than 150 million items.
- The library receives a free copy of every book, comic, map, newspaper and magazine published in the United Kingdom. This means it receives an average of 3 million items annually.
- The library building was mooted in the 1950s, but opened only in 1998, by which time it had cost three times its original budget.

❸ Madame Tussauds

One of London's most popular tourist attractions, Madame Tussauds offers you the chance to meet James Bond, see how tall actor-turned-politician Arnold Schwarzenegger really is and have your photograph taken with boxing legend Mohammad Ali – or at least waxwork models of these and more than 400 other famous people. A visit provides fun-packed entertainment for adults and children alike.

The displays proper start with the **A-List Party**, where you are in with the glitzy in-crowd. You can give Brad Pitt a squeeze or make J-Lo blush (you'll have to visit to find out how!), feature as part of an exclusive photo shoot with Kate Moss for a fictional "glossy" and you may even be interviewed on Madame T's TV.

Next comes the glitz of **Premiere Night**, with a lavish production of screen stars past and present, such as Marilyn Monroe and Zac Efron.

First Floor Displays

Upstairs on the **World Stage** there are models of religious leaders, members of the Royal Family, politicians and world leaders, as well as figures from the arts including Picasso, Beethoven and The Beatles.

From here you plunge into the **Chamber Live**, the most ghoulish section (unsuitable for children under 12). Torture, execution and murder are dealt with, together with lots of gruesome sound effects, the subject matter portrayed in

Opposite top: Hollywood actor Johnny Depp

Opposite: US President Barack Obama

Below: As if it were yesterday – John, Paul, George and Ringo, as they appeared at the start of their careers

FACTS AND FIGURES

- Early techniques involved casts being made of the model's head. Napoleon had to have straws stuck up his nostrils so that he could breathe as his cast was made, and was so distressed he held Josephine's hand throughout.
- All the hair used on the models is real and is regularly washed and styled.
- The wax used is similar to candle wax and the exhibition has no windows so that models don't melt in the sunlight.

graphic detail with live actors to add to the fear factor. There is an additional charge for this area.

More wholesome family entertainment is provided by the **Spider-Man** exhibition, where your task is to capture him on camera. In the **Spirit of London** section, you can take a ride through colourful tableaux of 400 years of London's history.

In Disney's inspired **Pirates of the Caribbean** experience you can join Captain Jack Sparrow (Johnny Depp) and his swashbuckling crew aboard the *Black Pearl*.

TAKING A BREAK

Try the dim sum at the hugely popular **Royal China** (40 Baker Street, W1, tel: 020 7487 4688).

➕ 196 B4 ✉ Marylebone Road, NW1 ☎ 0870 999 0046; www.madametussauds.com ⏰ Daily 9:30–5:30 🍴 Café for snacks, but a better choice in Baker Street near by 🚇 Baker Street 🚌 13, 18, 27, 30, 74, 82, 113, 139, 274, 205, 453 💷 Very expensive

MADAME TUSSAUDS: INSIDE INFO

Top tips The exhibition is hugely popular and you may have to wait up to two hours to get in during peak season. To avoid the wait, **book tickets online by credit card**, which allows you to enter by the Priority Access entrance. You also save 10 per cent compared to buying on arrival.

- The exhibition is quieter later in the afternoon: if you arrive by 4pm you'll still have time to see everything.
- Ticket packages are available if you plan to **visit other attractions**, such as the London Eye (➤ 99) and SEA LIFE London Aquarium (➤ 98).

4 Covent Garden

When London's wholesale fruit and vegetable market moved out of Covent Garden in the 1970s the scene was set for its transformation into one of the city's most lively, entertaining and popular districts. Weekends are best for exploring the superb shopping, market and entertainment area, with plenty of excellent bars, cafés and restaurants. There are some great museums, top London theatres and the world-renowned Royal Opera House.

The district's heart is the Piazza, the square surrounding the restored 19th-century market building that now houses small shops and the crafts stalls of the Apple Market. Close by is the revamped Royal Opera House and the indoor Jubilee Market (clothes, crafts and leather goods), while the Cartoon Museum (► 155) and London Transport Museum (► 155) will provide a good couple of hours' diversion.

Street performer in Covent Garden

One of the Piazza's highlights is the variety of street entertainers who congregate here, embracing everything from Chinese orchestras and South American pan pipe musicians to acrobats, mime artists and didgeridoo players. They generate much of the buzz and atmosphere of the place. The many

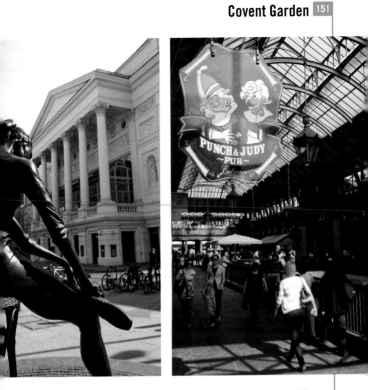

Left to right:
Bronze of a
ballerina outside
the Royal Opera
House; shoppers
in the markets

small streets, especially Neal Street and the area north of the Covent Garden Underground station, are also well worth exploring for their individual and unusual shops (➤ 159) and tucked-away cafés, bars and restaurants.

🚇 200 B4 🚇 Covent Garden 🚌 Along Strand 6, 9, 11, 13, 15, 23, 91, 176

COVENT GARDEN: INSIDE INFO

Top tips Don't leave Covent Garden without wandering down **Neal Street**. Interesting shops here include **The Tea House** (15 Neal Street, WC2, tel: 020 7240 7539), selling a huge range of teas and tea pots.

■ Don't miss **Neal's Yard Remedies** (15 Neal's Yard, WC2, tel: 020 7379 7222), where you can buy herbal remedies, top-quality aromatherapy oils and toiletries. The shop also has a good selection of books on herbal and alternative medicines.

■ For delicious English cheeses, try **Neal's Yard Dairy** (17 Shorts Gardens, WC2, tel: 020 7240 5700). Or stop at **Monmouth Coffee Company** (➤ 157), for one of the best cups of coffee in London.

Hidden gem Take time to go inside **St Paul's Church**, which dominates the western side of the Piazza, and pause in the delightful garden. It is known as the Actor's Church because of the many memorials of film and stage actors it holds.

At Your Leisure

5 Camden Markets

This conglomeration of markets, spreading out from Camden Lock along Chalk Farm Road and Camden High Street, draws many visitors to Camden Town. Sunday, when all the markets are open, is the best day to visit, though individual markets listed below are open on other days. The whole area is usually extremely crowded, especially in the summer. The market is particularly good for modern clothing, jewellery and crafts.

➕ Off map 197 E5 🚇 Camden Town

Camden Lock

Renovated warehouses beside the canal are packed solid with stalls selling arts, crafts, old and new clothing, and CDs, plus food and drink.

🕐 Daily 10–6

Camden Lock Village

This market, previously Camden Canal Market before a major fire destroyed it in 2008, is located to the north of the canal between Chalk Farm Road and Castle Haven Road. The new building opened in 2009, featuring more than 100 shops and many stalls.

🕐 Fri–Sun 10–6

Stables Market

This is the most northerly of the markets (off Chalk Farm Road). It sells pretty much the same range of items as Camden Lock, but with some furniture and antiques as well.

🕐 Sat–Sun 10–6; Mon–Fri 10:30–6, reduced number of stalls

Electric Ballroom Market

Selling second-hand clothes, plus some new items, this market has an emphasis on the weird and way-out.

✉ Camden High Street, just north of Camden Town Underground 🕐 Sun 9–5:30

Camden Market

Look here for old and new clothing, jewellery and audio cassettes.

✉ Camden High Street 🕐 Thu–Sun 10–5:30

6 Regent's Park

Regent's Park ranks alongside St James's Park as one of central London's loveliest green spaces (▶ 16–19). Fringed by the glorious Regency architecture of John Nash, it is loved by locals and visitors alike for its rose garden, its open-air theatre, boating lake and ZSL London Zoo (▶ opposite).

An oft-overlooked park attraction is a trip on the Regent's Canal. Built

Decorated shop front, Camden High Street

ZSL 7 London Zoo

6 Regent's Park

London Central Mosque

Open Air Theatre

Queen Mary's Garden

Boating Lake

Union Canal (Regent's Canal)

PARK ROAD

Lock. Or a stroll along the canal banks is a delightful antidote to the sights and sounds of the city.

➕ 196 B5

London Waterbus Company
☎ 020 7482 2660;
www.londonwaterbus.com
🕐 Apr–Sep daily 10–5.
Hourly departures

Jason's Trip
☎ 020 7286 3428; www.
jasons.co.uk 🕐 Apr–
Oct three times daily

Walkers Quay
(Jenny Wren)
Sightseeing trips from Camden
Town to Little Venice and return
(90 min) ☎ 020 7485 4433; www.
walkersquay.com 🕐 Apr–Oct 2
trips per day, 3 trips at weekends and
during school hols; Aug 4 trips per day

Madame Tussauds 3

Baker St

MARYLEBONE ROAD

University of Westminster

PADDINGTON ST

BAKER STREET

MARYLEBONE HIGH STREET

Wallace Collection 8

in 1820, it runs for 13km (8 miles) between chic Little Venice in west London to Limehouse in the Docklands, where it eventually joins the Thames. Little Venice is a particularly attractive enclave; the stretch of canal that runs through it is dotted with decorated houseboats awash with potted plants and flowers in summer.

Boat companies offer canal trips between Little Venice and Camden

7 ZSL London Zoo
Opened in 1828 as the world's first institution dedicated to the scientific study of animals, London Zoo was once the most fashionable place to be seen in the capital, and in its heyday in the 1950s attracted more than 3 million visitors per year. Today, conservation

Regent's Park in the spring

and study take preference over public display and changing fashions mean that the zoo is a much quieter place. Nonetheless, it is still a popular and important visitor attraction, offering the chance to see around 5,000 animals from 650 species, many of which are endangered in the wild.

Plan your tour around the daily events and get up close to reptiles, spiders and pelicans or see the keepers interacting with giraffes and gorillas. Aside from these creatures, visitor favourites are the big cats – Asian lions, tigers and leopards. The £5.3 million gorilla enclosure, Gorilla Kingdom, opened by HRH The Duke of Edinburgh in March 2007, is the zoo's most significant investment for more than 40 years.

🚹 Off map 196 C5 ✉ Regent's Park, NW1
☎ 020 7722 3333; www.zsl.org 🕐 Mar to mid-Jul daily 10–5:30; mid-Jul to Aug 10–6; Sep–Oct daily 10–5:30; Nov–Feb daily 10–4 (last admission 1 hour before closing)
💷 Very expensive

❽ Wallace Collection

This remarkable collection of objets d'art is made all the more alluring by its setting, Hertford House, a beautiful 18th-century mansion acquired in 1797 by the 2nd Marquess of Hertford. Its collection of artefacts was bequeathed to the nation on condition it should never be sold, loaned or removed from central London.

Every room is filled with treasures, though most people's favourite is the Great Gallery, where a wonderful collection of works by Titian, Rubens, Murillo, Van Dyck and others is on display. The collection's best-known work, Frans Hals's *The Laughing Cavalier*, is also here. The portrait of an unknown young man was painted in 1624. While obviously a figure of substance, the man in question is neither laughing nor a cavalier: the title was coined in 1888 when the picture was lent to the Royal Academy Old Masters Exhibition. Near by is another portrait of an unknown sitter, Velázquez's *Lady With A Fan*.

The collection's sheer variety is its principal charm, providing the opportunity to admire things you might normally overlook, be it Sèvres porcelain, fine furniture, detailed miniatures or 18th-century paintings. The displays of armour are some of the best in the country outside the Tower of London.

🚹 196 B3 ✉ Hertford House, Manchester Square, W1 ☎ 020 7563 9500; www.wallacecollection.org 🕐 Daily 10–5
🍴 Wallace restaurant 🚇 Bond Street
🚌 2, 13, 30, 74, 82, 94, 113, 189, 274 💷 Free

❾ Chinatown

The few blocks around Gerrard Street provide a magnet for London's 60,000-strong Chinese community. Many live elsewhere, but flock

Gerrard Street, at the heart of London's Chinatown, is crammed with good restaurants and shops

Transport Museum exhibits superb collection of 6,000 comics. Cartoon-related events include family fun days.

🔲 200 A5 ✉ 35 Little Russell Street, WC1

☎ 020 780 8155; www.cartoonmuseum.org

🕐 Tue–Sat 10:30–5:30, Sun 12–5:30. Library: Wed 10:30–1:30 🔳 Moderate

🚇 Holborn 🚌 7, 8, 19, 25, 38, 55, 98

here on Sundays when the area is most lively. The streets are full of Chinese signs, restaurants, grocers and bookshops. Even the telephone booths resemble pagodas.

🔲 197 F2 ✉ Around Gerrard Street, W1

🚇 Leicester Square 🚌 14, 19, 24, 29, 38, 176

🔟 Cartoon Museum

Opened in February 2006, this is London's first dedicated cartoon museum. Displayed are more than 1,500 of the finest original cartoons, caricatures and comics from top cartoonists and leading established artists from the 18th century to the present day.

Guaranteed to bring childhood memories flooding back, the collection features rare artwork on loan from *The Beano*, *The Dandy* and *The Topper* including, The Bash Street Kids, Roger the Dodger, Billy the Whizz, Desperate Dan, Beryl the Peril and Dennis the Menace.

Other key exhibits include cartoons in 3D, such as Gerald Scarfe's *Chairman Mao*, half dictator, half crimson leather chair, war cartoons like Sir David Low's *All Behind You Winston* and Captain Bruce Bairnsfather's two squaddies in a World War I trench

The reference library is open every Wednesday and by appointment, with some 5,000 books on cartoons and aspects of the art, as well as a

🔟 London Transport Museum

An expanded and transformed museum opened here in 2007 featuring new themes and exhibitions. The museum portrays the history of London over the last 200 years by looking at the way in which transport has affected the lives of people in the city. It also shows what it takes to shift millions of travellers around the capital daily. See how the transport systems were built, and there are displays illustrating current transport issues.

🔲 200 B4 ✉ Covent Garden, WC2

☎ 020 7565 7299; 020 7379 6344; www.ltmuseum.co.uk 🕐 Daily 10–6 (Fri 11–6), last admission 5:15 🍴 Café 🚇 Covent Garden 🚌 Along Strand 6, 9, 11, 13, 15, 23, 91, 176 🔳 Expensive; under 16s free

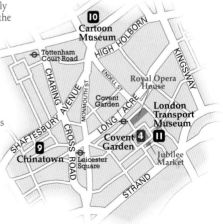

Where to...
Eat and Drink

Prices
Expect to pay per person for a meal excluding drinks and service:
£ under £25 **££** £25–£50 **£££** over £50

Alastair Little Soho ££

Everything about Alastair Little's eponymous restaurant is understated – from the bare aquamarine walls and stripped floorboards, to the casual but informed service and the fresh, deceptively simple food. An Italian influence sits well with the refreshingly seasonal ingredients, the quality of which shines through in every dish. The *prix-fixe* menus (there is no à la carte) are very good value for money.

🔢 197 E2 🔲 49 Frith Street, W1 ☏ 020 7734 5183 🔲 Lunch: Mon–Fri 12–3. Dinner: Mon–Sat 6–11 🔵 Leicester Square

Amphitheatre ££

Inside the Royal Opera House, this is a sumptuous place for lunch, or for pre-show or interval dining. The food is British with a modern twist: dinner dishes include royal breasts of pigeon with spinach and mushroom pithivier.

🔢 200 B4 🔲 Bow Street, WC2 ☏ 020 7212 9254; www.roh.org.uk 🔲 Lunch: Mon–Sat 12–3. Dinner: opens 90 min prior to performance (ticket holders only) 🔵 Covent Garden

Carluccio's £

Started by TV-chef Antonio Carluccio, this value restaurant, part of a small chain, offers a refined yet relaxed dining experience. There is also a food shop on the lower floor, stocking good deli items. The mouthwatering, classic Italian dishes, all made from the best fresh ingredients, include seafood linguine and gnocchi. Carluccio is a wild mushroom expert, so look for those on the menu.

🔢 200 A4 🔲 Garrick Street, WC2 ☏ 020 7836 0990; www.carluccios.com 🔲 Mon–Fri 8am–11.30pm, Sat 9am–11.30pm, Sun 9am–10.30pm 🔵 Leicester Square, Covent Garden

Christopher's ££

Set on two floors in a grand Victorian building, this lively restaurant serves some of the best classic American food in London. The steaks, specially imported from the United States, Maine lobsters, tasty grills and Maryland crab cakes are unmissable. Reservations are recommended. The café-bar has greater informality and a menu of salads and sandwiches.

🔢 200 B4 🔲 18 Wellington Street, WC2 ☏ 020 7240 4222; www.christophersgrill.com 🔲 Lunch: Mon–Fri 12–3, Sat–Sun 11.30–3.30 (brunch). Dinner: Mon–Sat 5–11.30 🔵 Covent Garden

Floridita ££

On the site of Terence Conran's old Mezzo restaurant, Floridita is his latest London venture, bringing the taste, excitement and sassy attitude of Cuba to W1. The Cuban and Latin American food is sensational with *langosta* (crayfish) the signature dish, but Floridita is as much about the cigars (separate cigar bar), the hot rhythms (with bands flown over from Havana), the daiquiris and late-night clubbing, as the dining experience.

🔢 197 E2 🔲 100 Wardour Street, W1 ☏ 020 7314 4000; www.floriditalondon.com 🔲 Mon–Wed 5:30–2, Thu–Sat 5:30–3 🔵 Piccadilly Circus, Tottenham Court Road

Fung Shing ££

Chinatown may be wall-to-wall with Chinese restaurants, and Lisle

Street a crowded, run-down part of it, but the long-standing Fung Shing remains one of the best places to eat. The quality Cantonese food here further distinguishes it from its neighbours. The staff are adept and patient at explaining the menu.

197 F1 ☒ 15 Lisle Street, WC2
☎ 020 7437 1539; www.fungshing.co.uk
☺ Daily 12–11:30 ☻ Leicester Square

The Ivy ££

The Ivy ranks as one of London's most fashionable eating places, with an almost cult status; regulars return again and again for their favourite dishes. What they enjoy is best described as classic brasserie food. Traditional British ideas are tempered by modern European and oriental additions. More than a dozen wines are available by the glass. Reserve well in advance.

197 F2 ☒ 1 West Street, Covent Garden, WC2 ☎ 020 7836 4751; www.the-ivy.co.uk ☺ Mon–Sat 12–3, 5.30–12, Sun 12–3.30, 5.30–11) ☻ Leicester Square, Covent Garden

J Sheekey ££

One of the oldest and best-known seafood restaurants in the capital, Sheekey's has been around since 1896. It is run by the team responsible for such gastronomic temples as The Ivy and Le Caprice. This is the place to go for traditional British fish dishes. A selection of modern creations add an extra dimension to the menu.

197 F1 ☒ 28–32 St Martin's Court, WC2 ☎ 020 7240 2565; www.j-sheekey.co.uk ☺ Mon–Sat 12–3, 5.30–12, Sun 12–3.30, 5.30–11 ☻ Leicester Square

Monmouth Coffee Company £

This is one of Soho's best-kept secrets. From the front it is nothing more than a shop selling bags of coffee beans, but at the back are eight tables. It's the perfect place to stop, relax and sample some great coffees and a delectable selection of pastries from the wide-ranging stock.

197 F2 ☒ 27 Monmouth Street, WC2 ☎ 020 7379 3516; www.monmouthcoffee.co.uk ☺ Mon–Sat 8–6:30 ☻ Covent Garden

Orrery ££–£££

This is one of the most prestigious restaurants in the Conran group, with just 80 seats, plus a shop and food store. However, the family design traits are all there: arched windows, lots of natural lighting, blond wood, a classy, stylish look. The short menu explores French classics, giving them a modern twist. The food bears many of Conran's trademark Modern European characteristics; raw ingredients especially have a true freshness and are of the highest quality.

196 B3 ☒ 55–57 Marylebone High Street, W1 ☎ 020 7616 8000; www.conran.com ☺ Lunch: daily 12–2.30. Dinner: daily 6:30–10.30 (Sun until 10) ☻ Baker Street, Regent's Park

Pâtisserie Valerie £

This cramped, but cosy, old-fashioned tea room is a Soho institution, with shared tables and motherly waitresses. The patisserie is superb (check out the window display) but there are also good salads, breakfasts, croque-monsieurs and savoury quiches to go.

197 E2 ☒ 44 Old Compton Street, W1 ☎ 020 7437 3466; www.patisserie-valerie.co.uk ☺ Wed–Sat 7:30–11, Sun–Tue 7:30–9 ☻ Leicester Square

La Porte des Indes ££

La Porte des Indes is a spectacular Indian restaurant filled with lush, tropical greenery and decked out in rich colours. The kitchen explores the relationship between France and its Indian colonies through such dishes as beignets d'aubergines – slices of aubergine (eggplant) filled with cheese and herb pâté. Lunch consists of a spectacular buffet, which offers one of the best-value deals in the area.

196 A2 ☒ 32 Bryanston Street, W1 ☎ 020 7224 0055; www.pilondon.net ☺ Mon–Fri 12–2:30, Mon–Sat 7–11.30, Sun 12–3.30, 6–10:30 ☻ Marble Arch

Quo Vadis £–££

Now owned by Sam and Eddie Hart, after a spell under the control of Marco Pierre White, this contemporary restaurant has moved to a classic British menu with a modern twist. Seafood and roasts are the stalwarts, but there are pasta, salads and egg dishes, too. Elegant yet simple decor, with sumptuous leather sofas, make for a sophisticated and relaxing dining experience. The set lunch and pre-theatre menu offer good choices.

✚ 197 E2 ⊠ 26–29 Dean Street, W1
☎ 020 7437 9585. www.quovadissoho.co.uk
Ⓖ Lunch: daily noon–2.45. Dinner: Mon–Sat 5:30–10:45 Ⓔ Leicester Square

Rasa Samudra £–££

Meaning a "taste of the ocean", this colourful venue for authentic Indian home cooking specializes in the cuisine of the coastal state of Kerala in the southwest of India, and in particular in its fish and seafood. Inside the bold pink exterior are bright silks and richly coloured oil paintings. Try crab *varuthathu* (fresh crabmeat stirfried with coconut, ginger and mustard seeds), accompanied by rice tossed in lemon juice, fresh curry leaves and mustard seeds.

✚ 197 D3 ⊠ 5 Charlotte Street, W1
☎ 020 7637 0222. www.rasarestaurants.
com Ⓖ Lunch: Mon–Sat noon–3. Dinner: daily 6–11. Closed two weeks in Dec
Ⓔ Tottenham Court Road

The Red Fort ££

This renowned Indian restaurant has been in Soho for more than 20 years. It features a menu of classic Mughal style dishes and some with a modern twist. A recent refurbishment has brought the style of the Red Fort in Delhi to Soho and offers a warm and intimate dining experience. Reservations are recommended for dinner from Thursday to Saturday.

✚ 197 E2 ⊠ 77 Dean Street, W1 ☎ 020 7437 2525. www.redfort.co.uk Ⓖ Mon–Fri 12–3, Mon–Sat 5:45–11:30 Ⓔ Leicester Square

Rules ££

A wonderfully quintessential British restaurant, Rules has an air of slightly aged grandeur. It is the city's oldest restaurant and offers up a mouth-watering selection of classic British dishes, with an emphasis on game, oysters and pies. It has been frequented by many famous characters throughout its long life, including Charles Dickens and Laurence Olivier.

✚ 200 A4 ⊠ 35 Maiden Lane, WC2 ☎ 020 7836 5314; www.rules.co.uk Ⓖ Mon–Sat 12–11.45, Sun 12–10:45 Ⓔ Covent Garden

Vasco & Piero's Pavilion ££

Dining out in Soho tends to be an overwhelmingly trend-driven affair, so it's heartening that this much-loved Italian restaurant is still going strong. The small space is nothing special in itself: peach-coloured walls hung with modern art, somewhat cramped tables and hard metal chairs. The daily changing menu is brief and reflects the owners' Umbrian heritage. The service is speedily efficient without rushing diners.

✚ 197 D2/E2 ⊠ 15 Poland Street, W1
☎ 020 7437 8774; www.vascosfood.com
Ⓖ Mon–Fri 12–3, 6–11, Sat 6–11 Ⓔ Oxford Circus

Wahaca £

At Wahaca you'll experience an authentic version of Mexican food based on the simple, flavoursome food sold at Mexico's markets. Everything is freshly made and many of the dishes are tapas-sized for a light snack or substantial dinner. Choose from street dishes such as organic chorizo and potato *quesadillas* with thyme or slow-cooked pork tacos with a spicy Yucatecan marinade. Larger mains include slow-cooked pork burritos with pink pickled onions served with green rice. It's canteen-style dining so booking isn't possible.

✚ 200 A4 ⊠ 66 Chandos Place, WC2 ☎ 020 72401883; www.wahaca. co.uk Ⓖ Mon–Sat 12–11, Sun 12–10:30
Ⓔ Charing Cross

Where to...
Shop

COVENT GARDEN

Traders in **Covent Garden**'s pedestrian-only Piazza (Tube: Covent Garden; ▶ 150–151). are keen to capitalize on the crowds and many shops stay open until 7 or 8pm. The Market itself is a good starting point. Stand and watch street performers or browse the arcades. **Peter Rabbit and Friends** (34 The Market, WC2, tel: 020 7497 1777) is a Beatrix Potter specialized gift shop. **Culpeper Herbalists** (8 The Market, WC2, tel: 020 7379 6698) stocks English herbs, oils, bath salts, pot-pourri and toiletries that make great gifts. **Benjamin Pollock's Toy Shop** (44 The Market, WC2, tel: 020 7379 7866) is an emporium of handmade puppets, puppet theatres and toys.

British designer **Paul Smith** (43 Floral Street, WC2, tel: 020 7379 7133) sells superb casual wear, sharp suits and unusual socks, ties and cufflinks. **Full Circle** (13–15 Floral Street, WC2, tel: 020 7395 9420) is stocked with cool, trendy clothing at prices in line with the high street.

BLOOMSBURY

The **British Museum**'s shop (Great Russell Street, WC1, tel: 020 7323 8000. Tube: Holborn, Tottenham Court Road, Russell Square) sells Egyptian artefacts and Michelangelo mementos, and hundreds of other historical replicas, alongside other usual museum gifts.

Bloomsbury is the traditional home of London's publishing houses, so there are bookshops galore here. **Charing Cross Road** (Tube: Leicester Square) is the place for bookworms: **Foyles**, **Books etc** and **Blackwell's** are the big three. **Any Amount of Books** (56 Charing Cross Road, WC2, tel: 020 7836 3697. Tube: Tottenham Court Road) sells second-hand books and has a bargain basement. **Ulysses** (40 Museum Street, WC1, tel: 020 7831 1600. Tube: Tottenham Court Road) specializes in first editions.

SOHO

Chinatown lies at the heart of Soho, and Gerrard Street is at the centre of Chinatown. It is the cultural and financial centre of Britain's Chinese community, with an amazing choice of restaurants and Chinese shops and supermarkets.

Soho is better known for its restaurants than for conventional shopping. Food, however, is a serious draw. **Berwick Street**

Market (Berwick Street. Tube: Oxford Circus), a Monday to Saturday fruit and vegetable extravaganza, is worth a visit. On Old Compton Street there are **I Camisa & Son** (61 Old Compton Street, W1, tel: 020 7437 7610. Tube: Leicester Square), which sells Italian deli foods, the **Algerian Coffee Store** (52 Old Compton Street, W1, tel: 020 7437 2480. Tube: Leicester Square) for a range of fresh coffees, and the wonderful **Patisserie Valerie** for delicious French cakes (▶ 157).

American Retro (35 Old Compton Street, W1, tel: 020 7734 3477. Tube: Leicester Square) is a great source of funky accessories. In Brewer Street, check out the **Vintage Magazine Shop** (39–43 Brewer Street, W1, tel: 020 7439 8525. Tube: Piccadilly Circus), a good place for old movie posters or rare film and music magazines.

London's clubbers help to keep places open later in Soho than in other parts of the capital.

Where to...
Be Entertained

This area of London is crammed with theatres, cinemas, busy clubs and crowded bars, and on a Saturday night it can seem as if the whole metropolis has squeezed itself into taxis or travelled on the Tube to surface at Leicester Square and Covent Garden. Late on a Friday or Saturday night, the streets are still thronged with people and the atmosphere is lively. There is much to take in when considering the choice of entertainment.

THEATRE

The choice ranges from the long-running blockbusters of Shaftesbury Avenue to Off-West End at the **Donmar Warehouse** (tel: 0870 060 6624. Tube: Covent Garden). You can go directly to individual theatre box offices, but you might be able to pick up a half-price ticket from The Society of London Theatres' ticket booth, **tkts**, in the clocktower building on the south side of Leicester Square (www.tkts.co.uk, open Mon–Sat 10–7, Sun 11–4). There is a service charge and tickets are for a performance on that day only. For a popular show, this is often your only chance of getting a ticket: be prepared to get there early to be as close to the front of the queue (line) as possible. There are other more expensive ticket booths in the square, so be careful to join the right queue. Never buy tickets offered by people who may approach you while waiting. They are working illegally and the tickets could well be fakes.

Ticketmaster (tel: 0870 4000 700) or **Keith Prowse/First Call** (tel: 0844 209 0381) may also help you find seats. However, there is a hefty service charge.

The **Official London Theatre Guide** (tel: 020 7557 6700, www.officiallondontheatre.co.uk) is a good source for special offers on shows. You can find details of all the offers on their website, along with more good advice on how to go about finding and buying tickets.

CLUBS

London is king of the hill as far as the music scene is concerned and its clubs cater for a wide spectrum of tastes, from mainstream pop acts, country and jazz, to techno, indie and hip hop sounds.

The listings magazine *Time Out* (published every Tuesday) is the most authoritative and comprehensive of all the London magazines. As music and themes vary from night to night, it is essential to check for up-to-date information.

Heaven (Under The Arches, Villiers Street, WC2, tel: 020 7930 2020. Tube: Charing Cross), a huge gay club with a laid-back, friendly atmosphere, is also popular with straight men and women.

Other popular club venues worth checking out:

The Enclave (25–27 Brewer Street, W1, tel: 020 7434 2911. Tube: Leicester Square) is a hot new club in the area. It has a late-night lounge bar feel upstairs, while there is a resident DJ and lasers downstairs to keep you dancing.

Café de Paris (3 Coventry Street, W1, tel: 020 7734 7700. Tube: Piccadilly Circus) is a glam dance hall, overlooked by a galleried restaurant.

Sound London (1 Leicester Square, WC2, tel: 0870 863 1010. Tube: Leicester Square) is a popular huge new venue, with three floors of eating, drinking and dancing offerings.

Excursions

Kew

Kew is an excellent day out. Not only is it convenient – just a short boat or train ride from central London – but its highlight, the Royal Botanic Gardens, is the world's foremost botanical garden and one of the loveliest spots in the capital.

The 121ha (300 acres) of Royal Botanic Gardens contain around 30,000 species of plants, including 13 species extinct in the wild. Keen botanists and gardeners will revel in the floral diversity, but non-experts can also easily savour the gardens' overall beauty. Visits outside the summer months can be especially rewarding – September to November produces wonderful autumn colours, camellias flower in January, and February to May sees the first blooms of spring. It would be easy to wander here for days, but to see the highlights visit the glasshouses in the order below. Their display boards offer entertaining information about some of the plants.

Previous page: The Palm House at the Royal Botanic Gardens

The famous landmark Kew Pagoda, completed in 1762 for Princess Augusta, mother of George III

The Princess of Wales Conservatory

The conservatory features 10 computer-regulated climate zones. Wander from orchids in the humid tropical zone to cacti in the dry tropical zone to appreciate the huge influence of climate on floral types. The most bizarre plants are the "living stone" lithops of Namibia, indistinguishable from stones until they produce brilliantly coloured flowers.

Palm House

This masterpiece of Victorian engineering was constructed between 1844 and 1848 with some 16,000 sheets of glass. Climb one of the wrought-iron spiral staircases to the raised walkways to view its lush rainforest interior containing tropical species such as coconut, banana and rubber from across the globe. Don't miss the basement with its marine plants and habitats, in particular the coral reef. Kew is one of the few places in Britain with living coral, something that is notoriously difficult to cultivate in captivity. The Waterlily House, by the Palm House, is Kew's most hot and humid environment, providing a habitat for tropical aquatic plants. In addition to beautiful waterlilies, you can admire spectacular lotuses, gourds and loofahs.

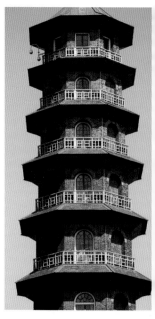

Temperate House

The largest of the glasshouses is an elegant Victorian structure that

The Palm House at Kew incorporates 16,000 panes of glass and took four years to build

took almost 40 years to complete. It is divided into various geographical zones. Its highlights include a Chilean wine palm, planted in the mid-19th century and now the world's largest indoor plant, and subtropical plants such as citrus trees, tea trees and Himalayan rhododendrons.

Evolution House

Just behind the Temperate House is the **Evolution House**, which traces the development of the most ancient plants. A bubbling primordial sludge has been recreated, replicating – it is thought – the earliest "soil". From here plant evolution is traced from the first bacteria through algae, mosses and ferns to conifers and flowering plants.

The 10-storey **Pagoda** is, sadly, not open to the public. During World War II it was used in research into how accurately bombs would drop. Holes were drilled in all 10 floors and models dropped from top to bottom.

Kew Gardens
✉ Victoria Gate, Kew, Richmond, TW9 3AB ☎ 020 8332 5655; www.kew.org
🕐 Daily 9:30–dusk (telephone for exact closing times). The glasshouses and galleries close earlier 🍴 Several cafés and restaurants in the gardens and other options near by 🚇 Kew Gardens 🚌 Kew Green (for Main Gate) 65, 391; Kew Bridge 237, 267, 391 ⛴ Riverboat to Kew Pier from Westminster, Richmond and Hampton Court 💷 Expensive; children free

---

INSIDE INFO: KEW

Hidden gem Tucked away within the gardens are **Queen Charlotte's Cottage Grounds**, named after George III's queen, who had a rustic "cottage" built here in the 1770s. The gardens are now a woodland nature reserve, specializing in British species.

Windsor

A visit to Windsor Castle is the obvious highlight of a trip to Windsor, but the town is attractive in its own right. There is also the chance to visit historic Eton College, traditionally a school for the sons of the rich and famous, and – a treat for the children – the modern theme park of Legoland.

Windsor Castle

Windsor Castle looks the part of a castle to perfection, with towers, turrets, battlements and even uniformed soldiers on guard. It possesses a grandeur that far outshines that of Buckingham Palace (► 50–51). The world's largest inhabited castle, Windsor was founded by William the Conqueror in about 1080, when it formed part of the defences around London. In time it became a royal residence, partly because of the opportunities for hunting afforded by the surrounding countryside. Henry I had quarters in the castle in 1110, and almost 900 years later the sovereign is still resident. Queen Elizabeth II spends most weekends here, as well as much of April and June.

A fire on the night of 20 November 1992, probably started by the heat of a spotlight too close to a curtain, destroyed much of the castle's interior. Several State Rooms, including St George's Hall, the Grand Reception Room, the State Dining Room and the Crimson Drawing Room were damaged. The fire burned for 15 hours and it took 1.3 million gallons (6 million litres) of water to extinguish the flames. Restoration took five years and cost £38 million, most of which was met by the Royal Family with money earned from the annual opening of Buckingham Palace and visitor admissions to the precincts of Windsor Castle.

Windsor Castle, seen across the river

Areas of the castle open to the public include the State Rooms (open all year except 16–19 June and certain other dates), Semi-State Rooms (open late September to March only) and St George's Chapel (open daily, all year except Sundays and 15–18 June). Their vast array of treasures includes Gobelin tapestries, ornate antique furniture and paintings by artists such as Van Dyck, Rubens, Gainsborough, Dürer, Rembrandt, Reynolds and Canaletto. The tour follows a set route.

Banners in St George's Chapel

Castle Tour Highlights

Queen Mary's Dolls' House is an entire house built on a scale of 1:12. Look especially for the tiny leather-bound books in the library, and the vacuum cleaner, crockery, kitchen equipment, miniature works of art on the walls and a sewing machine that actually works.

The **Grand Staircase** and **Grand Vestibule** provide a magnificent introduction to the State Rooms. Both are lined with statues, firearms, armour and huge cases filled with miscellaneous treasures – among them, in the Grand Vestibule, the bullet that killed Admiral Lord Horatio Nelson at the Battle of Trafalgar in 1805 (currently on display at the National Maritime Museum in Greenwich ► 177).

The opulent **Grand Reception Room** was designed for King George IV, a monarch with a passion for ornate French design, which is why everything from walls and ceiling to furniture and chandeliers is intricately gilded and adorned.

St George's Hall – superbly restored since the 1992 fire – is the grandest of the castle's rooms. More than 55m (180-feet) long, it is impressive for its size alone, but is also remarkable for its decoration – crests, busts and suits of armour – and the wonderful oak hammerbeam roof.

Ten monarchs are buried in **St George's Chapel**, a beautifully decorated space distinguished, among other things, by its choir stalls, altar and gilded vaulting. It also contains Prince Albert's Memorial Chapel, built in memory of Victoria's husband who died at Windsor in 1861. It's a startling work, laden with statues, Venetian mosaics and inlaid marble panels.

INSIDE INFO: WINDSOR

Top tips
■ The **Changing of the Guard** takes place at 11am daily (except Sunday) from May to July and on alternate days for the rest of the year.
■ **Buy a guide** on the way in, as little is labelled.

Tour Highlights

Almost next door to the castle on the High Street is the 17th-century **Windsor Guildhall**, where Prince Charles married Camilla Parker-Bowles in April 2005. It is open only on Monday from 10am to 2pm (closed public holidays).

If you've more time to spend in the area, **Eton College** lies a 15-minute walk across the river from Windsor. One of Britain's oldest private schools, Eton was founded in 1440, and pupils still wear formal dress. Today it is still highly prestigious; most pupils come from rich and influential families. More than 18 of Britain's prime ministers were educated here. The school yard, oldest classroom, museum and chapel are open to the public, and afternoon guided tours are available.

Legoland Windsor, a popular theme park just 3.2km (2 miles) from the town centre, is ideally suited to those with younger children. It mixes rides and displays with constructions made from the popular Lego bricks, together with live-action shows. A half-hourly shuttle bus operates to Legoland from stops close to Windsor and Eton Central and Riverside railway stations (tickets including admission, shuttle bus and rail travel are available from most major railway stations in Britain).

The Crooked House tea rooms in Windsor

Visitor Information Centre
✉ The Old Booking Hall, Central Station, Windsor, SL4 1PJ ☎ 01753 743900; 01753 831118 (recorded information) 🕐 Mon–Sat 10–5, Sun 11–4; extended hours in summer

Windsor Castle
☎ 01753 831118 (24 hour); 020 7766 7304; www.royalresidences.com 🕐 Mar–Oct daily 9:45–5:15 (last admission 4); Nov–Feb 9:45–4:15 (last admission 3). Closed Good Fri, Easter Sun morning. St George's Chapel closed to visitors Sun (subject to full or partial closure at other times). Opening times may change at short notice, check before you visit 💷 Very expensive

Eton College
☎ 01753 671177; www.etoncollege.com 🕐 Daily 2:30–4:30 school term time, 10:30–4:30 school holiday time (Apr–Sep) 💷 Moderate; tours moderate

Legoland Windsor
✉ Winkfield Road, SL4 4AY ☎ 0871 2222 001; www.legoland.co.uk 🕐 Mid-Jul to early Sep daily 10–7; late Sep to mid-Jul 10–6 (or dusk if earlier) 💷 Very expensive (2-day tickets available)

GETTING THERE
Windsor is 34km (21 miles) west of London.
Train (☎ 0845 748 4950) Direct trains to Windsor and Eton Riverside from Waterloo Station, every 30 min. Journey time approximately 55 min.
From Paddington Station to Windsor and Eton Central, changing trains at Slough, every 30 min. Journey time approximately 40 min.
Bus (☎ 0870 608 7261) Greenline service from Victoria Coach Station. Journey time 57 min. Telephone for times.

Walks and Tours

1 MAYFAIR SQUARES
Walk

Amid the noise and bustle of the surrounding streets, Mayfair (▶ 45–66) is an enclave of luxury and elegance. Originally laid out in the early 18th century by wealthy families such as the Grosvenors and Berkeleys, the area is the most expensive in London and retains evidence of past glories, including fine houses, both grand and humble, leafy squares, elegant shopping arcades and the old-fashioned alleyways and cobbles of Shepherd Market.

Look for commemorative blue plaques (▶ 22–25), indicating that a famous person is associated with the building, and for shopfronts carrying royal crests; the companies awarded crests supply a member of the Royal Family – read the small print to find out which one.

1–2
Leave **Piccadilly Circus** Underground station by the Piccadilly (South Side) exit and walk straight along Piccadilly past **St James's Church**, designed by Wren, Princes Arcade,

DISTANCE 5km (3 miles) **TIME** 2 hours. Allow extra time for window-shopping, refreshment stops and visiting churches **START POINT** Piccadilly Circus Underground station ✚ 197 E1
END POINT Oxford Circus Underground station ✚ 197 D2

lined with quality shops, and Hatchards, booksellers since 1797. You'll soon reach the high-class grocery and department store **Fortnum & Mason**, which was founded by a servant of Queen Anne in 1707. The store is very exclusive – some of the sales assistants even wear tailcoats.

2–3
Cross Piccadilly to Burlington House, an 18th-century mansion, now home to the **Royal Academy of Arts** (▶ 58). Just beyond is Burlington Arcade, built in 1819. This is the best known of the exclusive shopping arcades in the area, and the top-hatted officials enforce regulations against whistling, singing or hurrying.

The top-end Fortnum & Mason store on Piccadilly

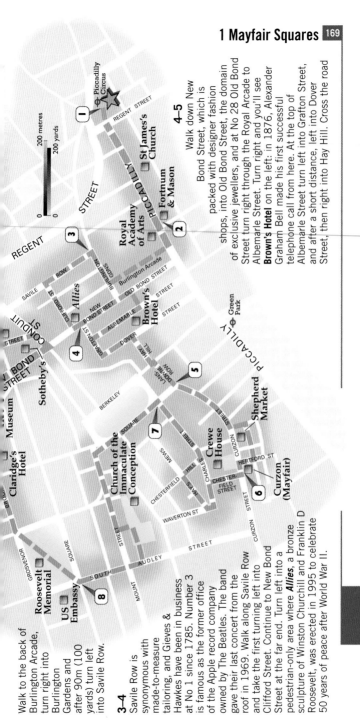

Walk to the back of Burlington Arcade, turn right into Burlington Gardens and after 90m (100 yards) turn left into Savile Row.

3–4

Savile Row is synonymous with made-to-measure tailoring, and Gieves & Hawkes have been in business at No 1 since 1785. Number 3 is famous as the former office of the Apple record company owned by The Beatles. The band gave their last concert from the roof in 1969. Walk along Savile Row and take the first turning left into Clifford Street. Continue to New Bond Street at the far end. Turn left into a pedestrian-only area where *Allies*, a bronze sculpture of Winston Churchill and Franklin D Roosevelt, was erected in 1995 to celebrate 50 years of peace after World War II.

4–5

Walk down New Bond Street, which is packed with designer fashion shops, into Old Bond Street, and at No 28 Old Bond Street turn right through the Royal Arcade to Albemarle Street. Turn right and you'll see **Brown's Hotel** on the left: in 1876, Alexander Graham Bell made his first successful telephone call from here. At the top of Albemarle Street turn left into Grafton Street, and after a short distance, left into Dover Street, then right into Hay Hill. Cross the road at the bottom into pedestrianized Lansdowne Row and walk through here to Curzon Street.

5–6

Walk straight along Curzon Street and after 183m (200 yards), you'll come to G F Trumper, Court Hairdresser and Perfumer, established in 1875. The building is considerably older, however, and with its original dark wood, glass and light fittings is one of London's finest 18th-century shops. Turn left through the covered entrance into **Shepherd Market**, built in 1735 by Edward Shepherd. Today its lanes are filled with outdoor cafés, small shops and restaurants; everything here is older and on a smaller scale than the surrounding area.

At Ye Grapes pub, at the far end of the passageway, turn immediately right through a pedestrian-only area. Cross cobbled Trebeck Street and turn right up Hertford Street past the **Curzon Mayfair** cinema to Curzon Street. Across Curzon Street stands **Crewe House** (now the Saudi Arabian Embassy), which Shepherd built in 1730 as his own home.

6–7

Turn left into Curzon Street and then right into elegant Chesterfield Street, left at the top into Charles Street, right at the Red Lion pub on to Waverton Street and right again into Hay's Mews, originally the stables for the coach horses of the wealthy, now converted into highly desirable homes. Take the next right into Chesterfield Hill and at the end turn left, back into Charles Street. Follow this road to its end at Berkeley Square.

7–8

Berkeley Square was made a household name through the song "A Nightingale Sang in Berkeley Square." It was originally laid out in the mid-18th century and retains its attractive, leafy feel, though these days the traffic roaring along the surrounding roads detracts from the prettiness and pollutes the air. Walk up the left (west) side of the square, which has kept the most character.

At the top left (northwest) corner turn left into Mount Street; after about 180m (200 yards) turn left into peaceful Mount Street Gardens where there is an entrance to the solemn **Church of the Immaculate Conception** (open to the public). Continue to the other side of the gardens and then turn right into Grosvenor Square. This leads to South Audley Street, one of London's largest squares, with the modern **United States Embassy** to the left – it's certainly assertive, although hardly in keeping with the square's period style. There are statues here of US presidents **Roosevelt** and **Eisenhower**.

Berkeley Square is a green oasis in an exclusive area

8–9

Walk diagonally right across the square and leave from the far (northeast) corner along Brook Street. Continue straight ahead past **Claridge's** (➤ 37), one of London's finest hotels, which is often patronized by visiting royalty. Number 25 Brook Street is where George Frederick Handel lived and died. Music lovers can visit the **Handel House Museum**, dedicated to the composer and his work, on the upper floors. Guitarist Jimi Hendrix lived next door at No 23 from 1968 to 1969.

9–10

At the next intersection turn right into New Bond Street. Along on the lef, where anyone can view the often fabulous articles waiting to be sold. Take the next turning left into Conduit Street and turn immediately left into St George Street, where the imposing bulk of **St George's Church** is ahead on the right. Built in 1724, it has long been a fashionable society wedding venue.

10–11

Carry on to the top of St George Street where the statue of William Pitt, who became prime minister in 1783 at the age of only 24, marks the entrance to Hanover Square. Take Princes Street from the top right (northeast) corner of the square out to Regent Street. Turn left and you soon reach **Oxford Circus** Underground station.

Church of the Immaculate Conception

TAKING A BREAK

Stop at one of the coffee shops or snack bars on Lansdowne Row or try one of the outdoor cafés or pubs in Shepherd Market.

WHEN TO GO

Weekdays are best, as on Sundays most shops are closed and on Saturdays weddings are often scheduled at the churches.

PLACES TO VISIT

Handel House Museum
➕ 196 C2 ☎ 020 7495 1685;
www.handelhouse.org ⏰ Tue–Sat 10–6,
Thu 10–8, Sun 12–6 💷 Moderate

St James's Church
➕ 197 E1 ☎ 020 7734 4511 ⏰ Daily 8–6:30.
Free lunchtime concerts (1:10) Mon, Wed, Fri.
Concerts most evenings Thu–Sat

St George's Church
➕ 197 D2 ☒ Hanover Square ☎ 020 7629
0874 ⏰ Mon–Fri 8–4, Sun 8–noon

2 THE CITY
Walk

The City of London (▶ 67–86), also known as the Square Mile, is a major world financial centre bursting with banks, corporations, financial institutions and trading centres. The wheeling and dealing takes place behind closed doors, and security concerns mean that most buildings are closed to the public. However, the streets have a real buzz during the week (they're dead at weekends) and this walk takes in towering landmarks, city churches, an art gallery and a Roman amphitheatre.

DISTANCE 5km (3 miles) **TIME** 2 hours. Allow extra time for window-shopping, refreshment stops and visiting churches **START POINT** Monument Underground station ♦ 202 A4
END POINT Bank Underground station ♦ 202 A4

1–2
Leave **Monument** Underground station via the London Bridge/King William Street (South) exit.

Walk straight ahead on to London Bridge for sweeping views up and down river; Tower Bridge to the east with **HMS Belfast** moored across to your right.

The Romans first bridged the River Thames at this point almost 2,000 years ago and there has been a succession of bridges here since. The one you're on dates from 1973, the previous bridge having been sold to American businessman Robert P McCulloch Sr for display in Arizona. Londoners joke that he thought he was buying Tower Bridge.

Guildhall

St Lawrence Jewry

CHEAPSIDE

St Mary-le-Bow

BOW LANE

WATLING

KING STREET

GRESHAM STREET

LOTHBURY

Bank of England & Museum

BARTHOLOMEW LANE

THREADNEEDLE ST

Royal Exchange

Bank ⊖

Mansion House

St Stephen Walbrook

WALBROOK

QUEEN VICTORIA ST

CANNON STREET

Cannon Street

Mansion House

BUCKLERSBURY

KING WILLIAM

Monument ⊖

OLD BROAD STREET

Tower 42

BISHOPSGATE

GREAT ST HELEN'S

St Helen Bishopsgate

30 St Mary Axe (The Gherkin)

St Lawrence Jewry

LEADENHALL ST

Lloyd's

Leadenhall Market

LIME STREET

PHILPOT LANE

GRACECHURCH ST

FENCHURCH STREET

EASTCHEAP

4

5

6

7

8

9

10

2–3

Walk back towards the Underground station and take the first road to the right, Monument Street, to **The Monument**. It was co-designed by Sir Christopher Wren, architect of St Paul's Cathedral, in the 1670s as a memorial to the Great Fire in 1666. It is 62m (203 feet) tall – the distance on the ground from its base to the place where the fire started in Pudding Lane – and there are 311 steps up to the viewing platform.

3–4

Walk up Fish Street Hill to Eastcheap at the top and turn right; the next road on the right is Pudding Lane, now lined with modern office buildings.

Cross Eastcheap into Philpot Lane and look ahead for a view of the dramatic **Lloyd's Building**. Designed by Sir Richard (now Lord) Rogers, it houses the Lloyd's insurance market, the world centre of insurance for over 200 years since it was founded in the coffee houses of the City. You'll either love or hate the steel-and-glass giant with the entrails of pipes and shafts exposed on the outside – it looks especially dramatic at night. Towering above the Lloyd's Building, just behind it, is **30 St Mary Axe**, home to Swiss

Re-Insurance company, designed by Sir Norman (now Lord) Foster and nicknamed **The Gherkin**.

At the end of Philpot Lane, cross Fenchurch Street into Lime Street and take the first street left, the cobbled Lime Street Passage, which leads into **Leadenhall Market** (▶ 80).

4–5

Leave the market through Whittington Avenue and turn right into Leadenhall Street by **Lloyd's Building**. Cross the road and head north across an open square to **St Helen Bishopsgate**, one of the few churches to survive the Great Fire of London. There are 38 churches within the Square Mile, many of them designed by Wren; with almost no resident parishioners and insufficient weekday worshippers to justify this number of buildings, the threat of closure hangs over many.

HMS *Belfast*

Thames

LONDON BRIDGE

0   200 metres
0   200 yards

Views across London from The Monument

5–6
Turn left at the church and along Great St Helen's to Bishopsgate. Look directly ahead to **Tower 42**. At 184m (604 feet) it is the City's tallest building.

Turn left in Bishopsgate and cross at the traffic lights into Threadneedle Street. At the intersection with Old Broad Street a small sign proclaims the London Stock Exchange; electronic dealing has replaced its old trading floor where deals used to be done in person.

Continue along Threadneedle Street and turn right down Bartholomew Lane where you will find the **Bank of England**. The bank's **museum** (▶ 82) gives an insight into its processes.

6–7
Carry on to the end of Bartholomew Lane, then turn left along Lothbury and into Gresham Street. To your right, behind **St Lawrence Jewry** church, is the **Guildhall**, the symbolic heart of the City. The original 15th-century building has undergone many reconstructions, but the main hall remains the highlight, decked with shields and banners and displaying figures of the legendary giants Gog and Magog.

Within the Guildhall complex is a curious Clock Museum, which includes a skull-shaped pocket watch that belonged to Mary, Queen of Scots; the Guildhall Art Gallery, where important paintings from the Corporation of London's 300-year-old collection are on display; and below ground, London's only Roman amphitheatre, discovered in 1988 and opened to the public in 2003.

7–8
With your back to Guildhall, cross Gresham Street into King Street and continue down to Cheapside where you turn right towards the huge steeple of **St Mary-le-Bow**. The church's

Guildhall is the symbolic heart of the City

original Norman crypt still exists, while the spacious elegance of Wren's work is obvious both in the fine lines of the spire and in the elegant arches and vaulted roof of the interior. Traditionally, only those born within the sound of Bow bells can call themselves true Cockneys (native Londoners).

Walk through Bow Churchyard next to the church where there is a statue of Sir John Smith (1580–1631), who married Native American princess Pocahontas and was a parishioner here. Walk around the back of the church and turn right into Bow Lane, where you will see Williamson's Tavern on the right. Turn left into Watling Street; Ye Olde Watling pub, at the bottom, dates from 1666 and, by tradition, Sir Christopher Wren used it as an office while building St Paul's Cathedral.

8–9
Walk along Watling Street to a large intersection and cross into Queen Victoria Street. Turn right into Bucklersbury to **St Stephen Walbrook** church, built by Wren (1672–79); the dome is thought to have been a trial run for St Paul's. The telephones in the church commemorate the founding in the rector's study on 2 November 1953, of the

first telephone helpline for the despairing, whicy became the Samaritans organization.

9–10

From the church turn along Walbrook and then right at the end towards the huge, temple-like building at the far side of the intersection. This is the **Royal Exchange**, first granted a charter to trade in all kinds of commerce by Queen Elizabeth I in the 16th century, although this particular building dates from 1844. It was the centre of futures trading, though this has now closed. The gardens in front are a good place for a rest, and if you stand with your back to the giant statue of the Duke of Wellington you will see a plaque that details the nearby buildings: the **Mansion House**, official residence of the Lord Mayor of London, is across to the left, and the solid bulk of the Bank of England, surrounded by its windowless walls, is on the right.

The walk ends here – Bank Underground station is near by.

TAKING A BREAK

The Place Below, Crypt of St Mary-le-Bow, (tel: 020 7329 0789), serves vegetarian food 7:30–3:30.

WHEN TO GO

Year-round.

PLACES TO VISIT

The Monument
➕ 202 A3 ✉ Monument Street, EC3 ☎ 020 7626 2717 ☻ Daily 9:30–5 💷 Inexpensive

St Helen Bishopsgate
➕ 202 B4 ✉ Great St Helen's, EC3 ☎ 020 7283 2231 ☻ Mon–Fri 9:30–5 (usually possible to visit church) 💷 Free

Bank of England Museum
➕ 202 A4 ✉ Bartholomew Lane, EC2 ☎ 020 7601 5545; www.bankofengland.co.uk/museum ☻ Mon–Fri 10–5 (last entry 4:45) 💷 Free

Guildhall
➕ 201 F5 ✉ Gresham Street, EC2 ☎ 020 7606 3030; www.cityoflondon.gov.uk ☻ Guildhall/amphitheatre: Mon–Sat 10–5. Clock Museum: Mon–Sat 9:30–4:45. Gallery: Mon–Sat 10–5, Sun 12–4 💷 Guildhall/Clock Museum free: Gallery/amphitheatre inexpensive; free fri and daily after 3:30

St Mary-le-Bow
➕ 201 F4 ✉ Cheapside, EC2 ☎ 020 7248 5139 ☻ Mon–Wed 7–6, Thu 7–6:30, Fri 7–4. Free lunchtime concert Thu 1:05 💷 Free

St Stephen Walbrook
➕ 202 A4 ✉ 39 Walbrook, EC4 ☎ 020 7626 9000 ☻ Mon–Thu 10–4, Fri 10–3 💷 Free

The Royal Exchange, founded in 1571

3 GREENWICH
Walk

Greenwich, 13km (8 miles) down the River Thames from central London, overflows with royal, maritime and astronomical associations, and is known across the globe for Greenwich Mean Time and the Greenwich Meridian where East meets West. Add to that the rolling parkland, superb views and lively weekend markets (Fri–Sat), and Greenwich begins to look unmissable.

DISTANCE 3.2km (2 miles) **TIME** 2 hours. Allow additional time for visits – you could easily spend a day here **START POINT** Greenwich Pier. Allow an hour from Westminster Pier to Greenwich by boat **END POINT** Greenwich Pier

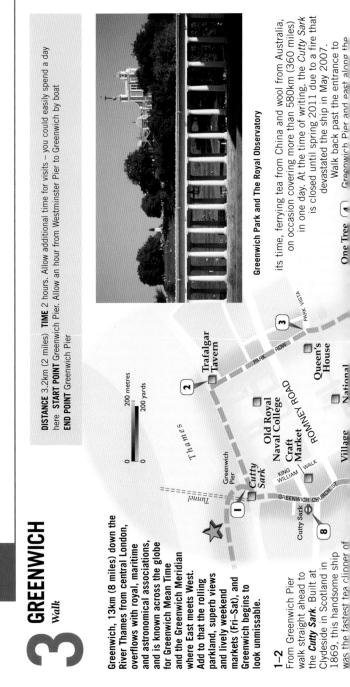

1–2
From Greenwich Pier walk straight ahead to the *Cutty Sark*. Built at Clydeside in Scotland in 1869, this handsome ship was the fastest tea clipper of

Greenwich Park and The Royal Observatory

its time, ferrying tea from China and wool from Australia, on occasion covering more than 580km (360 miles) in one day. At the time of writing, the *Cutty Sark* is closed until spring 2011 due to a fire that devastated the ship in May 2007.

Walk back past the entrance to Greenwich Pier and past along the

The Cutty Sark pub in Greenwich

footpath beside the river. The **Old Royal Naval College** is on the right, built on the site of the old Greenwich Palace where Henry VIII and his daughter Queen Elizabeth I were born. The college was built by architect Sir Christopher Wren, assisted by Nicholas Hawksmoor and Sir John Vanbrugh, starting in 1696. Generations of sailors, including Prince Charles, learned their trade here until its closure in 1995. The chapel and Grand Hall are open to the public and the latter contains the largest painting in the country, *The Triumph of Peace and Liberty* (a tribute to King William and Queen Mary). It was executed between 1707 and 1727 by James Thornhill (and several assistants) and measures 32m by 15m (105 feet by 49 feet). For this Thornhill was paid £6,685, a massive sum at the time. From the central gates there is a lovely view through the college to Queen's House, the elegant white building behind, and beyond to the Royal Observatory on the hill above. There are also excellent views down the river to the the O2, originally known as the Millennium Dome, and across the river to the stainless steel and glass bulk of Canary Wharf – at 243m (797 feet), it is London's, and indeed the UK's, tallest skyscraper.

Continue along the river path to Park Row and the Trafalgar Tavern.

2–3

The **Trafalgar Tavern** was built in 1837 and frequented by writer Charles Dickens: sample its fare or turn away from the river and walk along Park Row and cross the main road (Romney Road). There is an entrance to the National Maritime Museum and Queen's House on the right.

The **National Maritime Museum** is a treasure trove of naval instruments, charts, models, paintings and memorabilia; there's even a royal barge. The history of seafaring (exploratory as well as the military) is comprehensively illustrated in state-of-the-art exhibits and interactive displays. One whole gallery is devoted to Admiral Lord Horatio Nelson, victor of the Battle of Trafalgar in 1805. Exit back into Park Row and enter Greenwich Park.

Royal Observatory

General Wolfe's Statue

Park Café

BLACKHEATH AVENUE

Reservoir

Ranger's House

GROOM'S HILL

3–4

Follow the first path in front of the **Queen's House** until you can turn right, then take the second path to the left, which climbs steeply up One Tree Hill. Queen Elizabeth I often came here to enjoy the fine view, a custom commemorated in verse on the benches.

4–5

From **One Tree Hill** either follow the paths or cut across the grass towards the Royal Observatory, the regal red-brick-and-white building with the green dome on the next hill. You'll arrive at the **statue of General James Wolfe**; he was a local man who, in 1759, commanded the British army during the capture of Quebec, in which he was killed. There's another good view of London from here: look for St Paul's Cathedral, with the distinctive black bulk of Tower 42 (formerly called the NatWest Tower) close to it.

The **Royal Observatory** was founded in 1675 by King Charles II, with the aim of solving the problem of finding longitude at sea. Astronomers now study the skies away from the bright distracting lights of London, but the exhibits illustrate the history of astronomy and the challenges of measuring position and time. You can straddle the Prime Meridian, the line at 0° longitude from which all other longitudes are reckoned, and see the revolutionary chronometers with which John Harrison (1693–1776) solved the longitude problem.

5–6

With your back to General Wolfe, walk along Blackheath Avenue, with the **Park Café** on the left. At the small roundabout (traffic circle) turn right on to a path that follows a line of trees to a gate in the park wall. Turn left along the gravel drive to Croom's Hill.

The 17th-century **Ranger's House**, a 180m (200-yard) detour to the left, houses a splendid collection of medieval and Renaissance works of art.

6–7

As you walk down the hill, admire the 17th- and 18th-century houses. Towards the bottom of Croom's Hill, you will find the **Fan Museum**, the only one of its kind in the world, located in two 18th-century houses. Founded in 1990

The dome of the Old Royal Naval College features a compass

by Helen Alexander, whose personal collection of more than 3,500 fans is the basis of the exhibition, the museum displays stunning examples of the fan-maker's craft.

7–8

From the Fan Museum continue straight to the bottom of Croom's Hill, then walk ahead into Stockwell Street (the **Village Market** is on the right) and turn right into Greenwich Church Street. Continue along Greenwich Church Street and cross Nelson Road. The entrance to the main **craft market**, offering a varied selection of goods, is through a small alleyway to the right.

Return to Greenwich Church Street, turn right, cross College Approach, and after 90m (100 yards) you'll be back at the works on the *Cutty Sark*.

8–9

You can either return to central London by boat, or take the Docklands Light Railway (DLR; ▶ 34). There is a DLR station close to the *Cutty Sark*. Trains run on an elevated track, and you get some panoramic views of the futuristic landscape of Docklands on your way back into the city centre.

TAKING A BREAK

Trafalgar Tavern, afternoon tea in the Orangery of the Fan Museum (Tue and Sun from 3) and restaurants in Greenwich Church Street.

WHEN TO GO

Saturday or Sunday when the markets are open.

PLACES TO VISIT

Cutty Sark

⊠ King William Walk, SE10 ☎ 020 8858 3445; www.cuttysark.org.uk ⊙ Closed until spring 2011 following fire damage

Detail of the gate at the Old Royal Naval College

Old Royal Naval College

⊠ Entrance from King William Walk, SE10 ☎ 020 8269 4747; www.oldroyalnavalcollege.org ⊙ Daily 10–5 💷 Free

National Maritime Museum, Queen's House and Royal Observatory

⊠ Greenwich Park, SE10 ☎ 020 8858 4422; information line: 020 8312 6565; www.nmm.ac.uk ⊙ Daily 10–5 (last admission 4:30) 💷 Free

Ranger's House

⊠ Chesterfield Walk, Greenwich Park, SE10 ☎ 020 8853 0035; www.english-heritage.org.uk ⊙ Apr–Sep Mon–Wed (by guided tour only, at 11:30 and 2:30), Sun 11–5. Closed late Dec–Feb. Open other times by appointment only 💷 Moderate

Fan Museum

⊠ 12 Croom's Hill, SE10 ☎ 020 8305 1441; www.fan-museum.org ⊙ Tue–Sat 11–5, Sun 12–5 💷 Moderate

4 HAMPSTEAD
Walk

DISTANCE 5.5km (3.5 miles) **TIME** 3 hours. Allow more for refreshment stops and visiting the houses
START POINT Golders Green Underground station **END POINT** Hampstead Underground station

This walk through the charming village of Hampstead and across Hampstead Heath, 6.5km (4 miles) to the north of central London, offers some of the most rural scenery in the capital, a spectacular view from Parliament Hill, historic houses and delightful lanes. Hampstead has been a popular residential area, particularly with writers and artists, since the 18th century, when visitors flocked to drink the restorative spa waters. Famous inhabitants have included artist John Constable, poet John Keats, writers Ian Fleming and Agatha Christie, and actors Peter O'Toole, Elizabeth Taylor and Emma Thompson.

1–2
Catch the No 210 bus from outside Golders Green Underground station to Kenwood House – ask the driver to tell you where to alight. On the way look for Jack Straw's Castle. There was an inn on this site for more than 500 years until the latest pub (dating from 1962) was converted to apartments. Still serving pints of beer, however, is the 16th-century **Spaniard's Inn**, associated with the highwayman Dick Turpin and literary figures Dickens, Keats, Shelley and Byron.

There are two entrances to Kenwood House a few hundred yards after Spaniard's Inn on the right – **West Lodge** and **East Lodge**; both lead to the house.

2–3
Kenwood House dates from the 18th century and is famed for the work of the Scottish architect Robert Adam. The highlight of the interior is the fabulously ornate library and the Iveagh Bequest art collection, which includes a Rembrandt self-portrait, the *Guitar Player* by

HAMPSTEAD LANE

West Lodge

East Lodge

Kenwood House

Spaniard's Inn

0   300 metres

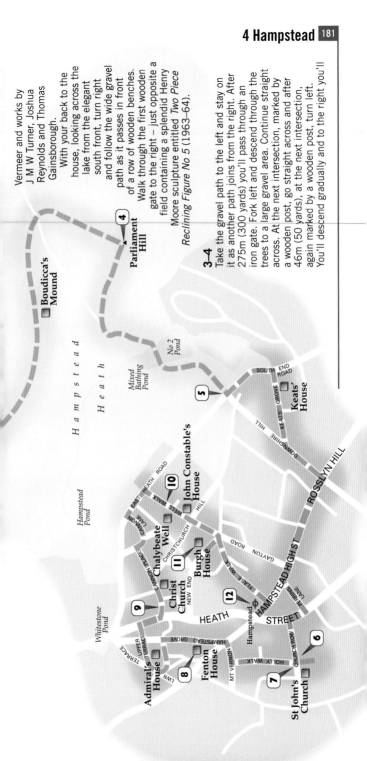

Vermeer and works by J M W Turner, Joshua Reynolds and Thomas Gainsborough.

With your back to the house, looking across the lake from the elegant south front, turn right and follow the wide gravel path as it passes in front of a row of wooden benches. Walk through the first wooden gate to the right – just opposite a field containing a splendid Henry Moore sculpture entitled *Two Piece Reclining Figure No 5* (1963–64).

④ Parliament Hill

Boudicca's Mound

Hampstead Heath

Hampstead Pond

Mixed Bathing Pond

No 2 Pond

3–4

Take the gravel path to the left and stay on it as another path joins from the right. After 275m (300 yards) you'll pass through an iron gate. Fork left and descend through the trees to a large gravel area. Continue straight across. At the next intersection, marked by a wooden post, go straight across and after 46m (50 yards), at the next intersection, again marked by a wooden post, turn left. You'll descend gradually and to the right you'll

⑤

SOUTH END ROAD

KEATS GROVE

Keats' House

KEATS HILL

DOWNSHIRE HILL

ROSLYN HILL

GAYTON ROAD

HAMPSTEAD HIGH ST

John Constable's House ⑩

EAST HEATH ROAD

WELL WALK

CANNON LANE

CHRISTCHURCH HILL

Chalybeate Well ⑪

Burgh House

NEW END

CHRIST CHURCH

Christ Church

HEATH

FLASK WALK

⑫

Hampstead

STREET

PERRINS LANE

Whitestone Pond

⑨

UPPER TERRACE

CANNON LANE

Admiral's House

Fenton House ⑧

LWR TERRACE

HAMPSTEAD GROVE

MT VERNON

HOLLY WALK

CHURCH ROW

St John's Church ⑦

⑥

see **Boudicca's Mound**, planted with trees and enclosed by a fence. Boudicca, Queen of the Iceni tribe, led her people against the Romans in the 1st century AD. Local legend claims this as her burial place. Follow the path straight through the next intersection of paths, then take the next path to your right and you'll spot Parliament Hill directly ahead, bare of trees and with benches on the skyline.

4–5

On **Parliament Hill** look for the plaque identifying the London landmarks laid out below. Facing the plaque, turn right and walk straight along the path that leads you between two of the many ponds on the Heath; the Mixed Bathing Pond is on the right and Hampstead Number Two Pond on the left. Follow the path left along the side of Hampstead Number Two Pond and out to the main road, East Heath Road.

Kenwood House

5–6

Cross East Heath Road at the pedestrian crossing and walk left down South End Road. Take the third turning right into Keats' Grove, with **Keats' House** along on the left. This is where the poet John Keats (1795–1821) lived for two years, wrote some of his best-known work and fell in love with the girl next door. The house contains many of his possessions and manuscripts.

Continue along Keats' Grove and turn left into Downshire Hill and then right into Rosslyn Hill. Turn left just after the King William IV pub into Perrins Lane, right at the end into Heath Street and then take the first turning left into elegant Church Row.

6–7

At the far end of Church Row enter the left gate of **St John's Church** and turn immediately left along the rough path. At the bottom of the churchyard on the left, behind a small iron fence, is the grave of Hampstead's most famous resident and artist, John Constable (1776–1837), together with his wife and their eldest son.

Walk up to the church, which has a pleasantly proportioned interior, fine stained glass and, at the front to the right of the choir, a memorial to John Keats.

7–8

Leave the church and, with your back to the church door, turn left and cross the churchyard. Now cross the road into Holly Walk to start the part of the walk through the back lanes of Hampstead village. On the right, the row of quaint cottages in Benhams Place dates from 1813. At the end of Holly Walk turn right into Mount Vernon, follow the path to the left of the last house and take the lower path to the left as it swings around to the

From Parliament Hill there are panoramic views across the capital

left on to Holly Bush Hill. At the top of Holly Bush Hill, the black-and-gold gates across the grass belong to **Fenton House**, one of the oldest and grandest Hampstead houses, with a large collection of early musical instruments.

8–9

Walk along the right side of Fenton House into Hampstead Grove and turn left into Admiral's Walk. Along on the right, the startling **Admiral's House** was turned into a facsimile of a ship by a former owner, who also used to fire cannons to commemorate naval victories. Continue along Admiral's Walk to Lower Terrace, turn right and then right again into Upper Terrace, and head straight across a small crossroads to the main road (Heath Street). Turn right and take the first left, a small lane, into Hampstead Square.

9–10

Walk across the top of the square, with **Christ Church** on the right, continuing straight into Cannon Place. At the end of the road turn right down the hill, left into Cannon Lane and you'll reach East Heath Road. Turn right and take the second road on the right, Well Walk.

10–11

To your right is the defunct **Chalybeate Well**, where the spring water, rich in iron salts, was discovered in the 18th century. Opposite the well is 40 Well Walk, one of the Hampstead homes of **John Constable**. Cross Christchurch Hill and at the end turn right into New End Square, where you will see historic **Burgh House**, on the right, which was built in 1703.

It now houses the local history museum and art gallery.

11–12

From Burgh House head back down New End Square. Take the first turning right into Flask Walk. This leads up to Hampstead High Street, where a right turn leads to Hampstead Underground station.

TAKING A BREAK

The Brew House Café at Kenwood House and the Buttery at Burgh House.

WHEN TO GO

Weekends are the best time to see kite-flying on Parliament Hill (shops are closed on Sunday).

PLACES TO VISIT

Kenwood House

🖾 Hampstead Lane, NW3 ☎ 020 8348 1286; www.english-heritage.org.uk ⊙ Daily 11:30–4 💷 Free

Keats' House

🖾 Keats' Grove, NW3 ☎ 020 7435 2062; www.cityoflondon.co.uk/keats ⊙ Jul–Oct Tue–Sun 1–5; Nov–Easter Fri–Sun 1–5 (times after Easter 2010 not available at time of writing, please check website) 💷 Moderate

Fenton House

🖾 20 Hampstead Grove, Windmill Hill, NW3 ☎ 020 7435 3471; www.nationaltrust.org.uk ⊙ Mar Sat–Sun 2–5; Apr–Oct Wed–Fri 2–5, Sat–Sun 11–5 💷 Moderate

Burgh House

🖾 New End Square, NW3 ☎ 020 7431 0144; www.burghhouse.org.uk ⊙ Wed–Sun 12–5 (Sat by appointment only) 💷 Free

5 THE NUMBER 15 BUS TRIP

Tour

This trip from Marble Arch to the Tower of London takes in many of the major London sights including Marble Arch, Piccadilly Circus, Trafalgar Square and St Paul's Cathedral, plus well-known thoroughfares – Oxford Street, Regent Street, Haymarket and the Strand. Sit upstairs on the bus and as close to the front as possible for the best views.

TIME 1 hour depending on traffic
START POINT Marble Arch Underground station ⊞ 196 A2
END POINT Tower Hill Underground station ⊞ 202 C3

1–2

Leave **Marble Arch** Underground station by the Subway 1 underpass, Marble Arch and Oxford Street North. Look across to the right to the huge marble edifice on the vast traffic island in the middle of the one-way system – this is the Marble Arch that gives the area its name. Built for the forecourt of Buckingham Palace, it was moved to its current incongruous site in 1851 when the front of the palace was remodelled.

Turn left out of the underpass and catch the No 15 bus at the second stop you come to, stop L. Ask for the Tower of London.

The bus goes along Oxford Street, one of London's busiest shopping streets, lined with department stores. Much of Oxford

Street is now shabby, but look for the grand frontage of **Selfridges** on the left. The store was built by an American, Gordon Selfridge, early in the 20th century and certainly rivals Harrods for its goods, if not fame and exclusivity.

2–3

At Oxford Circus the bus turns right into Regent Street, and a different world architecturally. Grand and unified, it is one remnant of the "Nash Sweep", a processional route running from St James's Park, through Trafalgar Square to Regent's Park, designed by architect John Nash (1752–1835). Most distinctive of the shops is Liberty (▶ 65)

Hop on the bus at Marble Arch

– look along Great Marlborough Street for the black-and-white mock Tudor entrance of this exclusive department store.

At the end of Regent Street, neon advertisements announce your arrival at **Piccadilly Circus**, with the fountain and *Eros* to the right (▶ 60).

3–4

The bus turns right down Haymarket, named for the market which sold hay for the royal horses stabled in the area until 1830, and then left and around the south side of Trafalgar Square. The **National Gallery** (▶ 54–57) is on the left, as Nelson on his **column** and the fine spire of **St Martin-in-the-Fields** rises ahead (▶ 53).

Below left: Marble Arch

12 crosses along the funeral route of his wife, Eleanor of Castile, from Nottinghamshire to Westminster Abbey, each cross marking the spot where her body rested on the solemn 12-day journey.

The bus passes along the Strand, once famed for its music halls (Vaudeville) and theatres, and arches around Aldwych, rejoining the Strand in the centre of the road, with the **Royal Courts of Justice** church in the centre of the road, at **St Clement Danes** on the left. In the centre of the road, the griffin statue marks the boundary of the City of London – the sovereign stops here on ceremonial occasions to ask the permission of the Lord Mayor of London to enter the City.

5–6

The road now becomes Fleet Street, which was once the publishing centre for the British

4–5

As the bus turns right along Duncannon Street, look towards the **Charing Cross** railway station forecourt with its highly ornate reproduction of an Eleanor Cross. In 1290, King Edward I built

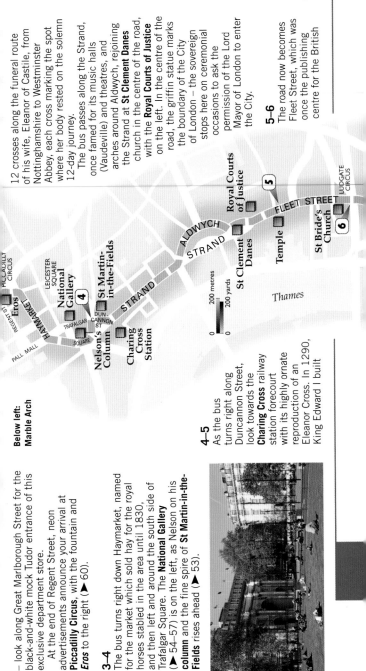

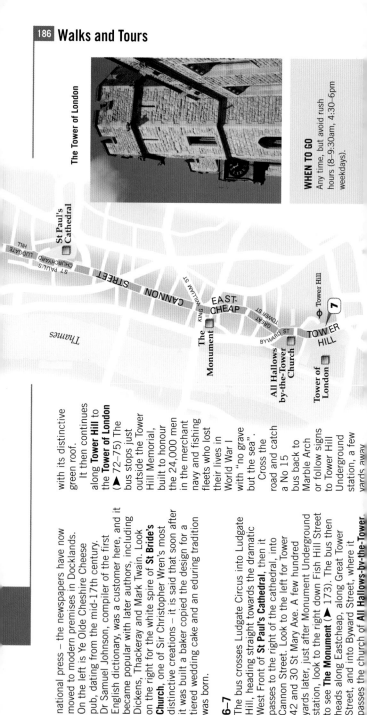

The Tower of London

WHEN TO GO
Any time, but avoid rush hours (8–9.30am, 4.30–6pm weekdays).

national press – the newspapers have now moved to modern premises in Docklands. On the left is Ye Olde Cheshire Cheese pub, dating from the mid-17th century. Dr Samuel Johnson, compiler of the first English dictionary, was a customer here, and it became popular with later authors, including Dickens, Thackeray and Mark Twain. Look on the right for the white spire of **St Bride's Church**, one of Sir Christopher Wren's most distinctive creations – it is said that soon after it was built a baker copied the design for a tiered wedding cake and an enduring tradition was born.

6–7
The bus crosses Ludgate Circus into Ludgate Hill, heading straight towards the dramatic West Front of **St Paul's Cathedral**, then it passes to the right of the cathedral, into Cannon Street. Look to the left for Tower 42 and 30 St Mary Axe. A few hundred yards later, just after Monument Underground station, look to the right down Fish Hill Street to see **The Monument** (▶ 173). The bus then heads along Eastcheap, along Great Tower Street, and into Byward Street, where it passes the church of **All Hallows-by-the-Tower**

with its distinctive green roof.

It then continues along **Tower Hill** to the **Tower of London** (▶ 72–75) The bus stops just outside the Tower Hill Memorial, built to honour the 24,000 men in the merchant navy and fishing fleets who lost their lives in World War I with "no grave but the sea".

Cross the road and catch a No 15 bus back to Marble Arch or follow signs to Tower Hill Underground station, a few yards away

Practicalities

BEFORE YOU GO

WHAT YOU NEED

		UK	Germany	USA	Canada	Australia	Ireland	Netherlands	Spain
● Required	Some countries require a passport to remain valid for a minimum period (usually at least six months) beyond the date of entry – check before you travel.								
○ Suggested									
▲ Not required									
Passport/National Identity Card		▲	●	●	●	●	●	▲	●	●
Visa (regulations can change – check before you travel)		▲	▲	▲	▲	▲	▲	▲	▲
Onward or Return Ticket		▲	○	○	○	○	○	○	○
Health Inoculations (tetanus and polio)		▲	▲	▲	▲	▲	▲	▲	▲
Health Documentation (► 192, Health)		▲	●	●	●	●	●	●	●
Travel Insurance		○	○	○	○	○	○	○	○
Driving Licence (national)		●	●	●	●	●	●	●	●
Car Insurance Certificate		▲	●	n/a	n/a	n/a	●	●	●
Car Registration Document		▲	●	n/a	n/a	n/a	●	●	●

WHEN TO GO

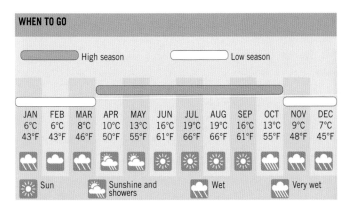

High season   Low season

JAN	FEB	MAR	APR	MAY	JUN	JUL	AUG	SEP	OCT	NOV	DEC
6°C	6°C	8°C	10°C	13°C	16°C	19°C	19°C	16°C	13°C	9°C	7°C
43°F	43°F	46°F	50°F	55°F	61°F	66°F	66°F	61°F	55°F	48°F	45°F

☀ Sun   ⛅ Sunshine and showers   🌧 Wet   🌧 Very wet

The chart above shows **average daily** temperatures for each month.
London experiences defined seasons. **Spring** (March to May) has a mixture of sunshine and showers, although winter often encroaches on it. **Summer** (June to August) can be unpredictable; clear skies and searing heat one day followed by sultry greyness and thunderstorms the next. **Autumn** begins in September, but clear skies can give a summery feel. Real autumn starts in October and the colder weather sets in during November. **Winter** (December to February) is generally mild and snow is rare, but expect the occasional "cold snap".
Be prepared for the **unpredictability** of the British climate – dress in layers and carry rainwear or an umbrella.

GETTING ADVANCE INFORMATION

Websites
■ British Tourist Authority
  www.visitbritain.com
■ UK Travel Guide
  www.londontown.com

■ London Tourist Board
  www.visitlondon.com
■ London Travel Service
  www.bridge-travel.co.uk

In the UK
Britain and London
Visitor Centre
1 Regent Street
London SW1Y 4XT
☎ 0870 156 6366

GETTING THERE

By Air Heathrow and Gatwick are London's two principal **airports**, handling worldwide scheduled flights. Charter flights also operate from Gatwick. Luton, Stansted and London City (Docklands) airports are increasingly busy, handling mainly European charter and business flights.

There are **direct flights** to London from most European, US and Canadian cities. Flights from Australia and New Zealand stop en route in either Asia or the US.

Approximate **flying times** to London: Dublin (1.25 hours), New York (7.5 hours), Los Angeles (11 hours), Vancouver (10 hours), Montréal (7 hours), Toronto (7 hours), east coast of Australia (22 hours), New Zealand (24 hours).

Ticket prices are lower from November to April, excluding Easter and Christmas. Check with the airlines, travel agents, flight brokers, travel sections in newspapers and the Internet for current special offers.

All **airport taxes** are usually included in the price of a ticket.

By Train An alternative option for travellers from Europe is the train. The Channel Tunnel offers a direct link between London and Paris or Brussels for foot passengers aboard "Eurostar" trains (tel: 0870 518 6186), while the car-carrying train, "Eurotunnel" (tel: 0870 535 3535), operates between Calais (France) and Folkestone (England).

By Ferry Passenger and car ferries operate from Ireland, France, Belgium, Netherlands, Germany, Scandinavia and Spain.

TIME

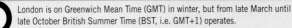

London is on Greenwich Mean Time (GMT) in winter, but from late March until late October British Summer Time (BST, i.e. GMT+1) operates.

CURRENCY AND FOREIGN EXCHANGE

Currency Britain's currency is the pound (£) sterling. There are 100 pennies or pence (p) to each pound. **Notes (bills)** are issued in denominations of £5, £10, £20 and £50. **Coins** come in denominations of 1p, 2p, 5p, 10p, 20p, 50p, £1 and £2. An unlimited amount of British currency can be imported or exported.

Sterling **travellers' cheques** are a safe way to carry money. They may be accepted as payment by some hotels, restaurants and large department stores.

Credit cards (MasterCard, VISA and American Express) are widely accepted.

Exchange You can exchange foreign currency and travellers' cheques at banks and bureaux de change. There are exchange facilities at larger travel agents, in large department stores and hotels, at most main post offices or at dedicated bureaux de change. Be sure to check the rate of exchange and the commission charged before any transaction as they do vary. It is possible to obtain local currency through automated cash machines (ATMs) using a debit or credit card. ATMs are found everywhere in Central London. Your bank will provide details of where your cards will be accepted in London.

In the USA
VisitBritain
7th Floor, Suite 701
551 Fifth Avenue
New York
NY 10176-0799
☎ 1-800-462-2748

In Australia
VisitBritain
Level 2
15 Blue Street
North Sydney NSW 206
☎ (02) 9021 4400

In France
VisitBritain
7–13 rue de Bucarest
75008 Paris
☎ (01) 5836 5066
(Not walk-in; contact by telephone)

WHEN YOU ARE THERE

NATIONAL HOLIDAYS

1 Jan	New Year's Day
Mar/Apr	Good Friday
Mar/Apr	Easter Monday
First Mon May	May Day Holiday
Last Mon May	Spring Bank Holiday
Last Mon Aug	Late Summer Bank Holiday
25 Dec	Christmas Day
26 Dec	Boxing Day

Almost all attractions close on Christmas Day. On other holidays some attractions open, although often with reduced hours.

Bear in mind that public transport services are likely to be less frequent on national holidays.

ELECTRICITY

The power supply in Britain is 230/240 volts. Sockets accept only three-(square)-pin plugs, so an adaptor is needed for continental European and US appliances. A transformer is also needed for appliances operating on 110–120 volts.

OPENING HOURS

- ○ Shops
- ● Offices
- ● Banks
- ● Post Offices
- ● Museums/Monuments
- ● Pharmacies

8am 9am 10am noon 1pm 2pm 4pm 5pm 7pm

□ Day   ■ Midday   □ Evening

Shops Many shops open for longer hours and on Sunday.
Banks High-street banks are also open Saturday morning and bureaux de change are open daily until late.
Museums Smaller museums may close one day a week.
Pharmacies When pharmacies are closed a window sign gives details of the nearest one that operates extended hours or is on 24-hour duty.

TIPS/GRATUITIES

Yes ✓   No ✗

Restaurants (if service not included)	✓	10%
Bar service	✗	
Tour guides	✓	£1–£2
Hairdressers	✓	10%
Taxis	✓	10%
Chambermaids	✓	50p–£1 per day
Porters	✓	50p–£1 depending on number of bags

GENERAL INFORMATION

- There is a smoking ban in all public buildings, including pubs, restaurants and Underground stations. It is strictly adhered to.

- Photography in public places is legal in the UK, but the police do challenge photographers, especially around sensitive sights.

TIME DIFFERENCES

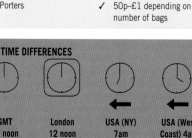

GMT	London	USA (NY)	USA (West Coast)	Sydney	Germany
12 noon	12 noon	7am	4am	10pm	1pm

STAYING IN TOUCH

Post Post offices are open Mon–Fri 9–5:30, Sat 9–noon. The only exception is Trafalgar Square Post Office, 24–28 William IV Street, open Mon–Fri 8:30–6, Sat 9–5:30. Poste restante mail may also be collected here.

Public telephones

Traditional red phone booths are now rare; instead they come in a variety of designs and colours. Coin-operated phones take 10p, 20p, 50p and £1 coins (20p is the minimum charge), but phones taking British Telecom (BT) phonecards or credit cards are often more convenient. Phonecards are available from post offices and many shops.

International Dialling Codes
Dial 00 followed by

Ireland:	353
USA:	1
Canada:	1
Australia:	61
New Zealand:	64
Germany:	49
Netherlands	31
Spain	34

Mobile providers and services The main mobile phone service providers are Vodaphone, Orange, O2 and TMobile. The cheapest way to make mobile calls during your stay is to buy or rent a local SIM card, from companies such as Go-SIM (tel: 0845 658 3410; www.gosim.com) and 0044 (tel: 0870 950 0044; www.0044.co.uk). They allow you to "Pay as you go", by topping up the card as necessary or paying monthly.

WiFi and Internet London is increasingly becoming wireless. The city business district is one big WiFi hotspot and you are likely to find a wireless network to use wherever you are. Many pubs, cafés and hotels now offer wireless services to attract customers; some networks require an access code, available from the staff, while others are open. British Telecom's Openzone is a popular one.

PERSONAL SAFETY

London is generally a safe city and police officers are often seen on the beat (walking the streets) in the central areas. They are usually friendly and approachable.

To help prevent crime:

- Bag snatchers operate on the Underground. Be careful when stopped at stations.
- Be wary of people approaching you or looking over your shoulder while using ATM machines. Check ATMs for any signs of tampering, as card skimming is a problem.
- Do not carry more cash than you need.
- Do not leave a bag unattended in public places.
- Beware of pickpockets in markets, on the Underground, in tourist sights or crowded places.
- Avoid walking alone in parks or alleys at night.

Police assistance:
☎ **999 from any phone**

EMERGENCY	
POLICE 999	
FIRE 999	
AMBULANCE 999	

HEALTH

 Insurance Nationals of Australia and New Zealand and the EU can get free or reduced-cost medical treatment in Britain with a passport or the EHIC (European Health Insurance Card). Medical insurance is still advised, and is essential for all other visitors.

 Dental Services Visitors qualifying for free or reduced-cost medical treatment (see Insurance above) are entitled to concessionary dental treatment, providing the treatment is by a National Health dentist. Private medical insurance is still recommended, and is essential for all other visitors.

 Weather The sun can shine a lot in July and August. Some sights involve being outdoors for prolonged periods when you should "cover up", apply sunscreen and drink plenty of water.

 Drugs Prescription and non-prescription drugs are available from pharmacies. Pharmacists can advise on medication for common ailments. Pharmacies operate a rota so there will always be one open 24 hours; notices in all pharmacy windows give details.

 Safe Water Tap water is safe to drink. Mineral water is widely available but it is often expensive.

CONCESSIONS

Students Holders of an International Student Identity Card may obtain concessions on travel, entrance fees and some goods and services. Information can be found at the National Union of Students' website (www.nus.org.uk).
Senior Citizens Senior citizens (usually those aged over 60) will find discounts on travel, entrance fees and some events and shows. You may be asked for proof of age.
Visitor Attractions Pass The London Pass (www.londonpass.com) covers around 55 attractions, restaurants and shops.

TRAVELLING WITH A DISABILITY

Provision is generally good for visitors with disabilities. Many of the capital's sights have access for wheelchair users but transport can be a problem; not all Underground stations have lifts (elevators) and ramps. Most public houses are not adapted for wheelchairs.
Go to www.visitlondon.com for more information.

CHILDREN

London offers a great deal of child-centred entertainment. Details of activities are given in *Kids Out* magazine. Baby-changing facilities are available in most family-orientated attractions. Under 16s pay half fare on public transport, while under 5s travel free.

TOILETS

The cleanest public toilets (restrooms) are usually found in department stores, hotels and restaurants.

CUSTOMS

The import of wildlife souvenirs from rare and endangered species may be either illegal or require a special permit. Before purchase you should check customs regulations.

EMBASSIES AND HIGH COMMISSIONS

USA	Ireland	Australia	Canada	New Zealand
020 7499 9000	020 7235 2171	020 7379 4334	020 7258 6600	0870 005 6962

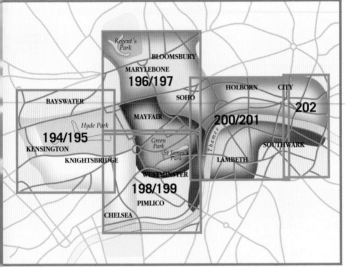

To identify the regions see the map on the inside of the front cover

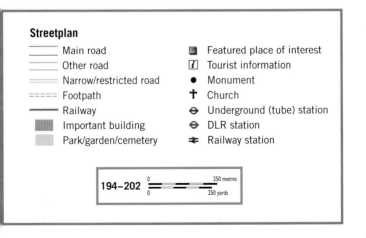

Streetplan

———— Main road	▣	Featured place of interest
———— Other road	*i*	Tourist information
═══ Narrow/restricted road	●	Monument
===== Footpath	†	Church
——— Railway	⊖	Underground (tube) station
Important building	⊖	DLR station
Park/garden/cemetery	⇌	Railway station

194–202   0 ———— 250 metres
         0 ———— 250 yards

Streetplan

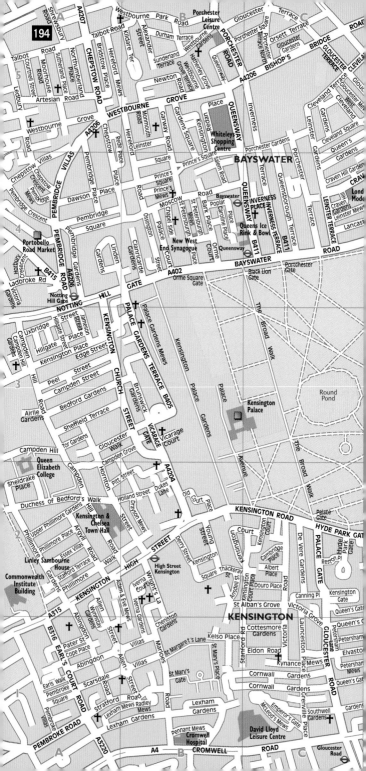

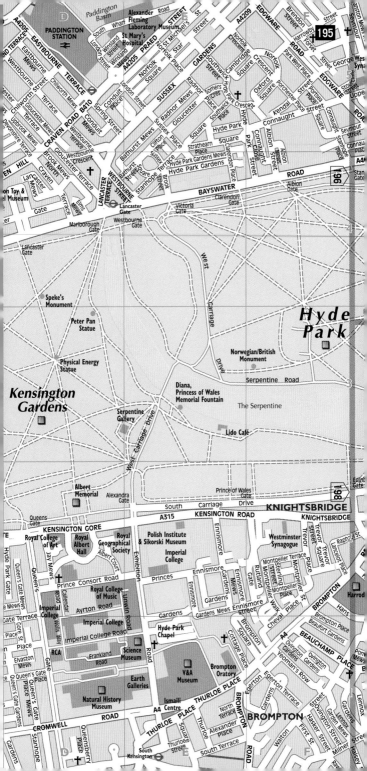

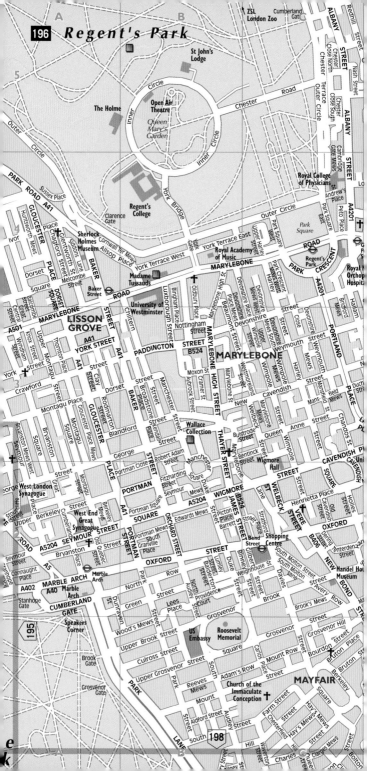

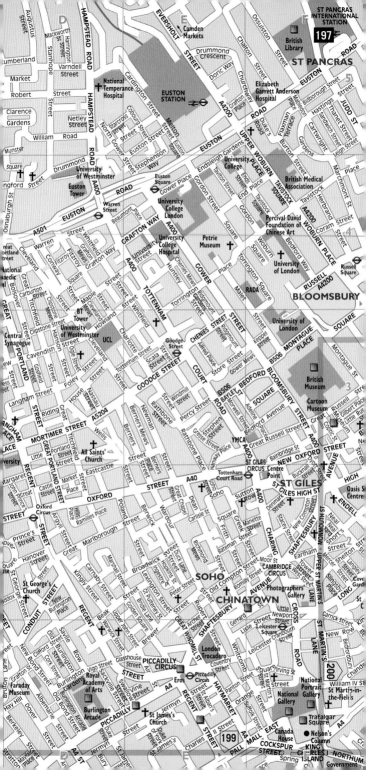

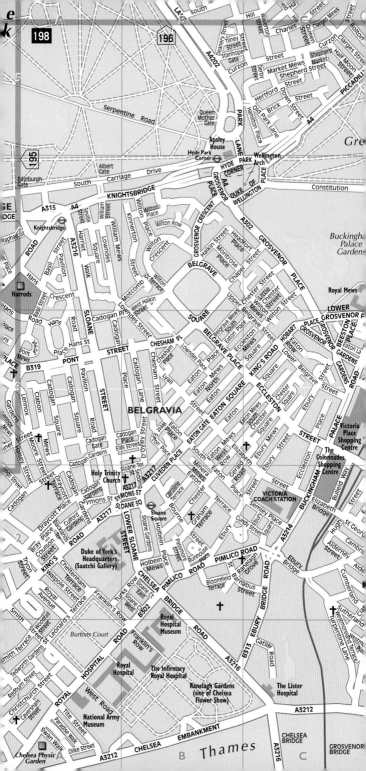

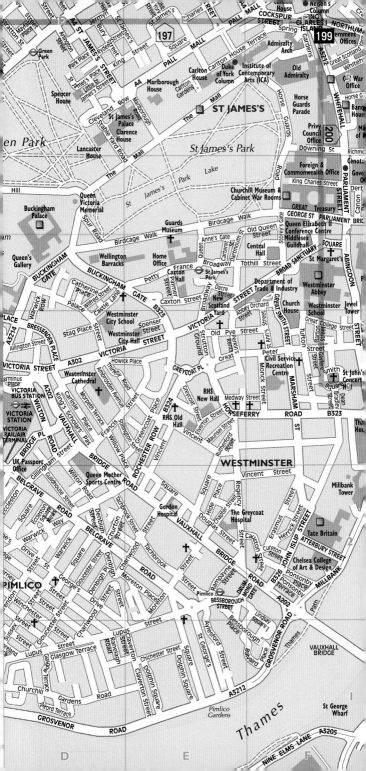

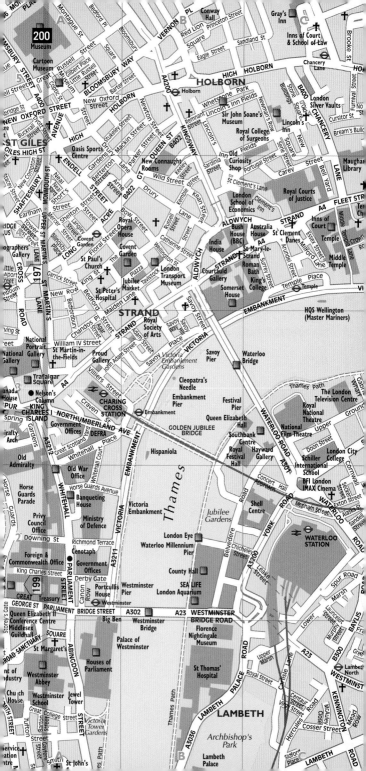

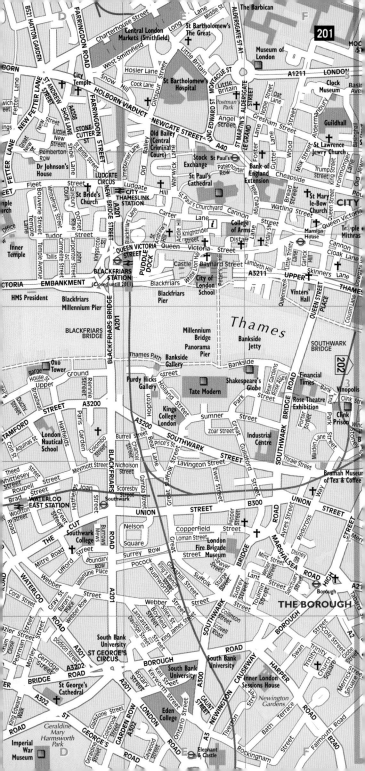

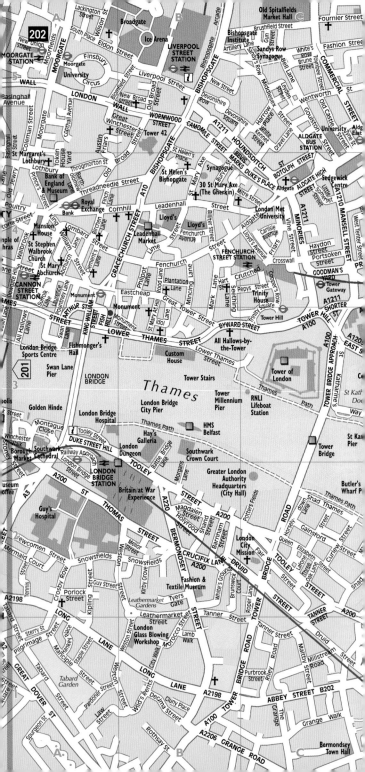

Picture credits
The Automobile Association would like to thank the following photographers, companies and picture libraries for their assistance in the preparation of this book.

Abbreviations for the picture credits are as follows: (t) top; (b) bottom; (l) left; (r) right; (c) centre; (AA) AA World Travel Library.

2 (i) AA/R Victor; 2 (ii) AA/S Montgomery; 2 (iii) AA/S Montgomery; 2 (iv) AA/S Montgomery; 2 (v) AA/J Tims; 3 (i) AA/J Tims; 3 (ii) AA/J Tims; 3 (iii) AA/N Setchfield; 3 (iv) Mark Hamilton/Alamy; 5l AA/R Victor; 5bc AA/M Jourdan; 5br AA/N Setchfield; 6/7t AA/C Sawyer; 7b AA/N Setchfield; 8/9 Alex Segre/Alamy; 9t Alex Segre/Alamy; 9cr AA/N Setchfield; 11l Jon Arnold Images Ltd/Alamy; 11r Arco Images GmbH/Alamy; 12/13b AA/J Tims; 13cr AA; 14l Fox Photos/Getty Images; 14/15t Fox Photos/Getty Images; 16 AA/N Setchfield; 19t AA/S Montgomery; 19c AA/J Tims; 19b AA/S Montgomery; 20l Gareth Fuller/PA Wire; 20/21c Nils Jorgensen/Rex Features; 21r Anna Gowthorpe/PA Wire; 22l AA/S Montgomery; 22r Illustrated London News; 23l Illustrated London News; 23r AA/S Montgomery; 24l Illustrated London News; 24r Illustrated London News; 26 Simon Stacpoole/Rex Features; 27 AA/N Setchfield; 28 AA/J Tims; 29t AA/S Montgomery; 29b AA/M Jourdan; 30 AA/J Tims; 31l AA/S Montgomery; 31bc AA/N Setchfield; 31br AA/J Tims; 45l AA/S Montgomery; 45c AA/J Tims; 45r AA/J Tims; 46 AA/S Montgomery; 48 AA/S Montgomery; 49t AA/J Tims; 49b AA/J Tims; 50 AA/J Tims; 51 AA/S Montgomery; 52 AA/J Tims; 53 AA/J Tims; 54 National Gallery, London/The Bridgeman Art Library; 55 AA/J Tims; 56 National Gallery, London/The Bridgeman Art Library; 57 AA/J Tims; 58 AA/M Jourdan; 59 AA/J Tims; 60 AA/J Tims; 60/61 AA/J Tims; 67l AA/S Montgomery; 67bc AA/S Montgomery; 67br AA/S Montgomery; 70t AA/S Montgomery; 70b AA/S Montgomery; 71 AA/S Montgomery; 72 AA/S Montgomery; 73t Photolibrary Group; 73b AA/S Montgomery; 74/75t AA/S McBride; 74b AA/S Montgomery; 75t David Levenson / Alamy; 75c AA/S Montgomery; 76/77 AA/J Tims; 78/79 AA/S Montgomery; 81 AA/S Montgomery; 83 AA/J Tims; 87l AA/N Setchfield; 87bc AA/J Tims; 87br AA/N Setchfield; 90 AA/J Tims; 91t AA/S Montgomery; 91b AA/J Tims; 92 AA/S Montgomery; 93 AA/S Montgomery; 94/95 AA/J Tims; 96 AA; 97 AA/J Tims; 98 AA/J Tims; 99 AA/J Tims; 100c AA/S Montgomery; 100b AA/S Montgomery; 101 AA/S Montgomery; 102 AA/J Tims; 103 AA/N Setchfield; 104 AA/R Turpin; 105 AA/S Montgomery; 106 AA/N Setchfield; 107 AA/J Tims; 111l AA/J Tims; 111c AA/N Setchfield; 111r AA/P Kenward; 114 AA/S Montgomery; 115t AA/J Tims; 115b AA/N Setchfield; 116 AA/S Montgomery; 117 AA/S Montgomery; 118 Edina van der Wyck; 119 Richard Waite; 121 AA/J Tims; 122 AA/J Tims; 123 AA/J Tims; 124 AA/M Jourdan; 125 AA/N Setchfield; 127 AA/S McBride; 128 Historic Royal Palaces; 129 2008 Charlie Hopkinson; 131t AA/M Jourdan; 131b AA/N Setchfield; 137l AA/J Tims; 137tc AA/J Tims; 137tr AA/J Tims; 140 AA/J Tims; 141t AA/J Tims; 141b AA/J Tims; 142 AA/J Tims; 143 AA/J Tims; 144t AA/J Tims; 144b AA/J Tims; 145 AA/J Tims; 146 British Library, London/© British Library Board. All Rights Reserved/The Bridgeman Art Library; 147 British Library, London/© British Library Board. All Rights Reserved/The Bridgeman Art Library; 148 AA/J Tims; 149t AA/J Tims; 149c AA/J Tims; 150 AA/J Tims; 151l AA/J Tims; 151r AA/J Tims; 152 AA/N Setchfield; 153 AA/J Tims; 154 AA/J Tims; 155 AA/J Tims; 161l AA/N Setchfield; 161tc AA/J Tims; 161tr AA/N Setchfield; 162 AA/N Setchfield; 163 AA/N Setchfield; 164 AA/W Voysey; 165 AA/W Voysey/The Dean and Canons of Windsor; 166 AA/J Tims; 167l Mark Hamilton/Alamy; 167bc AA/J Tims; 167tr AA/S Montgomery; 168 AA/S Montgomery; 170 AA/R Turpin; 171 AA/S Montgomery; 173 AA/J Tims; 174 AA/J Tims; 175 AA/S Montgomery; 176 AA/N Setchfield; 177 AA/J Hatts; 178 AA/N Setchfield; 179 AA/N Setchfield; 182l AA/S Montgomery; 182r AA/S Montgomery; 184 AA/S Montgomery; 185 AA/J Tims; 186 AA/S Montgomery; 187l AA/J Tims; 187tc AA/S Montgomery; 187tr AA/S Montgomery; 191t AA/S Montgomery; 191c AA/S Montgomery; 191b AA/M Jourdan.

Every effort has been made to trace the copyright holders, and we apologise in advance for any accidental errors. We would be happy to apply any corrections in the following edition of this publication.

SPIRALGUIDE
Questionnaire

Dear Traveller

Your comments, opinions and recommendations are very important to us. Please help us to improve our travel guides by taking a few minutes to complete this simple questionnaire.

You do not need a stamp (unless posted outside the UK). If you do not want to remove this page from your guide, then you can submit your comments and recommendations by email: travelguides@theaa.com

Send to: The Editor, Spiral Guides, AA World Travel Guides, FREEPOST SCE 4598, Basingstoke RG21 4GY.

Your recommendations...

We always encourage readers' recommendations for restaurants, night-life or shopping – if your recommendation is used in the next edition of the guide, we will send you a FREE AA Spiral Guide of your choice. Please state below the establishment name, location and your reasons for recommending it.

_____

_____

_____

_____

_____

Please send me AA Spiral _____

(see list of titles inside the back cover)

About this guide...

Which title did you buy?

_____ AA Spiral

Where did you buy it? _____

When? m m / y y

Why did you choose an AA Spiral Guide? _____

_____

_____

_____

_____

Did this guide meet your expectations?

Exceeded ☐   Met all ☐   Met most ☐   Fell below ☐

Please give your reasons _____

_____

_____

_____

_____

continued on next page...

Were there any aspects of this guide that you particularly liked?

_____
_____
_____
_____
_____

Is there anything we could have done better?

_____
_____
_____
_____

About you...

Name (Mr/Mrs/Ms) _____

Address _____

_____

_____ **Postcode** _____

Daytime tel no _____ **email** _____

Please _only_ give us your email address and mobile phone number if you wish to hear from us about other products and services from the AA and partners by email or text or mms.

Which age group are you in?

Under 25 ☐   25–34 ☐   35–44 ☐   45–54 ☐   55–64 ☐   65+ ☐

How many trips do you make a year?

Less than one ☐   One ☐   Two ☐   Three or more ☐

Are you an AA member? Yes ☐   **No** ☐

About your trip...

When did you book? m m / y y   **When did you travel?** m m / y y

How long did you stay? _____

Was it for business or leisure? _____

Did you buy any other travel guides for your trip? ☐ Yes ☐ No

If yes, which ones? _____

_____

Thank you for taking the time to complete this questionnaire. Please send it to us as soon as possible, and remember, you do not need a stamp (unless posted outside the UK).

The information we hold about you will be used to provide the products and services requested and for identification, account administration, analysis, and fraud/loss prevention purposes. More details about how that information is used is in our privacy statement, which you'll find under the heading "Personal Information" in our terms and conditions and on our website: www.theAA.com. Copies are also available from us by post, by contacting the Data Protection Manager at AA, Fanum House, Basing View, Basingstoke, RG21 4EA.
We may want to contact you about other products and services provided by us, or our partners (by mail, telephone) but please tick the box if you DO NOT wish to hear about such products and services from us by mail or telephone. ☐